A GUIDE TO SOCIAL SKILL TRAINING

A Guide to Social Skill Training

ROGER ELLIS and DOROTHY WHITTINGTON

CROOM HELM
London & Sydney

BROOKLINE BOOKS
Cambridge, Massachusetts

Croom Helm Ltd, Provident House, Burrell Row,
Beckenham, Kent BR3 1AT

Croom Helm Australia Pty Ltd, Suite 4, 6th Floor,
64-76 Kippax Street, Surry Hills, NSW 2010, Australia

Reprinted 1983 and 1986

British Library Cataloguing in Publication Data

Ellis, Roger
A guide to social skill training.
1. Interpersonal relations – Study and teaching
2. Life skills – Study and teaching
I. Title II. Whittington, Dorothy
302'.07 HM132

ISBN 0-7099-0929-2

Brookline Books, PO Box 1046,
Cambridge, MA 02238

ISBN 0-914797-25-5

Typeset by Jayell Typesetting, London
Printed and bound in Great Britain by
Biddles Ltd, Guildford and King's Lynn

CONTENTS

ACKNOWLEDGEMENTS

To: Owen Hargie, Christine Saunders, David Dickson and Sylvia Campbell who helped at various stages, particularly with the preparation of case-study material.

To: Lena Madden and Maureen Carswell who were the human face of information retrieval.

To: Valerie Barr, our secretary, who met illegibility, incoherence and indecision with unfailing technical and social skills.

To: all who have promoted the Ulster Polytechnic Social Skill Training Unit. They include the Rector, Derek Birley, who saw the point; the academic and professional colleagues who made it happen; the technical and secretarial staff who made it work; and the many trainees we hope it has helped.

INTRODUCTION

Social skill training, in some ways, is a very old rose by a comparatively new name. A concern with face-to-face behaviour and how it might be improved is as old as rhetoric and as pervasive as manners. The novelty of social skill training (SST) lies less in its substance than its approach which aspires to the rigour and system of science. Thus the methods of the natural sciences are brought to bear on describing how we behave to each other, how we achieve our social ends and, in particular, how behaviour might be changed and made more effective.

What are social skills? For most of us the majority of our waking hours is spent talking to, looking at, listening to, touching, and, perhaps, striving to avoid, other people. From a scientific point of view this behaviour is observable: it may be described, counted, classified and analysed. It has been labelled, in general terms, as social behaviour, face-to-face interaction, interpersonal behaviour, and, latterly, social skill. It includes such everyday actions as greeting, asking questions, explaining, encouraging, discouraging, persuading and resisting. At a more detailed level it includes the words we use, the nods of our heads and the winks of our eyes.

An obvious, but significant, distinction has been made between *verbal* and *non-verbal* behaviour as components of interpersonal communication. Thus we communicate our intentions and opinions not just through the words we use but also through facial expressions, gestures, bodily movements and posture. Some non-verbal behaviour – smiles, nods and gestures – may be as consciously controlled as words. Other behaviour may 'leak' our feelings unconsciously through, for example, the drumming of fingers or the crossing of legs. Verbal and non-verbal behaviour, conscious and unconscious: these are the ingredients of social skill and the material for SST training.

The scientific approach to social behaviour is given a special flavour by the use of the word 'skill'. At the everyday level to talk of social skill is to imply that our social behaviour may have an element of craft, accomplishment or expertise. Presumably such behaviour can be learned, improved and polished. Presumably also we can analyse it as we would an inefficient golf swing or a muddled piano scale; we can practise to make it better, if not perfect, and we can select or reject as appropriate. At a more technical level the notion of 'skill' allows us to analyse social behaviour using models derived from the psychology of skilled performance. These models have been developed in relation to such physical skills as assembling electrical components, playing tennis or driving a car. These skills concern man in relation to his physical environment. Social skill training transfers the approach to man in relation to man.

The 'skilled performance' approach to learning has a history (Welford, 1968) stretching back to the 1930s and has been extremely influential in military and industrial training. Skill is defined as the capacity to respond flexibly to circumstances in order to achieve a goal with maximum efficiency. Thus the skilled golfer adapts his swing to wind direction, lie of the ball and so on and with minimum effort executes a swing whereby the ball is likely to reach its target. The unskilled golfer, however, miscalculates and expends maximum effort and irritation to move the ball a few yards.

The difference between the two golfers is, in part at least, the result of learning. The skilled player is said to have built up a store of strategies and tactics relevant to the game of golf. These allow him:

(1) to pick out the most relevant aspects of the situation in which he finds himself (and his golf ball);
(2) to relate these perceptions to aims he has (e.g. for a hole-in-one); and
(3) to translate these plans and perceptions into action – a smooth and effective swing.

Significantly, after completing the stroke the skilled golfer reviews his performance and, in the light of its success or otherwise, modifies his approach to the game. Improvement is thus built into the process. This use of the results of action to modify subsequent action is known as feedback.

This basic model, involving perception, purpose, capability, action and feedback, has been applied to a wide range of physical skills (Annett, 1974; Fitts & Posner, 1967). Since the early 1970s it has also been applied to analyses of social behaviour (Argyle, 1967).

In both contexts principles of *training* have been derived. We will discuss these (and their application in SST), fully in Chapter 1. Briefly, the major components of training (Holding, 1965) are said to be demonstration, practice and guided feedback. Thus the novice golfer or social skill trainer must see skilled performance demonstrated, must try it out for himself and must be told how good or bad his attempts were.

The trainee is encouraged to concentrate separately (in the first instance) on individual aspects of the skilled performance. Thus the golfer practises gripping the club, addressing the ball and his back swing as separate exercises before attempting their integration in a full swing. The trainee teacher would be instructed to focus on, for example, asking questions or, more specifically, establishing eye contact rather than teaching a whole lesson.

Given that social behaviour may be conceived as a skill then training may be organised so that social skills may be acquired and developed in controlled circumstances. One broad social skill might be 'beginning a conversation with a stranger'. This skill could be broken down into component parts, e.g. 'using the right words', 'leaving pauses', 'smiling' and 'establishing eye contact'. The trainees' attention is drawn to these features during the so-called *'sensitisation'* phase of training. The trainee then practises the skill. He may do it at the level of conversing with a stranger or he may focus on a single component such as establishing eye contact. Practice takes place in a controlled and 'safe' setting where the trainee, it is argued, is able to experiment and take risks without any consequences for his self-esteem or relationships in real life. The practice may, for example, take place with a mock stranger who has been specially primed to be receptive to the encounter. A feature of this simulation is the recording which is made to provide feedback to the trainee. Conventionally, closed-circuit television is employed and the trainee has a record of the interaction in vision and sound. However, the record might be simply the structured notes of an observer. It is then available for scrutiny by the trainee, perhaps in collaboration with the trainers, so that he might modify his future behaviour. This cycle of sensitisation, practice and feedback applied to verbal and non-verbal social behaviour is the procedure known as social skill training.

This book aims to be a guide to social skill training. As such it has several interrelated themes.

A central purpose is to help those who wish to set up training programmes. In Chapter 2 we suggest questions which must be asked and decisions which must be made in planning a programme. At Ulster Polytechnic we have developed a social skill training unit unique in the number of trainees it accommodates and in the range of professions for which it offers courses. Describing and evaluating these developments in Chapter 4 provides a case-study element for the book.

We have tried to fill a notable gap in the existing literature by overviewing all current practices. In Chapter 2 we bring together, in outline at least, the different settings, purposes and procedures which can be described as social skill training. In order to make some sense of these diverse purposes we propose a continuum of social competence with specified entrance and exit points for trainees. At one end of the continuum social skill training is provided for those who are morbidly unskilled: the target would be to bring such persons closer to an average level of competence. At the other end of the continuum (and it is this place or thereabouts which professional training for such as social workers, teachers and therapists would occupy) social skill training is provided for those who are selected in the first place on the basis of their above-average capacity and who could be expected to reach a level of superior competence. This highly-developed level of social skill would be the professional's stock-in-trade whether he were salesman or social worker. Somewhere between these two extremes are the programmes which aim to accelerate normal learning, such as the social and life skills programmes for school leavers.

Using this continuum as a basis we propose three broad categories of social skill training: remedial, developmental and specialised.

Remedial SST is defined as programmes for those whose repertoire of effective social behaviours is deemed by themselves or others to be inadequate for everyday life. Programmes have been devised for such diverse groups as psychiatric in- and out-patients (Bellack *et al.*, 1976; Falloon *et al.*, 1977; McFall & Twentyman, 1973; Edelstein & Eisler, 1976; Hersen & Bellack, 1976a; Kaseman, 1976; Matson & Stephens, 1978; Matson & Zeiss, 1979; Williams, 1977), alcoholics and other addicts (Callner & Ross, 1978; Hirsch *et al.*, 1978; Jackson & Oei, 1978; Van Hasselt *et al.*, 1978), aggressive individuals (Brannigan & Young, 1978), homosexuals (McKinlay, 1978), and the hard-core unemployed (Shady & Kuc, 1977).

Developmental SST is defined as SST aimed at the acceleration and facilitation of developmental sequences which might be expected to occur without intervention, but more slowly or in a distorted form. Many programmes have been developed for individual children thought to be at risk of mental illness or behaviour disorder (Van Hasselt *et al.*, 1979; Oden & Asher, 1977; Bornstein *et al.*, 1977; Combs & Slaby, 1977; Rinn & Markle, 1979). Other programmes have been devised for more normal children who need help in producing behaviour appropriate to specific situations such as classrooms (Cartledge, 1978) or job interviews (Spence, 1979).

Specialised SST is defined as SST provided for trainees who are taken to have already achieved at least normal adult levels of skill but who have particular vocational objectives which necessitate sophisticated or specialised forms of interaction. These include a very wide range of vocational groups from teachers and social workers to managers and salesmen. Essentially anyone whose job entails working with people (and there are few which don't) might benefit from this type of SST. Programmes have proliferated accordingly although most acknowledge a debt to earlier work with one or other of the two original groups for whom specialised SST was developed. These were teachers (Allen & Ryan, 1969) and counsellors (Ivey, 1971).

As a feature of this overview we present in Chapter 3 comprehensive lists and brief descriptions of the social skills which trainers have identified. One complication with skills is that they can be described at different levels of detail. Thus 'making clients feel at ease' could be a skill but so could 'smiling'. The latter is clearly a small part of the former. Skills also differ with regard to the ease with which observers agree that they are taking place at all. Smiling is easy to identify; but how can we be sure that one person is making another feel at ease? Technically we would say that skills differ in 'grain of analysis' and 'inferential status'. 'Smiling' is at a finer grain than 'putting at ease'. Determining that smiling has occurred requires less inference from available evidence than being sure that someone has been put at ease. Given these problems of level and evidence, typical skills named by investigators include 'eye contact', 'asking questions', 'giving explanations', 'listening sympathetically' and 'closing interactions'.

We have tried, in Chapter 2, to clarify the different theoretical and practical antecedents of social skill training programmes. This we feel should be of particular value to would-be trainers who must be aware of the expectations and assumptions which they and others might bring to social skill training.

A strength of social skill training lies in its controlled environment where trainees may practise and develop social skills without the risks and stresses of real life. Using feedback they are able to contemplate and analyse their own behaviour and its effect on that of others. Final utility, however, must be measured in terms of transfer to real life and we consider, in Chapter 5, the question of generalisation from the simulated to the everyday.

Our own experience has been in the provision of social skill training for what we have called the interpersonal professions (Ellis, 1980), that is those professions such as teaching and social work whose primary method is face-to-face interaction. Such professions encounter SST as part of a larger curriculum. In Chapter 6 we present a model for the curriculum of these professions having analysed the problems inherent in attempts to integrate theory and practice. We have called this curriculum the 'action focus curriculum' for the fairly obvious reason that it makes professional action its central focus. Theoretical material is introduced as it assists in describing action, analysing action, planning for action and evaluating action. Earlier we described this curriculum model as addressing 'skills in context' which in part is intended to communicate the same message but which also emphasises that action and action-related theory should be placed in a wider context through more contemplative and critical studies. This curriculum has SST and associated theory as an important element.

SST's distinctiveness comes from the application of scientific method to an area of long-standing interest and concern. Part of this scientific approach must include the critical evaluation of SST's effectiveness. We review the literature regarding effectiveness in Chapter 7.

As a postscript we offer some predictions as to how social skill training might develop in the future.

We believe, obviously, that there is some logic to our chapters and their sub-sections in their present order. However, readers may wish to select or reorder these sections according to their needs. For their benefit we have provided questions which the chapters and the sections aim to answer.

Chapter 1: Approaches and Applications

(1) What are the theoretical assumptions which lie behind naming skills and devising training programmes?
(2) How do these theoretical assumptions influence the practice of SST?
(3) How does SST vary in principle and practice in the different settings in which it takes place?

Chapter 2: Planning the Programme

(1) What questions should an intending trainer ask before planning SST?
(2) How should he set about planning an SST programme?
(3) What decisions must he make about:

    (i) skills;
    (ii) training procedures;
    (iii) hardware, software and logistics;
    (iv) the evaluation of training?

(4) What resources are needed for SST?

Chapter 3: A Compendium of Skills

(1) What skills have been included in SST programmes?
(2) Which skills occur most frequently?
(3) How are skills presented for training?
(4) How are skills related to one another?

Chapter 4: SST at Ulster Polytechnic

(1) How has SST developed at Ulster Polytechnic?
(2) For whom are courses provided?
(3) What procedures are adopted for skill identification and training?
(4) What are the skills employed in different courses?
(5) How are material resources deployed?
(6) How has SST been staffed?

Chapter 5: Transfer of Training

(1) What evidence is there that the effects of training are maintained once the period of formal training has ended?
(2) How can training be modified to increase the likelihood of effects being maintained?

Chapter 6: The Curriculum Context

(1) What are the characteristic problems of education and training for interpersonal professionals?
(2) What approaches have been used to solve these problems?
(3) What is the action focus curriculum?
(4) How can SST help to foster the integration of theory and practice in such courses?
(5) How can SST be related to a wider curriculum?

Chapter 7: The Effectiveness of SST

(1) Does SST work? What evidence is there for claiming that it does?
(2) How adequate is the model of social interaction upon which skill identification and training is premised?
(3) What further research is needed?

1 APPROACHES AND APPLICATIONS

Introduction

The idea of social skill training is a simple one. Programmes are devised to enable trainees to become better at interacting with other people. At stages in the programme trainees are shown or told about social skill; they try the skills out for themselves; and they are told, or can see, how they have got on.

In the introduction we gave some brief indication of the skills social skill trainers have used, the procedures they have followed and the various groups for whom training has been provided. No doubt many readers will be impatient to gain further knowledge in these three areas. To them the content of this chapter may seem overly theoretical and too far removed from practical advice. However, we consider it most important that those organising social skill training should understand the different assumptions which trainers (and indeed trainees) may have regarding what social skills are and how they may best be learned. The major purpose of this chapter is to analyse positions which trainers have adopted either explicitly or implicitly with regard to the identification and acquisition of skills.

It is, we believe, differences in these assumptions and theoretical positions which have hindered communication between social skill trainers. They may well pose problems when a particular programme is being devised. We would, therefore, recommend that participants in training programmes should try to make their views on social skills and training explicit. Certainly we believe they should try to understand the scientific standards of evidence which have characterised social skill training. Those who are not psychologists by background will need to gain some understanding of the cybernetic model which underpins the training procedure, of the standards which characterise a behaviourist approach to evidence and of the approaches to the understanding of learning which are described as classical conditioning and operant conditioning. In our exposition of theoretical positions we have tried to include some introductory material from psychology for those who are not familiar with the area.

Notwithstanding these compelling arguments for readers confronting the analyses of this chapter, some will require grist rather than mill. For them we would commend the case studies in Chapter 4 followed perhaps by the skill compendium of Chapter 3 prior to tackling this chapter.

Within the simple framework of SST, many variations exist. The particular procedures adopted by a given socials skills trainer result from a number of factors including the characteristics of the trainee, the training objectives, the resources available and the trainers' expertise. It is hardly surprising, therefore, that while SST programmes do share certain basic characteristics they are in other aspects almost as diverse as they are numerous.

This diversity has proved a considerable hindrance to comparison across programmes. The combination of results from studies conducted in different programmes has frequently been rendered invalid by differences in detailed procedures, in skill categories and even in the definitions advanced (and translated into practice) for such basic components of SST as sensitisation, practice and feedback. The novice trainer is likewise in difficulty in trying to discern general principles for programme design and implementation and even the experienced practitioner finds debate with colleagues obfuscated by the lack of common terminology. Indeed, the authors have been struck by a kind of non-integrating parallelism between different social skill training ventures when attempts have been made at symposia.

In this chapter we aim to offer a framework within which existing programmes may be located. In the introductory chapter we offered a threefold categorisation of settings: remedial, developmental and specialist. The framework in this chapter emphasises the differing philosophies which underpin the ways in which trainers decide what social skills they will try to develop and the means by which they will be developed. Thus approaches are distinguished with regard to the *identification* and *acquisition* of social skills.

Those approaches most common in SST can usually be traced to well-established theoretical and methodological positions in psychology. Where appropriate we have offered an introduction to these positions for those readers who wish to explore or revise.

To note the variety of approach and imperfection of communication in SST is not, of course, to suggest that all programmes should be uniform in content, procedures and general approach. Indeed, if SST is to be a fruitful arena for the development and testing of basic hypotheses about social interaction it is vital that there be many varieties. It is, however, equally vital that the premises upon which new (or even well-established) varieties of SST are based and the theoretical antecedents from which their procedures have been derived be clearly identified and critically reviewed.

In this and the succeeding chapter a number of approaches or paradigms underlying the development of SST programmes will be isolated and the practical alternatives facing the tyro programme designer will be enumerated and discussed.

Approaches to SST

All social skill trainers accept, by definition, that social behaviour can be properly described as skilled, that skills can be identified and that these skills can be systematically taught. Obvious though it may seem, and tedious to repeat, a social skill trainer must know what social skills are and how he can arrange for his trainees to acquire or develop them.

The routes by which trainers arrive at this knowledge, however, vary considerably and are related at least in part to broader issues of truth, evidence and enquiry. There tends to be a consonance between approaches to the identification of skills, the kinds of skills described and the training programmes associated with them. Thus the trainer who accepts a generally behaviourist view might be expected to account for SST in terms of conditioning and to apply a rigorous empiricism to the identification of units of social behaviour. A more cognitively-oriented trainer might account for acquisition in terms of information theory and might be more prepared to discuss internal events such as plans and strategies in relation to skilled behaviour.

In producing signposts to this territory we have focused upon approaches to finding and naming skills on the one hand and to promoting their development (or acquisition) on the other. These two positions will be more or less consonant in a particular programme and may be implicitly or occasionally explicitly accidents of a coherent methodological and theoretical essence.

Paradigms for the Acquisition of Social Skills

Approaches to the acquisition of social skills and the way in which training programmes are conceived, planned, operated and evaluated, relate clearly to views of how learning occurs. Thus basic positions regarding human learning are reflected in the various social skill training programmes which exist. We have used four categories to describe these approaches and have called them *conditioning, cybernetic, experiential* and *teleological*.

For those who are familiar with the preoccupations of psychologists of learning, the theoretical and substantive background to the first two paradigms will be well-known. For those who do not have this background, a dispensable summary is provided.

The Conditioning Paradigm. A behaviourist view of learning implies that admissible evidence should be confined to features of the learner and his environment which are publicly observable. Thus the behaviour of the learner is legitimate subject matter whereas his subjective experience is not. The person adopting this approach would wish to confine his enquiries to evidence which is scientifically observable. He would also wish to avoid the introduction of so-called explanations which include notions which are themselves unobservable. For example an explanation of a person's behaviour in terms of his motives – 'he kissed the girl because he loves her' – would be criticised for explaining the observable (a kiss) by the unobservable (love). The provider of this explanation would be pressed to give evidence of *love* in terms of observable events. If the observable events are the very ones being explained (e.g. his love is revealed by his kissing) then the tautology stands revealed.

The behaviourist, therefore, would attempt to understand, for example, *learning* through observation and recording of publicly-accessible events and through the identification of recurrent patterns among these events. Thus kissing would be studied in relation to preceding, concurrent and succeeding stimulus conditions and behaviours. What other behaviours of the kisser precede, succeed or accompany the kiss? What environmental events go before, come after or co-exist with the kiss? Indeed what are the particular features of behaviour which constitute a kiss?

This rigorous approach to the observable bears obvious resemblance to that of the natural scientist. The biologist studying a beetle is unlikely to talk in terms of its motives. Rather there is a meticulous account given of its observable behaviour and the environment in which it occurs.

This approach to the study of learning has significantly increased our understanding of the mechanisms of learning and thus our ability to bring about those relatively permanent changes in behaviour which constitute learning. Two major approaches have emerged within this tradition and these are usually described as 'classical conditioning' and 'operant conditioning'. Both approaches try to understand learning in terms of observable behaviour and environmental conditions.

In crude terms classical conditioning is concerned with the ways in which a behaviour elicited by one stimulus may in time be elicited by another stimulus which has occurred close to the original stimulus. Thus, as Pavlov showed, a dog that salivates in response to meat may be 'conditioned' to salivate to a bell which closely precedes the meat. In human terms it might be suggested, by analogy, that a man who turns pale when threatened by a bully may turn pale at the bully's footsteps or the mention of his name.

The other major approach, operant conditioning, has concentrated on the way in which succeeding stimulus conditions may vary the probability of a particular behaviour recurring. Thus the rat which presses the bar in Skinner's famed experiment is more likely to press again if the bar-pressing is succeeded by a food pellet and the child whose questions are encouraged with smiles and attention is more likely to ask questions. Attempts to promote learning through procedures based on these two areas of work are usually described as 'behaviour modification'.

These approaches have defined learning in terms of relatively permanent changes in observable behaviour and have sought to identify the ways in which behaviour changes in relation to observable events. For the social skill trainer of this persuasion social skills would thus be described in terms of observable behaviour produced when interacting with another human or humans and training programmes would be based on the principles of classical or operant conditioning.

Historically it must be acknowledged that SST originated within such a behaviourist framework. Wolpe and Lazarus (1966) for example describe their procedures for Assertiveness Training as a variety of reciprocal inhibition in which a new association between responding assertively and the reward and support available from the therapist effectively demolishes an old association with unpleasant consequences. The procedure is precisely analogous to the technique for replacing one association with another demonstrated in classical conditioning experiments upon animals. A similar early identification of SST as a form of conditioning is to be found in McDonald (1973), who makes it clear that the origins of the first professional applications in microteaching were at least behaviourist in aspiration when he suggests (p. 73) that 'there is very little else about microteaching . . . that is worth studying. What is worth investigating is the application of behavioural modification principles that can be made when microteaching is used'.

More recent developments in SST which emphasise the specificity of skills and the manipulation of reward include the varieties of assertiveness training reported by Hersen and Bellack (1976a), Lange and

Jakubowski (1976) and many others. The third section of this chapter will trace the gradual development of such ostensibly behaviourist approaches and will show how far it has (and has not) been possible to maintain the purity of the model in its application. It should be noted at this point, however, that many of the necessary characteristics of SST as a procedure for skill acquisition can be traced back to the conditioning paradigm. Thus it is basic to SST that skills can be operationalised in terms of observable behaviour, that skills reduced to sub-skills are more easily acquired (and can be reconstituted by the trainee) and that reward (or at least association of appropriate responses with pleasant consequences) is an important aspect of training. Each of these premises can be traced back to the conditioning paradigm.

The Cybernetic Paradigm. This paradigm (see Figure 1.1) is essentially the skills model as proposed by Welford (1968, 1980), Holding (1965) and others and is briefly outlined in the introductory chapter. Its critical features include an emphasis upon the planned control of behaviour and upon the modification of plans (strategic or tactical) in the light of environmental feedback or knowledge of the results of action. The skills model is based upon a cognitive view of learning which explains it in terms of unobservable internal events which must, however, be reliably inferred from observable external events. Thus, in the example of the previous section the man who was observed to kiss the girl would be assumed to have perceived the girl as (a) present and (b) kissable, to have drawn upon a store of previous experiences of kissing and of potential female responses in forming a plan for the execution of the kissing behaviour and, possibly, to have fitted such a plan into a longer-term strategy for subsequent related behaviour. Observed evidence on the behaviours which preceded, succeeded and accompanied the kiss would be amassed as in the behaviourist model, but such evidence would then be related to the man's inferred thought processes or cognitions. Thus, if he was subsequently observed trying to kiss every girl who came within 100 yards it might be inferred that he was highly motivated towards kissing but lacking knowledge of normal social conventions and unlikely to be 'in love' with the first girl. Such inference is, of course, more fallible than pure observation and important safeguards are, therefore, built in to the cybernetic model. These are that the inferential leap which is made should be as parsimonious as possible, that the explanation advanced should account for all available evidence and that the explanation should only go beyond the evidence when it is unavoidable.

The skills model as represented in simplified form in Figure 1.1 incorporates evidence drawn from extensive laboratory and field studies of learning in animals and humans (Fitts & Posner, 1967; Annett, 1974; Welford, 1968) and has been particularly influential in the development of training programmes for the acquisition of motor skills from simple object assembly tasks to complex interactive skills like playing tennis (Bilodeau & Bilodeau, 1966). It was first extended to account for the acquisition of social skill by Argyle (1967) and, as indicated in the introductory chapter it has remained a potent influence upon the procedures adopted by social skill trainers.

Figure 1.1

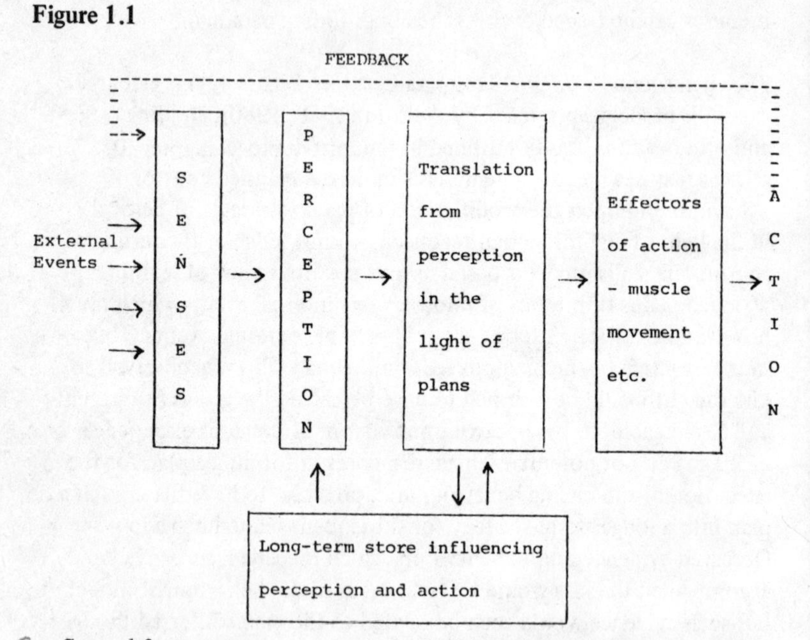

Several features are common to both this and the previous paradigm. Both, for example, assume that social behaviour is learned by processes similar to those by which motor or intellectual learning takes place; both suggest that learning takes place more easily if complex skills are reduced to simpler components; and both stress the importance for learning of associations between action and the consequences of action. The significant differences between this and the previous paradigm are threefold. First, as indicated, this paradigm explains skill acquisition in cognitive terms. Internal events (perceptions, plans, execution strategies etc.) are not only admissible but are essential to the model. Secondly, while knowledge of results is essential, such knowledge may be of negative results but still be useful. Learning from mistakes is taken to be a valuable aspect of skill acquisition although feedback which is in general positive is recommended. Thirdly, knowledge of results is taken to be motivating (even, according to Fitts and Posner (1967) to be the only source of motivation) and learners may, therefore, be expected to acquire skills without receiving rewards extrinsic to the task itself.

It might be argued that many of these differences are merely differences of degree. Certainly both paradigms aspire to the status of subsets of the empirical/scientific paradigm for the investigation and explanation of events although, as should be clear from the above, they differ in their respective criteria for the acceptability of evidence. It is perhaps this closeness which makes it difficult to distinguish between the practical acquisition procedures adopted by trainers who none the less claim to be operating in totally different paradigms. As indicated in the introductory chapter, the cybernetic paradigm for skill acquisition is the most obvious source of SST, particularly as it has been applied in the work of Michael Argyle and his colleagues. Trower *et al.* (1978a) for example make explicit (p. 11) the cybernetic and hierarchical nature of their model thus: 'social behaviour is organised heirarchically in that there are small behavioural elements, carried out more or less automatically, and larger units which are monitored according to a plan and ongoing feedback'. They also make clear the relationship of the phases of the SST sequence to the four critical variables in the acquisition of any skill, social or otherwise, namely practice, feedback, demonstration and guidance.

As will be detailed in the third section of this chapter many other SST programmes in remedial, developmental and specialised settings use acquisition procedures clearly within this paradigm although, interestingly, many do so without acknowledging their antecedents.

The Experiential Paradigm. Each of the previous paradigms has had a substantial influence upon the development of SST and while disagreement on detail exists, they can, between them, provide a coherent rationale for the entire acquisition procedure. The experiential paradigm has had a less direct but none the less significant influence. It underpins procedures such as role-plays, psychodrama and so on which in some respects resemble the practice phase of SST. Since many trainers come to SST following work in this tradition, reference to evidence from it is often made in discussion of the relative importance of the practice phase within SST (this topic is further discussed in Chapter

2, p. 64).

In the experiential paradigm individual trainees are taken to be unique (and uniquely worthwhile) organisations of purpose, intention and capacity for whom a personal set of solutions to the problems of skilful interaction will exist. These solutions may not be manifest in observable behaviour and indeed the trainee may be unable to provide a coherent verbal account of them. He can experience them and report that he has done so but, since they remain essentially covert, he must discover them for himself. Training consists only of exposing him to an appropriate range of problem situations.

A major difference between this and the previous paradigms is the emphasis upon individual uniqueness. Individual differences are acknowledged and, indeed are a focus for current research (as discussed in Chapters 2, 5 and 7) within both the conditioning and cybernetic paradigms, but it is there assumed that variation occurs within a framework of regularities in behaviour and cognition which are taken to be universal in humankind or, at least, in humankind as it registers for courses of SST.

The Teleological Paradigm. In the teleological paradigm it is assumed that analysis of and subsequent commitment to ends automatically generate effective means, and, furthermore, that explicit concern with means might inhibit creative and effective pursuit of ends. Thus a trainee would be encouraged to consider at length the purpose and patterns of effective interaction in his domestic, social or professional setting, but would be left to improvise his own technology of behaviour change to bring about improvement. This model may be derived from a consideration of everyday action, where the tactics of interpersonal behaviour are not usually themselves a focus for conscious analysis and selection but flow automatically from the motivation to achieve certain ends.

The prohibition against the analysis and systematic exploration of strategies for action thus enshrined in this paradigm might suggest that it could have no possible influence upon the acquisition procedures of SST. Indeed, within this paradigm reside the most trenchant criticisms of SST which is likened to a mechanistic and fundamentally inhibitory unpicking of the seamless garment of purposeful and freely-chosen action. As in the experiential paradigm emphasis is placed upon the uniqueness of each trainee and each interactional setting, but here training is stripped of its last vestige of control. The trainer denies his obligation to provide the trainee with a sequence of role-plays or other situations thought appropriate to his particular problems. In the remedial or developmental context this suggests that the trainee merely discusses hypothetical difficulties in hypothetical situations with resulting increase in insight and in the specialised context suggests merely that such discussion might best take place subsequent to exposure to professional practice through a lengthy period of placement.

Despite the apparent opposition of this paradigm to those with which SST is most closely related, namely the conditioning and cybernetic paradigms, traces of its influence can be detected in SST practice. Thus in the assertiveness training literature much time and print is devoted to discussion of the precise distinction between assertive and aggressive behaviours and upon the rights and obligations of 'oppressed' or 'minority' groups to over-assert until being black, female, homosexual or whatever no longer produces expectations of deference to non-minority interactors. Such discussion is obviously discussion of values and appropriate social 'ends' and since it is also encouraged (Lange & Jakubowski, 1976; Butler, 1976b; Minor, 1978) in groups of trainees, the assumption is made that trainees' capacities to devise 'means' for interaction will be enhanced – a clear instance of the teleological paradigm in application. Other such applications can be detected in the specialised SST literature as will be detailed later in this chapter.

Thus the practice if not the principle of SST reflects the influence of the teleological paradigm. Conversely, proponents of this paradigm rarely apply it in its purest form since exemplars (albeit hypothetical) are inevitably selected for discussion and, indeed, in the specialised setting particular forms and sequences of placement are generally specified and arranged.

Paradigms for the Identification of Social Skills

The conditioning, cybernetic and (in practice but not in principle) the experiential and teleological paradigms all require some analysis of social interaction and, by implication at least, identification of social skills. The techniques of analysis and identification employed, however, are not always epistemologically compatible with the acquisition model underlying the training procedure and separate categorisation is, therefore, appropriate.

Fundamentally, approaches tend to favour one side or the other of the classic rationalist-empiricist debate: that is the trainer identifies the skills by reflection or by observation. Further subdivision is, however, possible and the categories here proposed are the empirical, the analytical and the intuitive.

The Empirical Paradigm. The empirical paradigm for the identification of skills involves systematic observation, recording, categorisation and analysis of appropriate interaction to identify skills and groupings of skills. The relative importance of these skills and, after training, their relationship to desired outcomes is to be determined by observation and, where possible, quasi or full-blown experiment, with associated measurement and statistical analysis.

This traditionally scientific paradigm might be assumed to be necessary to the conditioning paradigm for skill acquisition, highly desirable in the cybernetic paradigm, useful but insufficient in the experiential paradigm and at best a necessary evil in the teleological paradigm. In fact, however, no training procedure adopts an exclusively empirical methodology in analysing and identifying skills. The behaviour analysis preceding some forms of individualised assertiveness training (Hersen & Bellack, 1977) or practised in the specialised industrial context by Rackham and Morgan (1977) comes closest to the ideal, but even there observation and analysis takes place within restrictions which were not themselves empirically derived. Thus Hersen and Bellack follow Wolpe and Lazarus (1966) and Zigler and Phillips (1960) in assuming that lack of assertiveness is the aspect of social skill deficit most handicapping and most amenable to treatment: an assumption based upon clinical judgement rather than strict empiricism. Rackham and Morgan (1977) do determine skills from raw observation of videotape without previously-determined categories but even they include (p.19) 'meaningfulness to the person being measured' as one of their criteria for skill identification – surely a source of bias reflecting the capacity of that individual for accurate or inaccurate perception of his own activities.

In microteaching the behaviourist originators of the technique set much store upon the eventual empirical identification of the component skills of teaching and while they (Allen & Ryan, 1969) were disarmingly frank about the non-empirical origins of their own set of skills, they did much to foster the burgeoning systems of classroom interaction analysis as a potential source of component skills. These systems for observation, recording and analysis (Simon & Bowyer, 1970) had a history (Medley & Mitzel, 1963) stretching back to the early years of the century and were ostensibly operationally behaviourist instruments (although the bona fides of some of the categories in relation to observable behavioural events were always dubious). Unfortunately attempts to relate the categories of skilled behaviour thus discerned to desired professional outcomes (pupil achievement for example) have (Rosenshine, 1971) proved rather disappointing. This, together with the inevitably painstaking nature of the analysis itself, has led to a situation in which component skills in microteaching (and micro-counselling) are less and less likely to be derived entirely within the empirical paradigm. Rather (as in assertiveness training) empirical analysis is likely to take place *within* skill categories traditional to the particular form of SST but themselves determined by reflection rather than observation. Macleod and McIntyre (1977) in a similar departure from pure empiricism advocate investigation (with an empirical basis where appropriate) of the long-term cognitive strategies which teachers employ as opposed to observation of large samples of possibly unique sequences of teaching behaviour. Behavioural analysis of teaching skills as exemplars of the broader strategies would then be undertaken and the results used for inclusion in the microteaching programme.

Thus the pure application of the empirical paradigm has been tempered not only by pragmatism but by the logical necessity for pre-empirical analysis and theorising.

The Analytical Paradigm. In this paradigm skills emerge from theory and analysis rather than from ostensibly atheoretical observation. The clear demarcation and systematic organisation of skills is stressed and it is assumed that the most effective method of determining the hierarchy of skills is the considered deliberation of rational men without recourse to specially undertaken observation and measurement. The technique is rarely advanced as an ideal by social skill trainers, but given the lack of immediately available empirical evidence all have used it.

The Intuitive Paradigm. In this paradigm systematic analysis is eschewed and the intuition of the experienced interactor is seen as the prime source of knowledge. Communication of skill is by interactional osmosis and identification and categorisation are anathematised.

Such a paradigm seems far removed from the systematic rigour of SST, yet within specialised settings it is endorsed by many professional tutors who approve of the opportunities for 'safe' simulated practice and greater access to student performance offered by SST but who can only accept the specific skills emphasis as an unfortunate concomitant.

The value of professional intuition is borne out by the fact that in some areas at least the ratings which professional tutors make of students' degree of skill do bear a close relationship (Rosenshine, 1971) to the capacity of such students to produce desirable professional outcomes. It has often (Simon & Bowyer, 1970) been stressed that one of the most valuable contributions empirical interaction analysis can make is in helping professional or otherwise experienced interactors to render their intuitions explicit. Thus a meta-language would be developed in which interaction might be discussed between trainees, trainers and other relevant interactors (e.g. classroom teachers, field-work supervisors, more advanced trainees). A further outcome of such a development would be its contribution to the identification of component skills for SST.

The Relative Influence of the Paradigms

The settings within which SST takes place were categorised in the introductory chapter as remedial, developmental and specialised. We have noted that practitioners within each of the settings have worked in relative isolation developing separate traditions and literatures. The separation is particularly clear between remedial and specialised SST while the developmental literature is both less extensive and less clearly demarcated from the other two traditions. Indeed, it might even be possible to subdivide developmental SST into programmes derived in emulation of remedial equivalents (and often developed for so-called 'at risk' children) and those derived in emulation of specialised trainings and more likely to be deployed with broad groups of children – school leavers, non-certificate pupils etc.

Given this relative separation of approaches, it is not surprising to find that the paradigms outlined above have had different degrees of influence in each setting. The extent of these influences will now be explored.

Remedial SST

The remedial use of SST was defined in the introductory chapter as the development of programmes for those whose repertoire of effective social behaviours is deemed by themselves or others to be inadequate for everyday life. It is generally associated with a hypothesised pathology. Programmes have been devised for a very wide range of trainees within the rubric and have been carried out in ward, out-patient and other settings, and in isolation or in combination (Phillips, 1980) with other forms of psychotherapy. Most authors in this setting acknowledge a debt to the work of Salter (1949), Wolpe (1958) and Wolpe and Lazarus

(1966) who developed assertiveness training as a direct derivative of classical conditioning. A widespread debt is similarly acknowledged to the work of Zigler and his colleagues (Zigler & Phillips, 1960; Levine & Zigler, 1973) who were primarily interested in the relationship between levels of social competence in psychiatric patients measured on admission to hospital and their success or relapse on release into the community after treatment.

Zigler's work is influential not so much for its recommendations for training as in its demonstration that social behaviour and empirically-identifiable social skills were both important predictors of patients' recovery and relatively ignored in treatment. Wolpe, on the other hand (with Lazarus, 1966) gave clear procedural guidelines for training and devised the first of several inventories and questionnaires (see Chapters 2 and 3) now available for the identification of non-assertive individuals and for the analysis of their specific difficulties.

Thus the acknowledged progenitors of SST for remedial purposes derived their training procedures from within the conditioning paradigm and developed skill identification techniques open to empirical validation. This was a logical conjunction of the conditioning acquisition paradigm with the empirical identification paradigm although the rigour of Wolpe and Lazarus' (1966) empiricism is open to question. No data on the reliability and validity of their questionnaire were presented and, indeed, the decision to focus upon assertiveness rather than any other subset of social competence was determined by clinical judgement and intuition rather than empirical enquiry.

It may be a result of Wolpe and Lazarus' failure to note the restrictedness of assertiveness training that their work has given rise to a major confusion in the literature wherein the expression 'social skills training' is commonly used where the narrower 'assertiveness training' would be more appropriate and, conversely, so-called assertiveness training often attends to skills and adopts procedures well outside the original canon.

However named, the clearest line of development within the conditioning and empirical paradigms is to be found in the work of Bellack and Hersen (1979) whose social skill training is a development of assertiveness training. Their acquisition procedures follow Wolpe and Lazarus and include demonstration, practice and feedback phases, while their techniques of skill identification include the equally traditional questionnaires and clinical interviews. As might be expected they stress the rigorous empirical evaluation of the work and, indeed, have helped to develop appropriately validated instruments for measuring the progress of individual trainees and of groups of trainees.

Despite the substantial endorsement of the scientific paradigm thus manifest, the fifteen years since Wolpe and Lazarus' original work have seen a softening of the behaviourist viewpoint advanced and it is now to some extent debatable whether this variety of SST can be said to fall within the conditioning paradigm for acquisition. A particular departure from the strict stimulus-response view of training is reflected in Hersen and Bellack's (1976) comment that (p. 575) 'behaviour therapists have increasingly recognised that intraorganismic processes must be taken into account if meaningful broad-reaching behaviour change is to occur'.

They develop the theme by discussing the increasing influence throughout behaviour modification (and hence upon SST practitioners) of the self-monitoring and self-rewarding techniques proposed by Kanfer and Goldstein (1975) and Kazdin (1975). In these techniques patients are encouraged to observe their own behaviour, compare it to some internalised criterion and give themselves rewards on the basis of the self-evaluation. The entire process could in theory happen without the intervention or even knowledge of the therapist, although in practice therapists discuss the specification and analysis of appropriate behaviour and help patients to set targets and establish reward schedules.

The application of these techniques in SST is an increasingly proposed (Hersen & Bellack, 1976a; Van Hasselt *et al.*, 1979; Zielinski & Williams, 1979) solution to the problems of ensuring generalisation of SST training to real-life settings. In particular it is suggested (Zielinski & Williams, 1979) that covert or imagined role-play can be successfully substituted for actual acting-out, that generalisation could be promoted by including covert role-play towards the end of a programme of overt role-play and (p. 862) that covert role-play 'has the potential to be used in future, unanticipated problem situations'.

Thus it is recognised (Bellack, 1979) that 'several factors . . . have not been adequately addressed . . . including the importance of assessing social perception skills and cognitions affecting interpersonal behaviour'. Emphasis is being placed upon patients' internalised store of problem-solving strategies and SST is seen, at least in part, as a process of modification of such strategies. This emphasis upon cognitive strategies is further elaborated in Meichenbaum's (1977) *Cognitive Behaviour Modification* which could be categorised as a form of SST in so far as behaviours are isolated, practised and the subject of feedback. A distinguishing feature, however, is the major emphasis upon trainees' internal dialogue.

Meichenbaum posits three processes of change, namely (1977, p. 218) '(1) the client's behaviours and the reactions they elicit in the environment; (2) the client's internal dialogue or what he says to himself before, accompanying and following his behaviour and (3) the client's cognitive structures that give rise to the specific dialogue'. Change is promoted by practising behaviours in role-play situations and developing new things for the client to say to himself as he prepares his responses. Notionally the new internal dialogue is less irrational and more likely to engender appropriate responses.

Meichenbaum's techniques (as reflected in their name) borrow from both the conditioning and cybernetic acquisition paradigms and the increasing reference to them and to similar methods in the assertiveness training literature thus represents a shift in remedial SST from simple adherence to the conditioning paradigm towards a more sophisticated amalgam of both conditioning and cybernetic approaches.

Other developments from assertiveness training include the looser developments of the technique in which trainers modify procedures to include much non-specific discussion of role-plays and skill structure and the development of trainees' insight into behaviour, while ostensibly maintaining a rigorous behaviourist viewpoint. It is arguable that such trainers have moved away from the conditioning paradigm in spite of themselves and that they have moved through the cybernetic paradigm to the experiential!

As indicated earlier in this chapter the most explicit exploitation of the cybernetic paradigm for acquisition in remedial SST is represented in the work of Michael Argyle and his colleagues (Trower *et al.*, 1978a). There is much emphasis in their procedures upon the hierarchical nature of skill and upon the manipulation of modelling and feedback modes and it is assumed that cognitive as well as behavioural changes can be usefully discussed and, indeed, pursued. Where appropriate (as in discussion of feedback) concepts and techniques are borrowed from the conditioning paradigm but these are subsumed within the broader cybernetic framework. They suggest (p. 125, our parentheses) that:

> both approaches are firmly committed to scientific evaluation and to meeting the requirements of experimental design, but the American studies [i.e. SST within the conditioning paradigm] have, we believe, generally ended up being too rigid in their methods, with a subsequent loss in appropriateness and relevance to daily life. The English studies [i.e. within the cybernetic paradigm] have been more

flexible in tempering experimental with real-life considerations, resulting in some loss of rigour but more meaningfulness.

The techniques for skill identification recommended by Trower and his colleagues (Trower *et al*., 1978) are necessarily more complex than those of Hersen and Bellack and others working in the assertiveness training tradition since the skill deficit to be identified and, if possible, remediated is not restricted to lack of assertiveness. Indeed, Trower makes it clear (1979) that for truly valid assessment a comprehensive model which applies to all social interaction may be a necessary precursor. Given the present lack of such a model the techniques recommended are best described as empirical where possible and rigorously analytical where not. (The techniques are more fully discussed in Chapters 2 and 3.)

Trower, Argyle *et al*. are, as noted, the chief proponents of the cybernetic acquisition model but one or two techniques embracing cybernetic principles have been developed in apparent isolation from Argyle's work. These include Goldstein's (1973) Structured Learning Therapy, Liberman's (1975) Personal Effectiveness Training and arguably (see above) Meichenbaum's (1977) Cognitive Behaviour Therapy. Interestingly skill identification is not rigorously pursued in any of these techniques. While lists of skills are presented and recommendations made as to how they might be operationalised for training purposes, it is clear that the personal intuitions of the trainee and the clinical judgement of the trainer make the major contribution to the isolation of skills for inclusion in any individual trainee's programme. Some questionnaires are used but data on reliability and validity are patchy or non-existent. Thus these programmes may be said to be derived from the cybernetic acquisition paradigm and from a mixture of the analytical and intuitive identification paradigms.

It might be argued that any form of psychotherapy is social skill training in so far as the intended outcomes of, say, Rational Emotive Therapy (Ellis, 1958) or even psychoanalysis would certainly include improved interpersonal relationships. Were such a broad approach adopted, remedial social skill training programmes devised entirely with the teleological and intuitive acquisition paradigms and incorporating skill identification exercises based exclusively upon analysis and intuition would assuredly be encountered. Such programmes would not, however, fall within the boundaries of SST as we have discussed and defined it. The exemplars of these paradigms which can be found in remedial SST are, as outlined above, instances where trainers have had recourse to the methodology *faute de mieux* and the most centrally-influential paradigms in remedial SST are clearly the conditioning and cybernetic paradigms for skill acquisition and the empirical paradigm for skill identification.

Developmental SST

Developmental SST programmes were defined in the introductory chapter as those aimed at the acceleration and facilitation of developmental sequences which might be expected to occur without intervention but more slowly or in a distorted form. Thus programmes have been devised for children and young adults who are well within the normal population or who are thought to be at risk of social incompetence but who, in either case, have yet to manifest major symptoms of such incompetence.

Social education in its widest form has been the subject of considerable attention in recent years. In part this is a reflection of the increased pastoral role adopted by the school and other agencies. In its turn this may reflect the increased isolation of so-called 'nuclear' families and, conceivably, an increased awareness of relationship between early childhood experience and subsequent performance in work, family and social roles. This increased awareness has been buttressed by a growing body of research demonstrating that levels of social competence in children can be reliably related to adult adjustment problems. Thus, social isolation in children has been associated with: juvenile delinquency (Roff *et al.*, 1972; Stott, 1966); dropping out of school (Ullman, 1957); and a wide range of other difficulties. Van Hasselt *et al.* (1979) review this research and conclude (p. 414) that:

> the aforementioned findings clearly indicate the importance of effective intervention for children who demonstrate poor social competence . . . approaches which enhance the interpersonal skills of these children may find some utility in the amelioration of current dysfunction and in the prevention of long-term aversive consequences of early skill deficits.

The pattern of normal social development has also been the focus of recent psychological and linguistic research as the importance of early childhood interaction (Schaffer, 1974, 1978; Waterson & Snow, 1978; Tizard, 1973; McTear, 1978, 1979) for language and communicative competence has been recognised. In part this recognition has reflected an increased capability for detailed analysis as the technology of video-recording and other varieties of 'baby watching' (Bower, 1977) has been improved.

In the later years of childhood, too, increased attention has been given to the development of aspects of children's social, moral and political awareness (Bronfenbrenner, 1967; Hess & Torney, 1967; Morrison & McIntyre, 1971, 1973) in the light of the possibly cataclysmic dangers of a world of international social incompetence.

The breadth of objectives for social education from the prevention of individual distress to the development of social and political awareness on a global scale has, inevitably, engendered confusion as to appropriate techniques for the achievement of such ends. Clearly no one technique is likely to be influential across the spectrum. Social education within the school curriculum well exemplifies this confusion: it has included everything from traditional social science teaching to fund-raising for lepers, preparation for job-seeking and aspects of human-biology teaching. It is perhaps not surprising in that context to find that the members of the Department of Education and Science's Further Education Curriculum Review and Development Unit refer (Annual Report, 1979, p. 5) to 'social and life skills' as 'a new and vaguely defined subject which has emerged without sufficient debate'.

Some of the confusion is the result of failure to distinguish between education for the accomplishment of very general long-term aims (e.g. that pupils should be capable of rational political judgement) and education for the achievement of very specific and fairly short-term objectives (e.g. that pupils should present themselves well in the first 60 seconds of job interviews). In the first instance the best promotion and prediction of pupils' eventual capabilities is probably still effected through traditional teaching and assessment techniques like essay-writing, question and answer exercises and so on. In the second, however, pupils' increased skills may be taught and measured closer to the anticipated real events for which they are being prepared. If the pupil performs well in a simulation interview exercise on Monday it is reasonable to suppose he has an increased likelihood of so doing in a real interview on Tuesday. Furthermore, it is easier in such an exercise to identify and promote specific behaviour thought relevant to the circumscribed conditions being simulated: such circumscription barely exists with respect to the first exercise and the gap between the specific behaviour taught (e.g. capacity to marshal facts for an essay, ability to argue logically in debate) and the ultimate aim is thus much wider.

It is clearly easier to develop exercises akin to SST in respect to specific situations and it has, indeed, been the case that SST in school settings has tended to be restricted to the more specific aspects of 'social and life skills'. However, some simulation exercises have been devised in which pupils have engaged in 'war games' or 'business games', the objectives of which have included both the accomplishment of specific short-term skills and the development of longer-term strategies for behaviour. If, indeed, it is argued (as it would be in the cybernetic paradigm) that the development of such strategies is an essential aspect of SST then the argument shifts from 'which technique is best – specific skill training, or the traditional procedures of reading, writing and disputation?' to 'which circumstances best engender behavioural and cognitive change – debate and disputation related to simulation exercises and skill training or debate and disputation in the traditional classroom?' This and similar issues will be discussed with specific reference to specialised SST in Chapter 6, but in the present context it will suffice to point out that SST may be necessary to the social education curriculum without also being sufficient to it. Thus straw-man arguments regarding the inappropriateness of 'training' in a value-laden area of 'education' may be avoided.

A further distinction which may help to clarify discussion of developmental SST (particularly as it takes place in school settings) is the distinction between SST where social development is a primary aim and SST where it is an incidental outcome or at most a secondary aim. Morrison and McIntyre (1971) make the point that all teachers are agents of socialisation and comment (p. 124) that:

> formal education becomes a potent means of social influence: it enables adults to deploy their social power with great effect as teachers of classes and as controllers of encounters between major categories of pupils; and it creates informal peer groups . . . which can operate with powerful and lasting effects on interpersonal behaviour.

Similarly Cartledge and Milburn (1978) make the case 'that social behaviours are taught informally all the time in the school classroom' and go on to review a large number of studies in which conditioning techniques have been applied as classroom management measures or in promotion of 'classroom survival skills' (Cobb, 1970). These skills include paying attention, volunteering or complying with directions and have been shown to be associated with academic achievement. Thus social skill training with clear short-term objectives takes place as a necessary strategy for maintenance of social order in individual schools and classrooms. Implicitly the assumption may be made that such training will be appropriately generalised to the world beyond that school or classroom but the main aim is classroom management.

Social education, therefore, subserves a wide spectrum of aims and objectives from the most far-reaching, long-term and value-laden, to the narrowest specifics of classroom convention and it is effected through a range of techniques from the formal to the informal and the behaviourally specific to the intuitively vague.

In spite of the diversity it is possible to detect a number of influences and to relate them to the paradigms outlined in the first section of this chapter. The conditioning paradigm for skill acquisition has, for example, been most influential in the area of overlap between developmental and remedial SST. That is in SST with individual children referred by parents or teachers or selected by trainers as at least at risk of social incompetence if not already displaying it. Van Hasselt *et al.* (1979) present a comprehensive review of some 30 published studies of this kind from which it is clear (p. 413) that 'applications of behavioural techniques to the evaluation and remediation of interpersonal skills' deficiencies in children have proliferated in recent years'. While the results of such studies are generally encouraging problems remain with regard to skill isolation and categorisation, to the generalisation and maintenance of positive results and to the optimum procedures to be followed. Procedurally, indeed, in the 30 studies reviewed by Van Hasselt *et al.* almost 30 different varieties are adopted and, apart from the basic emphasis upon behavioural specificity and the vaguely 'social' nature of the target behaviours it is difficult in this context to determine exactly what SST *is*.

The conditioning paradigm has also been a potent influence in developmental SST with children not 'at risk' or, at least, less obviously so since their 'selection' by teachers as targets for behaviour modification may imply the failure of regular classroom management methods. In this context the pioneering work of Becker and his colleagues (Becker, 1973; Becker *et al.*, 1967; Madsen *et al.*, 1968) provides a blue-print for a very large number of subsequent studies again varying in methodology but sharing the broadly behaviourist approach and tackling loosely 'social' behaviours. A defining feature of such work is the fact that it takes place in normal classrooms and is implemented by regular class teachers after short periods of training. Hops and Cobb (1973) divide such classroom studies into those which have specifically interpersonal target behaviours and those which have task-related behaviours as targets. Following this distinction Cartledge and Milburn

(1978) cite interpersonal programmes fostering increased encounter frequency and altruistic behaviour and decreased aggressive behaviour and task-related programmes fostering skills including paying attention, obeying rules and asking and answering questions.

Explicit acknowledgement of the cybernetic paradigm for developmental SST does not occur in frequency comparable to acknowledgement of the conditioning paradigm. This may be because it is not in fact applied or may be because it is so universally applied as to be worthy of neither note nor publication. Many of the simulation exercises in employment preparation schemes or in social and life skills training (Davies, 1979; ILEA, 1978; Spence, 1979; Priestley *et al.*, 1978; Saskatchewan Newstart, 1972) do specify skills and almost all go through a sequence of demonstration, practice and feedback strongly reminiscent of formal applications of the cybernetic paradigm. As indicated earlier, however, there is considerable confusion in the literature surrounding such schemes and, indeed, in the procedures adopted in relation to their stated aims.

In most cases the approach adopted is pragmatic as exemplified in Priestley *et al.* s introductory comment (1978, p. 5) 'we advocate the adoption of a jackdaw attitude towards anything at all that may be of value in particular problem-solving approaches'. True to their own prescription some of the techniques Priestley *et al.* describe are recognisably within the cybernetic paradigm but many others are experiential or teleological.

It is noteworthy that the more general social and life skills training (i.e. for groups of 'normal' or non-referred children in regular classroom settings) is much less likely to manifest acknowledgement of application of the more systematic and rigorous techniques of the conditioning paradigm than are the developmental programmes dealing with at-risk children. This may reflect the separate clinical and educational traditions to which the two types of developmental SST respectively relate. It is conversely clear that the experiential and teleological paradigms are much more manifest in the social and life skills literature than they are in developmental SST with at-risk individuals. Thus role-plays, experience schemes and much discussion and debate are central to the programmes described by the DES Social and Life Skills Unit in the Annual Report of 1979, the Schools Council Curriculum Project in Social Education and other such schemes. The unpredictability of social events and the uniqueness of each individual's experience are taken to render specific systematic training unprofitable, if not impossible, and the best that can be achieved is debate regarding the 'ends' of social action.

SST is not a sufficient answer to the problems of curriculum design in social education and the diversity of approaches outlined above might, therefore, be applauded. Less laudable, however, is the mismatch between curriculum objectives and procedures adopted. A carefully tailored programme of exercises in which pedagogic means are related to curricular ends is *not* the same as Priestley *et al.'s* (1978) 'jackdaw's nest'. This issue will be more fully discussed in Chapter 6.

As might be expected in a setting of such procedural diversity, exemplars of each of the three paradigms for skill identification (empirical, analytical, intuitive) can be detected in the developmental literature and, as in remedial SST, many programmes aspire to empirical identification but have recourse to analytic or intuitive methods *faute de mieux*.

In studies with at-risk children an initial screening procedure is generally adopted for the selection of children manifesting a specific deficit (e.g. 'isolated', 'emotionally unstable' or 'aggressive') which is itself selected as an important facet of social competence through analytical examination of the clinical and educational literature. Van Hasselt *et al.* (1979) comment upon the diversity of definitions of social skills in children which have been adopted – some of which stress rather negative or 'hostile' abilities while others stress co-operative, positive behaviours which would receive minus scores on the assertiveness scales. Similar inconsistencies occur in the assessment of social isolation (Gottman *et al.*, 1975; Gottman, 1977), where measures based upon frequency of interaction with peers have been shown not to correlate with measures based upon reported acceptability to peers, yet they are frequently taken to be alternative measures of the same variable. It is also surprising to note that little, if any, cognisance is taken of the growing literature (Waterson & Snow, 1978) in communicative development or indeed of the developmental literature as a whole. With a few exceptions it is assumed that, for example, children's social performance will be unaffected by their developing capacity to take the role of another or to consider simultaneously their own and other viewpoints. As Van Hasselt *et al.* (1979) conclude 'there are several problems requiring attention from researchers in the future' if a more satisfactory approach is to be made to the empirical goal.

In the more educational applications of developmental SST, the analytical and intuitive paradigms are more purposefully embraced and as implied in the previous discussion of acquisition paradigms pragmatism is at a premium. It is surprising to have to report that the available empirical procedures for the analysis of classroom interaction which have been influential in developing SST for teachers have not been exploited in its development for pupils. This is again an area for future research as is the entirely feasible application of behavioural observation and analysis (in any systematic form) to the often circumscribed areas (job-seeking; consumer complaint; interviews with public officials, etc.) which feature in the training programmes developed.

Specialised SST

Specialised SST is defined as SST provided for trainees who are taken to have already achieved at least normal adult levels of skill but who have particular vocational or professional objectives which necessitate sophisticated or specialised forms of interaction. All but the most isolated occupations demand interaction with others at times, but some jobs have skilled interaction as a primary focus and it is in training for these occupations that specialised SST programmes have typically been developed. They include what has been described (Ellis, 1980) as the interpersonal professions, i.e. teachers, social workers, counsellors, therapists, paramedical and medical personnel, salesmen and managers.

Microteaching now takes place in around 80 per cent of teacher training institutions in the UK and is also widely available in the USA, Australia, Africa and Western Europe (Hargie & Maidment, 1979). While programmes vary in format they share a basic model in which teaching skills are observed and analysed and component skills derived. These skills are then trained in a procedure involving modelling, practice and feedback. Such programmes are exemplars of the cybernetic paradigm in application but often without acknowledgement. Programme designers are more likely to refer to the origins of their procedures in conditioning and to resort to pragmatic arguments in justification of their departures from pure application of behaviourist methodology.

As already made clear the technique was originally based upon behaviour modification and thus upon the conditioning paradigm although McDonald (1973) also acknowledges an explicit debt to Bandura's social learning theory (Bandura, 1971) which might be regarded as a rather impure behaviourism.

Ellis and Whittington (1972) predicted the microteaching paradigm would spread to other professional groups and as outlined in Ellis (1980) programmes now exist for health visitors, social workers, speech therapists, counsellors, vocational guidance personnel, youth and community workers, nurses and doctors.

Many of these professional groups adopting SST had existing

traditions for the promotion of appropriate styles of client-professional interaction and, typically, these now co-exist with SST. Thus it is customary for teachers in training experiencing microteaching also to engage in traditional teaching practice. There, as Stones and Morris (1972) report, skills are identified intuitively by student, supervisor and class teacher, assessment categories lack behavioural referents and training is by a process of interactional osmosis. This experiential training paradigm is also reflected in the practicum elements of other professions adopting SST. Social work students for example typically experience procedures teleologically derived in the quasi-philosophical areas of their curriculum and experientially practised in role-plays, simulations, case discussions and finally, fieldwork placement. We have commented elsewhere upon the anomalous nature of such a hotch-potch curriculum and have proposed what we hope is a more coherent model (Ellis & Whittington, 1979) which is elaborated in Chapter 6.

SST in commerce and industry has been relatively uninfluenced by microteaching although the techniques derived are sometimes not dissimilar. The models most often acknowledged (Bradley, 1976; Mandia, 1974) are those derived from counselling techniques, notably Ivey and Authier's (1978) micro-counselling and Berne's (1976) transactional analysis. As in the public sector professions discussed above the major tradition in social skill training for managers and other personnel relies heavily upon on-the-job learning and tutelage to experienced supervisors. Where simulation techniques have been used these have generally derived from extensions of psychodynamic theory (Cooper & Mangham, 1971) and have focused upon individual self-awareness rather than behaviour change.

Recent developments towards more systematic procedures, however, include Rackham and Morgan's (1977) work with airline personnel and the elaboration of assertiveness training (O'Donnelly & Colby, 1979; Shaw & Rutledge, 1976; Onoda & Gassert, 1978) for industrial and commercial purposes. These authors acknowledge the origins of their acquisition techniques within the cybernetic (Rackham & Morgan, 1977) or conditioning paradigms.

As previously noted, the skill identification paradigm first endorsed in specialised SST was strictly empirical but the results of attempts to relate the skills isolated to appropriate professional outcomes were not encouraging. In part as a result the skill identification techniques now typical in specialised SST continue to aspire to the empirical but are in fact substantially analytical and, at times, intuitive. As Hargie and Maidment (1979) point out, the original skills proposed by Allen and

Ryan (1969), the analytical origins of which were entirely obvious, have survived the rigours of ten years' application in hundreds of diverse microteaching programmes. Similarly the component skills of micro-counselling advanced by Ivey (1971) have continued to enjoy popularity despite their lack of rigorous empirical validation by disinterested investigators who have not already invested time and effort in programme design based upon the very skills they seek to validate.

In the professional areas where SST is novel, such as speech therapy and medicine, lists of component skills do not come readily to hand from popularised training programmes. Arguably, therefore, SST should not take place until empirical observation and analysis of appropriate professional interactions have been undertaken and component skills isolated therefrom. In practice, however, discussion with experienced professionals together with rigorous application of the analytical paradigm can produce apparently useful lists of skills and, indeed, a number of skills (see Chapter 3) seem to have generic validity across a wide range of professions. Some advances have, none the less, been made in the analysis of professional interaction in these newer areas (Korsch & Negrette, 1972; Ley, 1977; Oratio, 1977) and ultimately these must surely provide the basis for skill identification.

Rackham and Morgan (1977) provide a detailed account of the application of behaviour analysis to the tasks undertaken by airline personnel and describe the effect of feedback from such analysis upon training but their work is unique in private-sector SST.

Specialised SST can thus provide exemplars of each of the seven paradigms in application and it is not unusual for individual trainees to experience a variety of approaches during their novitiate.

Conclusion

The diversity of approaches to SST can thus be seen to originate sometimes in high-minded principle, sometimes in scurrilous pragmatism and more often in half-understood contingency. The novice trainer will no doubt be similarly influenced in devising programmes, but it is a central thesis of this book that trainers should *know* when decisions are being made on principle and when upon baser grounds. Without such awareness development is always haphazard and systematic evaluation difficult, if not impossible.

2 PLANNING THE PROGRAMME

Social skills training has many variations. The skills used are a function of settings, clients and purposes; the learning experiences devised reflect available time, space and staff; and both are fundamentally determined by the theoretical approaches to skill identification and acquisition favoured by the programme designer. The intending trainer, therefore, might select from a variety of possibilities. No doubt those who have turned to this book for guidance would appreciate detailed advice regarding the skills they should focus upon and the procedures they should follow to develop such skills in their trainees. Those who seek such information will find it in Chapters 3 and 4.

We believe strongly, however, that programmes of social skill training should reflect local needs. In particular we would commend a negotiation between interested parties to arrive at an appropriate set of skills and procedures. In this chapter, therefore, we try to clarify the questions which might be asked and the decisions which must be taken. Guidance is offered based on the literature and on our own experience.

Questions

If the training programme is to meet local needs the intending trainer must establish what these are. Specifically he must pose questions about the trainees, about the context of training and about available resources including trainers.

We have recommended negotiation with fellow trainers as a first step in planning, but the initiator would do well to pause before taking this step in order to consider the best ways to draw his colleagues into discussion. Fellow trainers may be involved as organisers of training, as tutors involved in selected phases of the training cycle (e.g. in feedback sessions) or as associates of training who help with homework and other exercises designed to foster the extension of training into real life. They are likely to be varied in background. In the specialised setting they would typically include the initiator of training (who may be assumed to have some degree of expertise), professional tutors approaching SST for the first time and fieldwork supervisors who may never have heard of SST. These fieldworkers may even be unable to visit the unit for training or discussion. In remedial SST participants would include clinical psychologists (the typical initiators), nurses, occupational therapists and other paramedicals. If training is being given to out-patients, spouses, colleagues and other significant members of the trainee's social circle might take part.

We discuss our own experiences of the induction and training of fellow trainers and associates in the latter part of Chapter 4. In this chapter we have suggested the questions which we recommend the initiator of training should ask before and during the negotiation and planning of his programme. We have also identified questions about context and resources which the negotiating team should ask before embarking upon detailed planning. The questions are as follows:

(1) Tutors and Associates

Knowledge and experience	What knowledge and experience of the setting and of typical trainees do they have? What knowledge and experience of SST do they have? What teaching experience do they have? What organisational experience do they have?
Theoretical orientation	What is their explicit or implicit orientation to skill analysis and acquisition?
Social skills	How socially skilled and analytical concerning their own behaviour are they?

(2) Trainees

Ability	What is their present level of skill and what, if any, are their specific deficiencies?
Situation	What particular personal or professional role are the skills intended for?
Motivation	Why are they undergoing training and how does it relate to their personal needs and aspirations?
Attitudes	What are their attitudes towards SST and towards themselves as trainees?

	Do they believe the exercise to be worthwhile and do they think they can succeed in it?
(3) Context	
Realism	How closely can the programme approximate to the conditions of relevant real-life interaction? How can it be extended into exercises conducted outside the training unit?
Related learning	How can the programme be integrated with concurrent learning experiences such as other areas in the curriculum or other forms of therapy?
(4) Resources	
Time	How much is available and how can it be used?
Space	How much accommodation is there and how can it be used?
Equipment	What equipment and materials can be used and how can they be most effective?
Staff	How many staff are available as organisers or tutors? How many can offer supportive teaching or assistance outside of the unit? What are their attitudes to SST? How can they be best deployed?

Decisions

Having answered these preliminary questions, the initiator is ready to work, with the planning team, through a sequence of decisions which will determine the programme. Broadly the sequence falls into phases concerning skills, training procedures, hardware and software, logistics and evaluation. These phases, of course, interrelate. For each phase we have given typical but not exhaustive questions which must be answered.

(1) Skills

Identification	What skills are appropriate for these trainees in the situations specified?
Operationalisation	How will these skills be reliably identified?
Selection	Which of the skills are most suitable for training?
Sequence	In what order should the skills be presented? Will each skill include skills of a finer grain?

(2) Training Procedures

Sensitisation	How will skills be presented to the trainees? Should model tapes be made? Should trainees use observation schedules? How will the skills be justified to trainees? What theoretical material should trainees encounter?
Practice	What familiarisation will trainees be given with closed-circuit television (CCTV), if used, to overcome the cosmetic effect? What form will practice take? Will 'real' clients be imported? Will actors, drama students, etc simulate clients? Will trainees simulate clients? Will role-play instructions be given? How long will trainees prepare for practice?
Feedback	What form will feedback take – audio, visual, or paper record? How will trainees view the record? How will their viewing be systematised (e.g. using observation schedules)? Who will work with trainees during feedback (e.g. tutors, peers)?

	Will feedback be followed by further practice?
Optimising transfer	How will controlled practice relate to real life? Will trainees have practical 'home-works'? Will intermediate controlled experiences be devised?

(3) Hardware and Software

Audio	How will the practice be recorded? What arrangement of microphones will be used? What kind of recorder will be used? Where and how will students hear recordings?
Video	How will practice be recorded? What kind of cameras will be used? Where will cameras be located? How will cameras be controlled? What kind of recorder will be used? Where and how will trainees view recordings?
Model tapes	Which skills need recorded models? How will these be produced? Are any commercial tapes suitable? How will trainee groups view/hear the tapes?
Observation schedules	Do suitable schedules exist? Who will devise schedules? Will schedules use categories or signs? Will schedules involve counting or rating?
Written materials	Are there suitable textbooks or off-prints for sensitisation and linked theory? Will handouts be produced?
Tapes	How many video/audio tapes or cassettes will be needed? How will tapes be stored? How long will records be kept?

(4) Logistics

Group size	How will trainees be grouped for sensitisation, practice and feedback?
Timing	How will the stages of training be timed given numbers, group size, accommodation, tutors, clients and equipment?
Clients	How will clients be brought in, instructed, occupied (e.g. school children)?

(5) Evaluation

Assessment	How will trainee achievement, practically and theoretically, be recorded and assessed?
Monitoring	How will the work of the unit be monitored and evaluated?
Modification	How will skills, procedures, logistics and evaluation change to reflect evaluation?

These questions are, we would stress, exemplary, not exhaustive: there are many others to be posed and answered if a programme is to be mounted. However, we hope the sequence offers a framework for programme planning. We have focused the guidance provided in this chapter on: skills; training procedures; programme evaluation; contexts of training and logistics.

Guidance for Planners

Skills

Determining the Skills. As has already been suggested, approaches to skill determination vary, and, as Chapter 4 will make clear, the lists of skills actually adopted by trainers working within a particular approach are also subject to considerable variation. Techniques for skill determination can, however, be usefully dichotomised. First, there are techniques which allow a skills sequence to be tailor-made for an individual trainee. In contrast, there are those which produce an off-the-peg predetermined list thought appropriate for an entire group of trainees. These approaches may be labelled, respectively, *clinical* and *curriculum* approaches.

Within each of these categories the empirical, analytical and intuitive approaches to skill identification can be found: often as indicated in Chapter 1, in combination within the practice of one programme designer. The empirical approach, it will be recalled, requires systematic observation, recording and analysis of appropriate interaction to determine skilled behaviour. The analytical approach rests upon 'armchair' analysis of agreed aims, statements of purpose and imagined needs. Thus we might *deduce* from the aims of education that the ability of teachers to 'explain clearly' is one skill even if we were never able to observe an actual teacher. If skills are chosen by trainers because they seem right – they feel appropriate – then a more intuitive approach has been adopted.

Individual 'clinical' skill sequences are most often devised in remedial settings. The assumption is made that while regularly occurring deficits in social skill do exist, they are sufficiently idiosyncratic in their expression in individual trainees to merit individualised remediation programmes.

The techniques used for the determination of skills in such settings are, typically, the classic instruments of clinical psychology namely, the psychological test coupled with behavioural observation and clinical judgement. As such they are implicitly based upon a model of competent social behaviour and are designed to find the degree of mismatch between the clients' behaviour and the implicit norm. The explication and elaboration of such models presents difficulties and the literature reporting remedial social skills training is studded with appeals (Van Hasselt *et al*., 1979; Trower 1980) for sounder models and better empirical data on normally competent social behaviour.

Some remedial programme designers (Goldstein *et al*., 1976; Liberman, 1975; Trower *et al*., 1978a) have worked on the premise that social skill deficit might be found and remedied at any point in the entire repertoire of social behaviour and have, therefore, devised very comprehensive assessment procedures. Others, however (Wolpe & Lazarus, 1966; Hersen & Bellack, 1977; Rathus, 1973; McFall & Lillesand, 1971; Lange & Jakubowski, 1976) have developed skill programmes essentially derived from Wolpe and Lazarus' (1966) observation that lack of assertiveness is a common characteristic of the anxious patient and that 'the person plagued with interpersonal anxieties is unable to respond assertively even when most necessary' (p. 39). Programmes of assertiveness training are thus predetermined in so far as they are limited to the development of behaviours regarded as 'assertive'. Within that category, however, individualised programmes of great variety have been developed and there is now a substantial literature on the observation and analysis of assertiveness. Other areas of social behaviour such as supportiveness, bargaining, or non-assertiveness, might profit from similarly enthusiastic investigation.

In both assertiveness training and the broader forms of remedial SST, assessment and skill determination techniques employed include both self-report and behavioural assessments. Most popular among the self-report measures are the various social skill inventories and the behavioural interview. They are usually used in conjunction.

The first inventory to be used specifically for the determination of component skills for SST was the Wolpe-Lazarus Assertiveness Questionnaire (1966) which consists of a series of questions apparently related to assertiveness, e.g. 'Are you able to contradict a domineering person?' 'Are you inclined to be over-apologetic?' which Wolpe and Lazarus present as a questionnaire 'intended to reveal specific areas and degrees of assertive and non-assertive interaction'. It is not a standardised instrument and it is intended as an accompaniment to a life-history questionnaire and a probing interview in which the therapist uses his clinical judgement to determine the major areas of skill deficit and potential remediation. Lange and Jakubowski (1976), in reviewing the range of assertiveness questionnaires which have succeeded the Wolpe-Lazarus Questionnaire, comment on the fact that several of them permit respondents to 'fake good' or present socially desirable responses but conclude that Galassi *et al.*'s (1975; Gay *et al.*, 1975) Adult and College Self-expression Inventories 'seem to be the most useful for measuring a wide range of different types of assertive behaviour'.

More general inventories have been developed by Goldstein *et al.* (1976) and Trower *et al.* (1978a). Goldstein's is a rating scale in which both the trainee and people who know him well or have had ample opportunity to observe him are invited to rate him on each of the 32 basic skills which constitute Goldstein's system. The programme subsequently devised is based upon the deficits apparent from the inventory and from the accompanying interview. Trower's inventories are part of a larger package of assessment techniques but comprise a relationships scale, which taps patients' social life-history, and a social situations scale which assesses the situations in which least and most discomfort are experienced. In a separate section, the social situations in which patients tend not to participate are identified. Again, the therapist is encouraged to follow up response in interview and to use his judgement in devising the specific skills programme.

As befits the behaviourist/cybernetic provenance of SST, measures of actual social performance are a feature of individualised assessment. Techniques employed include naturalistic observation in kindergarten, school and hospital ward settings (Durlak & Mannarino, 1977; Kirby & Toler, 1970; Berger & Rose, 1977) and behaviour charting (Goldstein *et al.*, 1976). In each of these, significant categories of behaviour are selected for observation and a record kept of frequency and rate of occurrence. Skill deficit is then determined from the observational profile.

Naturalistic observation assumes access to real-life social situations. In many cases such access cannot be obtained or can only be obtained in restricted areas of trainees' social behaviour such as school or hospital interactions. A more easily contrived variant of behavioural measurement is the role-play or simulated-situation measure. In this method the trainee is put in a simulated situation likely to require socially competent behaviour and his performance is recorded for subsequent analysis. A number of such role-plays are available in the literature (McFall & Marston, 1970; McFall & Lillesand, 1971; Eisler *et al.*, 1973a) but many trainers have devised their own on the basis of previous interviews or self-report tests with their trainees.

Two elaborations of the simulated-performance measure are Eisler's (1973a) Behavioural Assertiveness Test and Trower *et al.'s* (1978a) Social Interaction Test. Eisler's technique involves playing an audio-tape to the trainee which describes a series of interpersonal situations which finish with a prompt line to which the patient is asked to respond. One such situation follows (Eisler *et al.*, 1973b):

Narrator: You're in a crowded grocery store, in a hurry, and have one item to check out. You're next to be waited on when a woman with a cart full of groceries tries to cut in front of you.

Prompt: You don't mind if I cut in here do you? I'm in a hurry.

This technique is also used with the prompt given by a confederate present in the room with the trainee in which case video as well as audio-tape recording is made of the patient's response.

Trower's Social Interaction Test (1978a) is a standard simulation in which the patient is simply asked to keep conversation going with two confederates, one of whom is primed to respond positively to the trainee and one of whom is primed to respond negatively. Again, the entire performance is video-taped. Evidence on the extent to which trainees' performance in these simulated situations relates to performance in natural settings (Van Hasselt *et al.*, 1979; Bellack *et al.*, 1978) or to self-report measures (McFall & Lillesand, 1971; Friedman, 1971;

McFall & Marston, 1970) is unfortunately mixed. None the less numerous training programmes have been devised from these simulations and patients have shown at least short-term improvement.

Before programmes are derived from the BAT or SIT record, this record must, of course, be analysed. The techniques employed are the typical techniques of naturalistic observation, namely category and rating systems. These systems present the analyst of the tapes with a number of explicit aspects of behaviour which he is asked either to count or to rate. Eisler *et al*. (1973a) for example suggest four categories of non-verbal behaviour said to be significant components of assertiveness namely: duration of looking; duration of reply; loudness of speech (rated on a five-point scale); and emotional tone of voice (rated on a five-point scale). A variety of other rating scales has been proposed purporting to measure the presence or absence of assertiveness in the trainee's verbal response to BAT role-plays. Trower *et al*. (1978a) present (p.150) a much more comprehensive system for the analysis of SIT tapes which is subdivided into an 'elements' sub-test and a general impression sub-test. The 'elements' test is a system of fairly detailed behaviour categories (e.g posture tonus, posture position, gaze, gesture) within which the analyst checks the variety of behaviour present and awards a score accordingly. Posture tonus for example gets 0 for 'normal relaxed' and 4 for either 'extremely slouched, very unpleasant' or 'extremely rigid, immobile, symmetrical, very unpleasant'. The general impressions test comprises 13 bipolar adjectives (e.g. warm/cold; emotional/unemotional; masculine/feminine) with seven-point scales between them on which the analyst rates the trainee's performance . The analyst's free comment on the performance is also invited.

Outside of the remedial context this level of detailed assessment and analysis of individual competence and incompetence is rare. Rather it is assumed that a heterogeneous group of clients (e.g. school children in the developmental context or students in the specialised context) bring to training a diversity of talents and deficiencies and leave training having achieved either a minimum acceptable level of competence or a minimum acceptable degree of improvement or indeed both. Minimum levels of competence in interpersonal skill are likely to be the goals of pre-service teacher training for example where the ultimate criterion might be 'Would this student be positively harmful in the classroom?', whereas minimum acceptable degree of improvement might be the goal in a management training scheme where the organisation investing in the scheme uses a crude cost-benefit analysis, viz. 'Was it worth taking the man out of his usual role? Has he changed?' In either case it is assumed that exposure to a fixed sequence of skills – a curriculum – is the optimal technique. Such a technique is, of course, easier to derive in the sense that once determined any number of trainees may undertake the programme before it is modified and work with large groups may be possible. (Some group training is undertaken in the remedial context but either programmes tend to be less individualised or group support is only before and after training.)

The problem faced by the designer of the predetermined programme is, of course, the problem faced by the designer of the off-the-peg garment – has he got it right for the market? The risk he runs if he makes a mistake is far greater than that run by the designer of individualised programmes. It is clear, therefore, that the determination of skills for inclusion in a predetermined programme of SST is as important, if not more so, than the assessment procedures for the remedial setting discussed so far. It follows logically from their predetermination that such skills are easier to list and to adopt for use in many settings than are the skills of individualised SST. In many cases, therefore, the novice designer of SST programmes simply copies a skill list from some previous context deemed relevant to his own and modifies it as he sees fit. In microteaching, for example, Hargie (1980) reports from an international survey of institutions using microteaching that there was (p. 62) 'a tendency to accept *en bloc* the total Stanford package' and that 'only a very small percentage had conducted any original research into the analysis and development of skills'. The problems the trainer faces in modification are not, however, unlike those which would be faced by the desert-island designer who set out to derive a skills list from first principles.

We assumed at the beginning of this chapter that the trainer had some idea of the type of behaviour he wished to promote and, indeed, that most trainers in developmental and specialised settings are already involved in some other more haphazard form of skill training. All teachers would agree that social education of a kind occurs in their classroom; all social work trainers would agree that they aim to improve their students' ability to make and sustain appropriate relationships with clients. The questions to be put by the trainer in selecting or modifying skills are 'Yes, but what do I *mean* by social education or by making and sustaining appropriate relationships?' The emphasis is firmly upon analysis of competent behaviour rather than upon the detection and analysis of deficits. Not surprisingly, therefore, the techniques of skill identification here employed vary somewhat from those previously discussed.

The major tradition in specialised SST is, of course, the microteaching tradition and it is to microteaching that one might, therefore, look for the most sophisticated approaches to the identification, selection and ordering of skills. Turney *et al*. (1973) suggest that 'the skills which microteaching is designed to develop are, ideally, classroom behaviours that are specific, definable, observable, demonstrable, quantifiable and known to be causally related to desired pupils learnings'. The most cursory acquaintance with educational theory and research will, however, reveal the problems manifest in deciding what 'desired pupil learnings' are, or once defined, how they are 'causally related' to teachers' classroom behaviours. There is a very long history of research into effective training and just as the model of normally competent social behaviour implicit in the individualised programmes discussed above is imperfect, likewise the model of effective teaching (or effective action in any other professional area) needs further refinement and elaboration. It is important to recognise, therefore, that the merit of SST is not that it is based upon a perfect model of competent behaviour, but rather that skills are selected which *seem* in the light of available evidence to be significant components of competent behaviour and that these skill programmes are subject to constant evaluation and modification. There is in fact a reciprocal relationship between SST and the development of models of competent social behaviour. As the models improve so more useful lists of skills will be derived and as empirical data is amassed in the context of SST so models of competent social behaviour will improve.

The very much copied (Hargie, 1980) list of skills (see Chapter 3) suggested by the originators of microteaching, Allen and Ryan (1969), was on their own admission, derived entirely by discussion and analysis among a particular group of teacher researchers. It included, however, skills such as reinforcing, defined (p. 5) as 'the use of incentive by the teacher to reward desirable behaviours', for the importance of which considerable support can be found, not only in the commonsense view of 'good teaching' but in the literature of educational psychology. Thus it was assumed, without renewed observation and analysis of classroom interaction, that reinforcement might be taken to be an important aspect of teaching skill. Surprisingly, however, such research as has been undertaken on classroom reinforcement as it relates to pupil achievement and pupil attitudes gives a very mixed set of results (Turney *et al*., 1973; Rosenshine, 1971) nicely illustrating the dilemma of the programme designer in determining his skills.

Similarly in micro-counselling (Ivey & Authier, 1978) the identification of skills has evolved from (p. 326) 'the attempt to operationalise and teach skills *considered* to be *facilitative to counselling*' (our italics). In other words the *starting point* for the empirical analysis of competent behaviour is the rational analysis of that behaviour by people of experience and expertise. Thus the first publication describing micro-counselling (Ivey *et al.*, 1968) dealt with three skill areas (attending, reflecting feeling and summarising feeling) which had commonsense validity and were supported by a considerable literature in counselling theory. They have *subsequently* been subject to considerable empirical investigation in simulated micro-counselling sessions and in real counselling interviews.

If, then, skills are to be selected, in part at least, on the recommendations of 'experts' (whether practitioners, researchers or both) who may well disagree (Stones and Morris, 1972) the question arises 'How do you pick your expert?' Some researchers have approached this problem by analysing the perceptions of groups of individuals thought to be experienced in the area. Thus Oratio (1977) has factor-analysed the perceptions of 'effective therapy' displayed by experienced and novice speech therapists and by speech-therapy clients and has derived a list of 'technical' and 'interpersonal' skills in speech therapy on that basis. Likewise, Crowley and Ivey (1976) have factor-analysed practitioners' ratings of videotaped counselling sessions to derive sub-skills in the broad skill areas of empathy, warmth and genuineness.

Some specialised SST areas, however, do not have a significant tradition in the training of interpersonal skills and experts would, therefore, be hard to find. Empirical scrutiny of the interaction for which training is to be developed has thus been a prerequisite. Interestingly, the skills eventually derived have in some cases borne some resemblance (see Chapter 3) to those already identified in more traditional areas. Thus, Rackham and Morgan's (1977) very careful analysis of appraisal interviewing in British Airways' executives yields skills of supporting, summarising, giving and seeking information which would be very familiar to designers of micro-counselling programmes. Rackham and Morgan (p. 261) give six steps in devising their training programme which are echoed in Nuttall and Ivey's (1978) account of the development of a training programme for the sales representatives of a large pharmaceutical company. The steps are:

Step 1 Develop behaviour analysis system.
Step 2 Identify performance criteria; devise measures.
Step 3 Assess performance.

Step 4 Identify high/low performers.
Step 5 Compare the results of 4 and 5 to identify crucial behavioural dimensions.

In both cases the behaviour analysis systems of Step 1 were akin to those existing in the more extensive literatures (Simon & Bowyer, 1970) on the observation and analysis of teaching behaviour and used the basic methodology and techniques of naturalistic observation.

In summary, the strategies for skill selection and operationalisation available to the designer of individualised or predetermined programmes are (1) doing what has been done before, (2) analysing the views of 'experts' and (3) empirical observation and analysis of relevant interaction. These strategies can be amplified as follows:

(1) Doing What Has Been Done Before.

(i) Trainers may adopt an existing skills package, e.g. the Stanford microteaching skills (Allen & Ryan, 1969); Ivey's micro-counselling's skills (Ivey & Authier, 1978); Goldstein's Structured Learning Therapy (Goldstein *et al.*, 1976); Lange and Jakubowski's group version of Assertiveness Training (Lange & Jakubowski, 1976). A number of institutions have developed unpublished packages for use with a wide range of interpersonal professions and discussion with their designers would be helpful to new trainers in related areas.

(ii) Published assessment procedures for the analysis of skill deficits (e.g. Wolpe-Lazarus Assertiveness Questionnaire (1966); Behavioural Assertiveness Test (also available in a version for children, Eisler *et al.*, 1973a, 1975); Galassi *et al.*'s (1975) Adult and College Self-Expression Inventories; Trower *et al.*'s (1978a) Social Interaction Test and related procedures) may be used.

(2) Analysing the Views of Experts.

(i) Relevant judges may view videotapes of relevant interaction, rate them for effectiveness, and assist in the isolation and analysis of the behavioural components of effective and ineffective performance. (Oratio (1977) and Crowley and Ivey (1976) give an account of factor-analysis in this exercise while Saunders and Saunders (1977, 1979) describe a statistically less-sophisticated version of the same technique).

(ii) The literature relevant to competent performance and its training and assessment may be reviewed. Most professional areas do have a literature on interpersonal skills and many explicitly train and assess them. Assessment schedules for fieldwork, clinical practice etc. may be a useful starting point for the development of a profession-specific package.

(iii) Pilot lists of skills should be exposed to the scrutiny and discussion of relevant groups – including potential trainees.

(3) Empirical Observation and Analysis.

(i) Naturalistic observation of relevant interaction and the development of appropriate observation schedules in related areas may be a useful starting point.

(ii) Observed interaction events may be related to performances deemed effective or ineffective in the light of outcome measures (e.g. pupil learning; sales made; clients' attitude change) or of the ratings of experienced judges.

Note that (i) and (ii) are expensive, time-consuming and difficult if undertaken on the large scale probably necessary for analysis of effective behaviour across, say, an entire profession. For smaller scale or more specific interactions or where the success of interactions can be measured in some concrete way (e.g. sales made) Rackham and Morgan's (1977) techniques can be recommended. *Some* observation and analysis is a necessary accompaniment to the development of adequate schedules for feedback. It could also be argued forcefully that the experience of developing a relevant observation schedule is the best training for trainers who want to be sure that their skills are in fact 'specific, definable, observable, demonstrable and quantifiable' (Turney *et al.*, 1973).

Whichever strategy (or combination of strategies) the programme designer uses to identify and operationalise the components of competent performance, he is left with further questions regarding the usefulness of these components as skills to be inculcated in a training programme. Some components may, for example, be easier to train than others and might, therefore, be particularly motivating for trainees; others may be significantly related to appropriate outcomes but so 'reduced' (e.g. eyebrow position in displaying counsellor warmth) as to seem irrelevant and even farcical to trainees. Likewise questions must be put regarding the order in which skills are trained – should they be arranged from small-scale to large-scale or vice versa or, indeed, should they all be on the same scale? Should they be discrete or mutually overlapping and inclusive as, say, reflection of client feeling, eyebrow position and paraphrasing might be for a counsellor? A good observation system has discrete categories which do not overlap in this way, but all training programmes seem to develop heavily overlapping skills.

The evidence on the arrangement of skills in programmes is very patchy and while certain traditions have emerged controlled studies comparing different skill orders are almost totally absent in the literature. Several commentators on microteaching (Young & Young, 1972; Brown, 1975) do recommend the gradual integration of skills and lengthening of the practice period so that the simulated sessions become increasingly realistic. Likewise, assertiveness trainers (Wolpe & Lazarus, 1966; Lange & Jakubowski, 1976; Butler, 1976a,b) recommend progression from least to most anxiety-provoking but again, evidence in the area is scant.

General criteria for the determination of skills can be borrowed from the language of psychometrics in that the useful list should be both reliable and valid. Some consideration of these criteria may be helpful.

(1) Reliability. Reliability is defined by Anastasi (1978, p. 28) as 'the consistency of results from a given measure'. Put crudely, in the context of SST, a skill is reliably observable if observers can agree that it has occurred. Such reliability is easier to obtain the closer the skill is to specific behavioural events, viz. 'warmth' is more difficult to agree upon than 'smiling'.

(2) Validity. Anastasi (1978, p. 27) defines validity as 'the degree to which a test measures what it purports to measure'. The subsets of validity which she proposes are useful in the context of skill determination as:

(i) *Construct Validity*. Are the skills related to the theoretical 'constructs' or models of competent interaction present in the relevant literature?
(ii) *Concurrent Validity*. Are those individuals demonstrating the skills also rated by expert judges as 'competent performers'? Do they score highly on other acceptable measure of competent performance?
(iii) *Predictive Validity*. Does good performance on the skills predict good performance after training? Does training generalise? (This is a larger problem which will be further discussed later in this chapter and in Chapter 6.)
(iv) *Face Validity*. Are the skills acceptable at face value by relevant groups, e.g. trainees, other staff involved with trainees?

Training Procedures

SST was tentatively defined in Chapter 1 as a sequence of activities including sensitisation, practice and feedback. Each of these components has, however, been the subject of considerable investigation and although almost all SST programmes include them, forms of SST exist in which they are given very different relative weightings.

Sensitisation. The sensitisation phase in SST includes the period where patients, clients or students are first introduced to the total procedure and, more traditionally, the period in which they are exposed to each of the sequence of skills before practising it themselves. The earlier general sensitisation phase will be dealt with in the section of this chapter called 'Considering the Clients' and this section will, therefore, be confined to skill sensitisation as such.

The systematic promotion of behaviour change stretches back at least as far as Miller and Dollard (1941) and Chittenden (1942) and probably a good deal further since imitative play has always been a notable feature of children's learning and development. In SST its inclusion in the sequence derives in part from its known efficacy (Holding, 1965) in the acquisition of motor skills and in part from the work of Bandura (1969, 1971) on the effect of modelling procedures upon maladaptive behaviour. Bandura (1971) suggests that observation of a model who behaves appropriately can encourage the display of similar behaviour, discourage the display of dissimilar behaviour, and reduce anxieties about the display of the behaviour. He describes a variety of techniques, but points out that whatever the precise method, the modelling sequence will include an attention phase, a retention phase and a reproduction phase. The observer must note the significant features of the model, must be able to store them and relate them to his existing understanding of his own behaviour and must be able to translate them into plans and executive strategies which allow him to produce the new behaviour.

Marlatt and Perry (1975) in discussing modelling procedures in psychotherapy use Bandura's three phases as an organiser for their review of research findings. The significant aspects of the attention phase they suggest are the extent to which the observers are given cues as to the most important features of the model, the extent to which the model's performance contains elements of uncertainty or suspense and the extent to which the observers are sufficiently relaxed to pay appropriate attention. Retention of the model is facilitated if observers participate in the modelling session by discussion or problem-solving and if they are given incentives. Reproduction on the other hand is significantly influenced by the observers' motivation which is in turn influenced by the characteristics of the model. Observers are most likely to want to imitate models if they are people for whom they have respect, if they are only slightly more skilled than they are and if there are several of them.

Each of these phases has also been explored and the findings to some extent replicated in the context of SST programming. Some studies (Wagner, 1973; Goldthwaite, 1969) even suggest that the sensitisation phase by itself is a more effective procedure than the entire package of sensitisation, practice and feedback.

Definitions of modelling in SST vary considerably as do the terms describing different varieties of model. Briefly, the alternative procedures are:

(1) Live modelling by trainer or other person.
(2) Recorded modelling by trainer or other person (audio-tape, videotape or film).
(3) Live description of the skill and instructions for its performance.
(4) Recorded description of the skill and instructions for its performance (audio-tape, videotape or film).
(5) Any combination of the above.

For the purposes of this book confusion between the terms symbolic, perceptual, conceptual, formal and informal (diversely used in the literature) will be avoided and 1 and 2 above will be termed live and recorded *demonstrative* models and 3 and 4 termed live and recorded *descriptive* models.

In spite of the terminological confusions some conclusions can be drawn. There is a wide literature in microteaching (Turney, *et al.*, 1973), micro-counselling (Ivey & Authier, 1978), assertiveness training (Lange & Jakubowski, 1976; Hersen & Bellack, 1976a; Bellack & Hersen, 1980) and other forms of social skill training (Trower *et al.*, 1978a; Sarason & Ganzer, 1973; Goldstein *et al.*, 1976), to suggest that sensitisation is an active and useful component of the sequence. It should be noted, however, that the most useful form of model may depend upon the skill being trained. In microteaching, for example, Orme (1966), Koran, J. (1969) and Koran, M. (1969) found that aspects of higher-order questioning were more effectively trained using demonstrative models rather than descriptive ones, whereas Koran, J. (1971) found that other aspects of questioning which he suggests are 'easily described' were better trained using descriptive models. Similarly in micro-counselling (Ivey & Authier, 1978; Kuna, 1975; Fyffe & Oei, 1979; Goldberg, 1970) the more difficult and less specific skills such as 'reflection of feeling' or 'empathising' seem to need demonstrative models while the simpler more specific skills such as 'smiling' or 'restatement of clients' contribution' can be trained using descriptive models. Hersen and Bellack (1976a) in reviewing the literature on remedial social skills training also point out that demonstrative models are not important in so-called 'analogue' studies where trainees are intelligent undergraduates, but are important in clinical or experimental psychiatric studies where trainees are (presumably) less intelligent patients. Goldstein (1973) also makes much of the use of demonstrative models in his advocacy of Structured Learning Therapy as a 'psychotherapy for the poor' who (again presumably) may be less articulate than either undergraduates or the more fortunate middle-class patients who, he suggests, are typical of psychoanalytic or client-centred practice. These results should be interpreted with caution since other aspects of the procedures adopted (e.g. nature of recording, use of cueing, subjects' participation) vary across studies, but it may, none the less, be inferred that the more difficult it is (as a function of the skill or of the subjects) for the descriptive model to be understood and translated into behavioural terms (and responses) the more useful a demonstrative model (alone or accompanied by a descriptive equivalent) is likely to be.

Descriptive models are, of course, cheaper to produce than demonstrative ones but the latter (whatever the skill) may be more acceptable to clients (Borg, 1970) and may facilitate long-term retention of the skill (Kissock, 1971). Live models, likewise, are cheaper to produce (whether demonstrative or descriptive) than recorded models and have additional advantages of flexibility which may be particularly useful where individualised SST is being carried out. Recorded models on the other hand have advantages of uniformity of treatment and in the opportunity for editing and replay they afford.

In confirmation of Marlatt and Perry's (1975) comments on modelling *per se* there is evidence in the SST literature to suggest that the identity of the person delivering the model and the content of the model influence its effectiveness. Thus Berliner (1969) stresses the importance of student teachers being able to identify with the teachers they observe in microteaching models while Koran, M. (1969) suggests that student models may be superior to qualified teacher models. In assertiveness training Lange and Jakubowski (1976) indicate the complexity of the relationships involved but suggest that models should at least be of the same race, sex and social class as the trainees. Evidence on the appropriate content of model tapes (e.g. positive demonstration – 'how to do it' – or negative – 'how not to do it') is mixed, but all programmes offer more positive exemplars than negative. Meichenbaum's (1977) suggested observation of a model who 'copes' by first making errors and then recovering from them is beginning to be influential however and some remedial SST trainers also recommend the use of a 'sliding model'. This model begins by modelling simple skills appropriately but erring on the more complex ones and gradually 'slides' into more competent performance in a progression analogous to that of the trainee but just a few steps ahead of him. The use to which trainees are asked to put the model also seems to be significant. There is a wide literature (Lange & Jakubowski, 1976; Eisler *et al*., 1973b; Young, 1967; Jensen & Young, 1972; Claus, 1969; Borg, 1970; Bjerstedt, 1967) suggesting that providing cues for the trainee so that he may organise and reorganise the 'message' presented by the model and having him participate in discussion or other problem-solving exercises relevant to the model assists him in the retention and reproduction phases.

In summary the steps to be taken in designing the sensitisation phase of the SST sequence includes consideration of the following questions.

(1) Should live or recorded models be used?
Live models offer flexibility but recorded models offer more control. Cheapness and access to recording facilities may be the determining criteria.

(2) Should demonstrative or descriptive models be used?
Although there is some evidence favouring the use of descriptive models for simpler skills it is probably safer (at least in a new programme) to use both.

(3) Who should the model be?
Ideally the model should be someone sufficiently like trainees to facilitate identification but he or she should also be someone who can be respected by them.

(4) Should the model's content be positive, negative or 'coping'?
Despite the growing body of evidence favouring the coping model it is probably easier for novice trainers to use positive models until they develop greater experience of their particular group of trainees. The errors of a coping model should reflect trainees' earlier patterns.

(5) How long should the model be?
Descriptive models should be as short and easily comprehended as possible. Fifteen or 20 minutes discussion or two pages of written description is ample for any one training session. Evidence on the length of demonstrative models is unsystematic but 5-10 minutes is general practice unless a demonstration of skill integration is being presented.

(6) How should cues to demonstrative models be presented?
Evidence on methods of cueing is very scant. The possibilities include instruction before viewing or listening, prerecorded commentary, and stopping the recording for discussion with a live trainer. The novice trainer is best advised to experiment with different techniques until he finds those which best suit his models and his trainees.

(7) How should trainees participate in sensitisation?
Again, beyond the injunction that trainees should participate, no clear advice can be given. Possibilities include discussion, paper or pencil exercises and use of observation schedules.

(8) How should trainees be motivated?
The characteristics of the model are themselves motivating if trainees can identify with them. Additional incentives can be given in the form of praise for contribution to discussion or problem-solving and, in particular, for extension of the model by relating it to relevant personal experiences.

Practice. Like modelling, the use of practice as an aid to learning has an honourable history in both the psychology laboratory and the commonplace classroom. The question is not so much 'does practice make perfect?' as 'which practice makes most perfect?' In social skill training the inclusion of a practice element in the programme has been prescribed from a number of theoretical and pragmatic perspectives. Wolpe (Wolpe & Lazarus, 1966) for example argues explicitly that assertiveness training works as a process of counter-conditioning in which the practice of an assertive response in the relaxed, rewarding atmosphere of the assertiveness training clinic creates a new association (being assertive goes with being relaxed and rewarded) which eventually becomes stronger than the previous negative association (being assertive goes with anxiety and punishment). Without practice, (or as it is called by Wolpe, behaviour rehearsal), no counter-conditioning could take place.

Allen and Ryan's (1969) model for microteaching similarly emphasises the importance of the practice phase, but stresses the scaled-down safe environment in which it takes place. Micro-practice is not a substitute for no practice at all (as it might be for Wolpe's patients) but a substitute for the threateningly unfocused hurly-burly of teaching practice in a real classroom. This idea of practice in a simulated environment before tackling reality is, of course, commonplace in the training of motor skills where dangers to life and limb as well as psyche are involved: the pilot practises in a mock aircraft; the surgeon on a cadaver. Again, in micro-counselling each of these ideas is adopted (Ivey & Authier, 1978), but added to them is the notion that simulated scaled-down practice offers an arena for the development of new plans, strategies and ideas about the client, the counsellor and the business of counselling. The emphasis is neither upon the diminution of anxiety nor upon the firm establishment of appropriate responses but rather upon the development of new ways of thinking about and planning for the interpersonal encounter. Thus, in this model, the student who has a thoroughly anxiety-provoking, disastrously mishandled micro-counselling practice but comments sensibly on it and learns from his mistakes would be said to have had a successful session. This more cognitive model is also advanced in the looser forms of role-play first suggested by Moreno (1959) and commonplace in both psychotherapy and the training of counselling and social work personnel. George Kelly (1955) suggests that the very enactment of a new role (he used both fixed and exaggerated versions of the roles thought appropriate for his clients) inevitably alters patients' constructs or ways of thinking about themselves and others and that for many patients it might be the best way of achieving a more positive viewpoint. A variation on this strategy also used (Lange & Jakubowski, 1976) in group versions of assertiveness training involves reversing roles so that patients have an opportunity of changing their view of assertiveness by responding to it as well as displaying it.

A few investigators have explored the possibility of SST without practice and, indeed, as indicated in the previous section several micro-teaching studies have stressed the relatively superior potency of the sensitisation phase. It has also been demonstrated in related forms of psychotherapy (Kazdin, 1976; Flowers, 1975) that covert or imagined practice can show effects just as beneficial as actually acting out the appropriate role. Zielinski and Williams (1979) recently demonstrated that this technique works in assertiveness training with 'underassertive individuals from the community'. They concluded, however, that while patients displayed more appropriate behaviour change after covert practice than they did after overt acted-out practice, they also consistently preferred overt practice and had more faith in its ultimate generalisation to real life. This corresponds with microteaching research where both Borg (1970) and McIntyre and Duthie (1977) report that students preferred modelling plus practice to modelling alone.

The precise techniques employed in organising the practice element of the SST programme vary considerably and the literature reveals few studies comparing one such technique with another. The novice trainer must, therefore, make his own judgement as to the following.

(1) *Introducing Trainees to Practice*. There is evidence from specialised SST that first exposure to practice (and, particularly, feedback on practice) can be highly anxiety-provoking and it has become standard (Hargie, 1980) to allow trainees a first session in which no skill as such is practised. They are merely allowed to do what they normally do and receive feedback (at this stage, exclusively positive) upon it. Other techniques (Lange & Jakubowski, 1976; Goldstein *et al*., 1976; Trower *et al*., 1978a) are used in remedial SST, but it is clear that however it is effected it is important that trainees enter into SST in as supportive and friendly an atmosphere as possible. It is one of the advantages of the system that trainer and trainee can be seen as involved in a joint exercise in the observation, analysis and modification of the trainees' behaviour.

(2) *Tasks or Situations in which the Skill is to be Practised*. The focus in SST practice is upon skills, but skills cannot be practised *in vacuo*. In remedial SST the nature of clients' difficulties to some extent dictates situations as well as skills and the behavioural interviews carried out should certainly explore the areas of the patient's life in which he is most likely to experience difficulty. Whether this is possible or not it is certainly important to ensure that the situations chosen for skill practice bear some relationship to the everyday life of the trainee. Otherwise the entire exercise may lose its validity.

In specialised and developmental SST likewise, it is important that the tasks to be used for practice be relatively lifelike. A danger in this kind of SST, however, is that trainees (and trainers) may begin to focus on content rather than skill. The trainee social worker may thus be distracted by his ignorance of Supplementary Benefit regulations or the trainee teacher by his ignorance of French verbs. It might be suggested that careful discussion of the possible content with other trainees or with trainers should be undertaken *before* skill practice. Brown (1975), indeed, makes lesson planning an integral part of the microteaching programme.

(3) *Other Interactors to be Involved in the Practice*. Interpersonal skill practice, by definition, needs other persons upon whom to practise. Basically there are three alternatives. Skills may be tried out on other trainees (peers), on appropriate groups brought in to the SST unit (e.g. pupils for microteaching, interviewees for vocational guidance counsellors), or upon confederates brought in by the trainers to role-play 'others' significant in the situation. Social skill training with parents (Twentyman & Martin, 1978; Patterson, 1973) provides a further alternative in that practice is undertaken *in vivo* with the actual children concerned although undertaken in the artificial setting of the clinic.

Evidence on the relative efficacy of these strategies is patchy, but in microteaching it appears that (Hargie & Maidment, 1979) while some 40 per cent of microteaching units in the UK use peers only, many students (Hargie, 1980) report difficulty in accepting the relevance of practice with peers. Trower *et al*. (1978a) recommend that initial training with psychiatric patients be undertaken using trainers' confederates, but that as progress is established the patient may be introduced to group work. Working in groups at some point (i.e. not necessarily during the role plays) in the progress of the course allows trainees to share difficulties and explore ideas about their own and other people's performance. Supportively used it can therefore be a useful adjunct.

(4) *Number, Length and Disposition of Practices*. Evidence here is again patchy and few explicit investigations have been undertaken. Trower *et al*. (1978a) and Lange and Jakubowski (1976) stress the establishment of a hierarchy of difficulty and suggest that patients be allowed to practise a particular skill as often as is necessary for the development of competence before progressing to a more difficult one. Resources, however, often prevent such a scheme and indeed almost all predetermined programmes predetermine not only skills but the number of practices. Classically (Allen & Ryan, 1969) the microteaching programme included one teach, feedback, and one reteach, but in the UK at least (Hargie & Maidment, 1979) many institutions use a cycle of only one teach plus feedback.

The length of practice also varies widely and, indeed, little comment is made on it in the remedial and developmental literatures. In the specialised context however (Turney *et al*., 1973; Hargie & Maidment, 1979) it seems clear that trainers vary the length of practice according to the skill being dealt with. Thus simpler skills (e.g. counsellor restatement) might be practised in the originally standard microteaching/microcounselling 5-minute period while a more complex skill (e.g. reflection of feeling) might be given up to 15 or 20 minutes. Likewise, towards the end of a programme where several skills are being integrated in an increasing approximation to real life, a longer session might be thought necessary.

Evidence on the appropriate disposition of practice sessions is almost entirely lacking and programmes vary from intense 2-3 hour sessions two or three times a week (Liberman, 1975) to one hour per fortnight (Hargie & Maidment, 1979). Some authors (Trower *et al*., 1978a) refer back to the findings on motor skill acquisition which suggest that small amounts of practice spread out are superior to one large block of it, but again no evidence from SST itself one way or the other is cited. It seems that this is a decision the trainer must make in the light of his own circumstances and predilections.

Feedback. As indicated in Chapter 1 the feedback or knowledge of results which a learner obtains is an essential element in the cybernetic model of learning. There is therefore much emphasis upon feedback in SST derived within that model. Likewise since the manipulation of reinforcement contingencies is an essential feature of the operant conditioning model it is not surprising to find that the more behavioural programme designers are much conerned with the rewards which follow on performance.

Unfortunately summary of the investigations which have been undertaken presents difficulties, since the other features of the programmes vary considerably and comparison between studies is in many cases impossible. Tucker and Acheson (1971) even suggest that modelling and feedback are so closely related that it is impossible to determine which of two or more feedback methods is more effective. The function of feedback is to provide information to the learner which both motivates him to further effort and gives him guidance for the modifications and improvement of his performance. It is, therefore, important that he be able to relate it to his previous understanding of the model performance. It is in this context that the importance of the model being someone with whom the learner can identify and compare himself without anxiety (cf. comments on p. 63 about 'coping' models) become apparent.

Whatever the characteristics of the model and whatever the trainee's acceptance of it, his capacity to use feedback may, of course, relate to the way in which it is presented. It is possible to misconceive SST as entirely an exercise in the provision of one particular form of feedback presentation, namely the video-playback. In fact, however, many other forms have been investigated and there is evidence to suggest that video-playback alone effects little change in behaviour (Lane, 1973; Ellett & Smith, 1975) and that spontaneous comments in such circumstances are related to self-image (Waimon & Ramseyer, 1970). Fortunately for the many institutions which have invested in CCTV equipment, however, there is also evidence to suggest (Turney *et al.*, 1973; Hargie, 1980) that video-playback used by trainees who know what they are looking for is singularly potent.

Feedback in SST can vary in the type of record of performance from which it is derived, in its source, in its content and in the extent to which the trainee is given assistance in using it. Records may be made while performance takes place on video-tape or audio-tape, by means of an observation schedule or, less formally, by peers or trainers watching and subsequently remembering what they have seen. Such records may then be used by the trainee by himself, in discussion with peers or in discussion with the trainer. Additional feedback may be obtained from other participants in the practice be they school pupils, trainers' confederates or other trainees. In some specialised contexts change in client behaviour is measured (e.g. did microteaching pupils learn anything from the microlesson? Did they enjoy it?) and provides obviously relevant information on the performance.

Evidence on feedback source is very contradictory, some studies finding that the presence of a trainer during feedback has no effect upon behaviour (Perrott, 1972; Tuckman & Oliver, 1968; McIntyre, 1973) although trainees *preferred* them to be present, whereas other studies (Authier & Gustafson, 1976; Berliner, 1969; McKnight, 1971) suggest that the trainer's presence during feedback is superior to both isolated feedback and feedback from peers or other participants in the interaction. Turney *et al.* (1973), Ivey and Authier (1978), Griffiths *et al.* (1977) and Hargie (1980) all conclude that the value of trainer guidance during feedback depends upon other variables in the programme and upon the way in which the guidance is given.

In particular, there is some evidence (Hargie, 1980) that the most important feature of the feedback system is the extent to which it is made specific and is linked into the development of the trainee's capacity to identify and discriminate skills. Thus the importance of the trainer in feedback is in facilitating such discrimination. If it has been effected during the modelling phase there may be no need for further guidance during feedback; if not, the presence of the trainer helping the trainee to look at his record, use an observation schedule or comment upon significant aspects of his performance may be invaluable.

In summary it is suggested that feedback, in whatever form, be specifically related to observed features of the record, and provided in a generally supportive framework. These principles should guide decisions as to the following.

(1) *Record of Performance*. Should trainees obtain feedback from video or audio records, from observation schedules or from informal observations? Should some combination of records be used?

All of the above have been successfully employed. Since the video-record is most complete it can be argued that it offers more opportunity for subsequent analysis and comment. Its disadvantage is that it must be analysed – by itself it is non-specific and distracts trainees from consideration of skills as such.

(2) *Source of Feedback*. Should trainees obtain feedback from the trainer, from peers, or from other participants?

Again, all have been successfully used but the important variable seems to be not source but method. Trainees do, however, prefer trainers to be present and it may be that they interpret this as a general expression of support and involvement.

(3) *Content of Feedback*. Feedback should be generally positive but should highlight significant features of performance whether positive or negative. If positive feedback cannot be provided the task is too difficult and should be changed. Feedback should always offer guidance as to how subsequent performance might be modified. There is evidence to suggest that this is best facilitated where a more objective record (e.g. videotape, observation schedule) is available for consultation and confirmation by trainer and trainee together. Indeed, the presence of such a record may be sufficient to lead the trainee to pick out significant features of his performance without any comment from the trainer.

(4) *Timing of Feedback*. Experimental psychology might suggest that immediate knowledge of results is important but apparently (Turney *et al*., 1973) where a video-tape record is used this is not so

and replaying the tape 'reinstates the performance' (Turney *et al*., 1973, p. 24). Otherwise, however, it is important to provide feedback at least while the performance is fresh in the trainee's mind.

Programme Evaluation

Chapter 7 will discuss the evaluation of SST in general. Monitoring and evaluation of specific programmes for specific trainees is, however, an integral part of each SST system. Ideally it should include systematic analysis of performance for each trainee before and after training. If records have been made for feedback purposes this is not a difficult exercise, although the behaviour analysis undertaken for monitoring purposes should probably be more sophisticated than that undertaken during feedback. Ratings of real-life interactions and self-report inventories can also be administered before and after training as an aid to evaluation as can relevant attitude scales or indeed, scales designed to measure aspects of mental health not directly related to SST. Longer-term evaluation is more difficult since the results of training may be masked by other intervening events. We would recommend however that trainers explore the transfer of their results at least as far as the first subsequent approach to real life, e.g. teaching practice, professional placement or return to the ward or hostel.

The records of behaviour change, attitudes to training etc. obtained through these procedures afford insight into the extent to which training works. It is debatable however whether they offer insight into how it works. Stufflebeam *et al*. (1971) discussing management training contrast evaluative procedures designed to *prove* that training is effective with procedures designed to *improve* its effectiveness. He stresses that evaluation for improvement is often less formal and more individualised. Applying the distinction to the SST system it should be possible to institute discussions with trainees, fellow trainers and people working with trainees outside the training unit. Their impressions and evaluations can provide useful hints for subsequent systematic evaluations or, alternatively, for immediate modification of the programme. If every single trainee reports that a particular observation schedule is incomprehensible, it is hardly necessary to carry out comparative trials between it and three other forms of feedback. It is our impression that most SST programmes (including our own) are subject to a great deal of such informal evaluation and modification.

Ideally, of course, evaluation should include formal, informal, short-term and long-term measures and results should contribute not only to the monitoring of programmes in a particular unit but also to the refinement of SST procedures as such. It might also be possible to devise investigations designed to illuminate basic models of social interaction. The explicit recorded nature of SST may thus be exploited, not only for its own internal evaluation, but for the extension of knowledge for its own sake.

Contexts of Training

The context of training has so far been explored as it influences each phase of programme planning. Some aspects of context however merit separate consideration.

Trainee Characteristics. Consideration of client characteristics has been implicit in several of the foregoing sections, particularly where individualised programmes have been considered. In an obvious sense all programmes are individualised since in the end an individual either changes or doesn't change his behaviour. Given the extent to which individual differences in IQ, personality, learning style and so on can be shown to influence learning in other forms of training it is reasonable to hypothesise that SST may work better for some trainees than others and that even the most standardised programme might do well to allow some flexibility to accommodate individual variations.

Research on individual differences in response to SST remains scant. This is in part because trainees tend to be preselected. Thus in remedial SST trainees are only admitted to training if they are diagnosed (usually by clinicians other than those responsible for training) as socially incompetent or if they are said to suffer from some wider disorder with which social incompetence is associated. Conversely in specialised SST, trainees are only admitted to training if they are judged to be potentially extraordinarily competent.

Some investigations have been undertaken, however (Austad, 1972; Hargie *et al*., 1979) in respect of personality characteristics and behaviour change in microteaching and several reviewers (Hersen & Bellack, 1976a; Van Hasselt *et al*., 1979) comment upon individual difference as a factor in the design of assertiveness training programmes. It can be inferred from these studies that some individuals are more nervous and more antipathetic throughout their SST experience than others but that there is no clear relationship between these differences (Austad, 1972; Freeman & Davis, 1975) and degree of behaviour change at the end of the programme. Studies are few in number, however, and vary in their design and in their specification of 'behaviour change' so results must be interpreted with caution.

Despite the scarcity of directly relevant investigation it may be surmised that individual trainees will vary in their capacity to perceive and discriminate aspects of social behaviour, in the accuracy of their self-perception, in their general capacity for learning and in their attitudes towards SST in totality and in its elements. The following strategies may be useful in helping individual trainees to obtain maximum benefit.

(1) The programme should be carefully introduced to trainees and something of its rationale should be explained.
(2) Trainees should be allowed ample time for 'practice' practices so that any cosmetic effect of video or other feedback can be got over.
(3) Models should be as closely related to individual trainee characteristics as possible.
(4) Trainees should participate as much as possible in the sensitisation phase and every effort should be made to accommodate individual learning differences in the activities provided.
(5) Practice talks and situations should be readily comprehensible and should have face validity for trainees.
(6) Feedback should be at an appropriate intellectual level and should have a supportive emotional tone.

Relationship to Other Trainee Experiences. SST does not take place *in vacuo*. Trainees spend the intervals between training sessions involved in social interaction of some kind, even if (as with psychiatric in-patients) that interaction is not the interaction of normal daily life. Thus, SST unlike training in the more restricted motor skills (e.g. dinghy sailing) is subject to interference from the trainees' experience of 'wild' practice between the sessions of practice in the confines of the SST unit.

In developmental and specialised SST a potentially more damaging source of interference may be the possible mismatch between SST and other elements of the school or professional training curriculum. Thus the social work trainee whose SST programme focuses upon individual casework while other aspects of his curriculum suggest that effective social work is the facilitation of large-scale social change through community action has problems unless steps are taken towards curriculum integration.

Ultimately, of course, it is the aim of the SST programme, along with other measures (other teaching, therapy or medication) to provide the trainee with skills which will transfer to real-life situations. These issues of interference, generalisation and transfer will be fully discussed in Chapter 5, but two comments may usefully be made at this point. First, many SST programmes totally ignore the context in which they take place and still show useful short-term outcomes. Secondly, whatever the context, trainers should explore connections thoroughly so as to (1) avoid unnecessary conflict and (2) exploit it where possible.

Appropriate strategies for exploring and exploiting contexts might include the following:

(1) Relating models and practice tasks as closely as possible to real-life situations.
(2) Tailoring the programme so that skills and practice situations gradually approximate to real life (this may include using less reduced skills and longer practices and focusing specifically upon skill integration).
(3) Making links with other teaching or therapy.
(4) Giving 'homeworks' or 'wardworks' to be undertaken between sessions. These may be practical and the trainee may be asked to obtain feedback from real-life 'others' for discussion when he returns to the unit. Alternatively, they may be conceptual exercises, e.g. writing up a logbook or undertaking further analysis of videotape. Again these should be discussed or written comments should be provided.
(5) Involving other personnel, teachers, family, caretakers, as appropriate, so that they understand the programme being followed by the trainee(s).
(6) Ensuring a gradual entry to 'real-life' interaction. This might involve a gradual diminution of the number of sessions in the unit, an accompanied trip to some 'difficult' place or, in specialised contexts, the use of obviously SST-related values and techniques in, for example, teaching practice or fieldwork supervision.

Logistics and Systems Amplification

The case studies of Chapter 4 will exemplify the detailed logistics of selected SST programmes and will discuss staffing and equipment. It should be clear from the foregoing sections, however, that there is sufficient doubt about the optimum strategies in programme implementation for trainers to feel confident about designing their programme within the resource constraints of their own situation. The best argument for increased institutional investment in SST is the actual demonstration of its success with the relevant clients and of its acceptability to other personnel working in contingent areas.

Cost-benefit analyses of SST have not been undertaken in any systematic way but it seems likely (Bellack & Hersen, 1980; Cohen, 1969; Kennedy, 1975) that it is less expensive than alternative forms of therapy or training. At its simplest SST need involve only the trainers' time, some paper and pencil and a room with chairs. Given those limited resources, skills could be modelled and practised with appropriate feedback. Indeed, it should be noted that the procedures described by Lange and Jakubowski and reflecting extensive practice are just as simple. Short-term costs begin to mount when large groups (or many groups) are involved and (for example) accommodation must be given over exclusively to SST or when the stages are amplified as indicated in Table 2.1. Costs have been categorised under hardware (equipment, accommodation, etc.), software (consumables, e.g. paper, tapes etc.) and people. These costs do not include the research and investigation costs of skill identification and determination of individual assessment or of long-term evaluation.

Conclusion

This chapter has presented a model of the SST programme and has indicated the decisions to be made by designers of such programmes. It has essayed a statement of criteria for such decision-making and has in places been firmly prescriptive. The reader should now be in a position to sketch out the possibilities for programme design in his own environment and, it is hoped, should be more aware of both pitfalls and potential.

Table 2.1: Potential Costs of Amplifying SST Stages[a]

Stage	Hardware	Software	Personnel
Sensitisation	Videotape recorder(s) and monitor(s) Video camera and microphones[b] Audio-tape recorder(s)	Videotape Audio-tape	Technician assistance in preparation of models
	Film projector Film camera and microphones[b]	Film Hand-outs/ Workbooks	Trainer involvement in lectures, group discussion, individual guidance
	Accommodation and appropriate furniture	Commercially-produced model tapes etc. Textbooks (for trainers and/or trainees)	
Practice	Video and/or audio equipment. Accommodation and appropriate furniture including 'props' relevant to situation (e.g. blackboard for microteaching, office desk for assertiveness training with managers) One-way mirror for observation by peers/trainers	Video/audio tape Software 'props' (e.g. paper and pencil for microteaching pupils) Observation schedules	Technician availability for equipment failure. Trainer availability for logistic and/or personal support. Confederates in interaction[c] (pupils, interviewees etc.)
Feedback	Video and/or audio playback equipment. Accommodation with appropriate furniture (should allow relaxed atmosphere). Calculator for data-analysis	Video/audio tape. Observation schedules. Paper and pencil for trainee's personal note-taking	Technician availability for equipment failure. Trainer role in cueing feedback and for general support

Notes:
a. The costs outlined are, of course, optional costs and it is likely that very few institutions (in the UK only Ulster Polytechnic, the New University of Ulster and the University of Stirling) have all of the facilities mentioned.
b. Only if models are to be 'in-house' rather than commercial.
c. There may be associated costs in the transport and caretaking of such individuals, e.g. of pupils in microteaching.

3 A COMPENDIUM OF SKILLS

Introduction

One ambition which sustained the authors in the preparation of this text was the desire to produce a 'bumper book of social skills'. Such a compendium would, for the first time, include under one cover lists of all the skills focused upon by current social skill trainers. This would be informative in itself and would provide raw material for comparison, contrast and analysis. The list would enable any person bent upon developing a social skills training programme to borrow and modify accordingly.

We have noted in even the most assertive social skill trainers a violet-like reluctance to divulge the actual skills which they use, matched only by their curiosity and rapacity concerning the skills used by others. Strangely this modesty is sustained in many published papers where skills are relegated to an appendix or mentioned as available, presumably under plain cover, to those who communicate directly with the author.

This chapter, therefore, is a compendium of skills. We have organised the various lists according to the settings in which they have been used and thus in relation to the types of trainee for whom they have been thought useful. Given the speed with which the literature on SST is expanding and the above-mentioned modesty of many trainers, the compendium is no doubt incomplete. However, we do believe it to be the most comprehensive produced so far.

It should be possible for intending trainers to determine from these lists the major focuses of training to date. They should also be able to discern which skills have been most widely used and are thus more generic. This comprehensive view should provide a context for whatever skills, whether derived analytically or empirically, the trainer may intend for his own area. Obviously the prospective trainer will be interested in what the skills are. But he might also ask how the individual skills relate to each other. Are they, for example, hierarchically organised according to grain of analysis? Do major skills include several smaller components? How do the skills relate to each other sequentially? Does, for example, one skill always initiate a sequence and another terminate it? How do verbal and non-verbal skills integrate?

Questions should also be asked about the inferential status of each skill. How would we know if it were there? Is it like eye contact, obviously a piece of behaviour, or must it, like empathy, be inferred from unspecified behaviour?

Related to this is the question of the evidence for the skill. How do we know that this behaviour is part of social skill? What does the originator of the skill mean by social skill anyway?

Finally, and crucially, the prospective trainer should consider how the skills might best be arranged and presented to trainees.

We have organised the presentation of skills in relation to settings and clients. We had considered a more ambitious multi-dimensional presentation. Rejecting this as a method we would still wish to identify certain dimensions along which skills appear to vary. There are four such dimensions.

(1) *Low-inference: High-inference*

A low-inference skill is easily observable as behaviour (e.g. head-nodding); a high-inference skill requires inferences to be made from behaviour, e.g. sincerity.

(2) *Molecular: Molar*

The most molecular skills would be irreducible elements of interaction (e.g. angle of gaze): molar skills would be an amalgam of more molecular skills (e.g. explanation).

(3) *Situational: Generic*

This dimension concerns the extent to which the skill is specific to a particular situation or is applicable in a range of situations, e.g. refusing offers of drugs versus questioning.

(4) *Explicitly Interactive: Implicitly Interactive*

This dimension concerns the extent to which the skill requires the person to mesh his behaviour explicitly with the behaviour of others.

The Remedial Setting

Skill programmes in the remedial setting are largely designed for individual patients whose difficulties are determined through self-report questionnaires, structured role-play procedures and clinical interviews. Certain skills do recur however and attempts have been made to relate the more popular skills (or skill deficits) to other psychiatric symptomatologies. Thus lack of assertiveness has been frequently related to depressive illnesses (Lewinsohn & Shaffer, 1971; Libet & Lewinsohn, 1973; Weissman & Paykel, 1974; Hayman & Cope, 1980).

In this setting a skill such as assertiveness is, in the first instance, judged to be important on the basis of sheer intuition. Empirical support is sought *post hoc* through studies such as those on depression cited above. Similar pursuit of logic rather than data has led to the more recent development of so-called 'positive skills' including 'the ability to express tenderness' and 'friendliness' (Bellack, 1979). These no doubt help to rebut criticisms of assertiveness training as presenting pushiness and hostility as both healthy and virtuous, but are just as lacking in empirical warrant as was assertiveness when first suggested as a training target by Wolpe and Lazarus (1966).

It would be a mistake, however, to assume that 'assertiveness', 'friendliness' or any of the other remedial SST skills listed below are identical wherever they are mentioned in the literature. Definitions of, for example, assertiveness abound and the translation of that quality into precisely-observable behavioural units or even into focuses for rating seems to vary with each practitioner and each reference consulted. Further difficulties in identifying skill components emerge from the fact that as traditionally practised (Hersen & Bellack, 1977) the stress in assertiveness training (as opposed to assessment) is less upon the sub-skills of assertiveness and more upon the role-plays within which they can be trained. Thus the fixed sequence of skills through which trainees progress which typifies specialised SST and which was implicitly assumed in Chapter 2 is absent from this form of SST. Instead the trainer chooses role-play scenes (probably from one of the role-play assessment instruments such as the BAT) and the trainee progresses through the sequence within which (Hersen & Bellack, 1977, p. 157) 'attention is directed to the specific components of social skill'. No indication is given of how 'attention is directed', of the order of skill treatment or indeed of the relationship of skill components to role-play scenes. Group studies of assertiveness training relying upon self-report or structured role-play ratings of the outcomes of training are particularly guilty of failing to describe how skills are focused upon during sensitisation (where cueing (see Chapter 2) of skill components is especially important) and practice.

Clinical studies using single-subject methods provide some clues as to the sub-skills used as targets for improvement during role-plays. Their methodology necessitates behaviour counts before and after training, but it is still difficult to discern how these are related to role-plays. The sub-skills of assertiveness mentioned in these studies are usually very specific and can be objectively observed. They include, for example, loudness of voice, response latency and ratio of speech disturbance time to total speech time – all of which can be precisely measured.

Assertiveness training thus varies somewhat unpredictably in the degree of emphasis given to skill specificity. Skills vary from the precisely observable, where (Rosenshine, 1971) little or no inference is needed to determine their occurrence, to more global skills (such as assertiveness itself) where a very great deal of inference is required before agreement can be reached.

Assertiveness training also varies with respect to situational emphasis, some skills being clearly related to very restricted situations (e.g. ability to refuse offers of drugs) and others being much more generically applicable (e.g. smiling, giving praise, etc.). Confusingly, Bellack (1979) lumps assertiveness together with heterosexual dating skills and ability to perform well on job interviews and terms the category 'molar skills' as opposed to the 'molecular' skills such as eye contact and response latency. The confusion is between the inference dimension and the situational dimension and is no doubt related to the way in which assertiveness training emphasises role-plays at the expense of systematically-sequenced skill practice. In our dimensional model assertiveness is high-inference and generic; smiling is low-inference and generic; but dating skill is high-inference and situational.

Thus we would subdivide Bellack's (1979) molar and molecular categories into sub-sets of molar-situational, molar-generic, molecular-situational and molecular-generic.

As will be seen from the lists which follow, the skills employed in other remedial programmes also vary in both inference level and situational reference but several programmes at least recognise the distinction between the dimensions.

Trower *et al*. (1978a) for example assess patients through a Social Situations Interview designed to discover the social situations which give the most difficulty. They also use a Social Interaction Test in which patients are rated on skills thought to be important across a wide range of situations (e.g. greetings) or, indeed, all interaction (e.g. meshing one's contribution with the other person's). Patients are then taken through a sequence of exercises determined by the skills in which they are thought deficient. Skills are sequenced as thought best for learning (generally from low-inference to high-inference and from generic to situational) and the sequence of exercises is a consequence of the skill sequence thus determined. These programmes are thus more like specialised SST in their approach to organising skill practice.

It is widely acknowledged throughout the remedial setting that the skills promoted are neither isolated nor discrete. Attention has recently been paid (Fischetti *et al.*, 1977; Trower, 1980a, 1980b; Bellack, 1979) to the timing, sequencing and organisation of behaviour in smooth performance but so far this concern has not been reflected in actual training. Most skills are treated as if they were entirely discrete although it is patently obvious that, for example, assertiveness is made up of lesser components such as speaking, gesturing, organised in some yet-to-be-established way.

Most skills are also rated or otherwise determined by exclusive reference to the behaviour of the trainee thereby ignoring the fact that the trainee's influence upon his colleagues in interaction may be a potent test of skill. Interestingly Lewinsohn (1975) defines assertiveness in terms of the trainee's capacity to provoke reinforcing behaviour in others. He presents a set of diagnostic categories for social skill deficit in depressives which includes reference to the number of responses the patient can elicit from others in proportion to his own contributions. He also includes a measure of the number of others with whom he can interact at once. These diagnostic categories do not, however, appear to have been translated into skill programmes.

The lists of remedial skills which follow have been divided initially into those derived as part of a programme of assertiveness training and those derived in more general social skills training programmes. As previously noted there is much confusion in the use of these terms 'assertiveness' and 'social skill'. As a rule of thumb if a programme called social skills training none the less makes heavy reference to the assertiveness literature or uses, for example, self-report of assertiveness to measure improvement we have included its skills under the assertiveness heading.

Assertiveness Skills

(1) Low-inference Skills. These include Bellack's (1979) 'molecular' skill components and feature widely in reports of clinical studies using single-subject methodologies where they provide baseline measures:

(1) duration of eye contact;
(2) response latency;
(3) loudness of voice;

(4) speech fluency;
(5) smiles;
(6) number of questions used;
(7) duration of responding.

These skills are generally the subject of objective measurement, e.g. of minutes spent looking, decibels produced or ratio of time in speech errors to total speech, but are sometimes also (or only) rated. Measurement of a skill itself induces greater specificity and precision. 'Response latency' for example is usually a measure of pauses between the other person stopping speaking and the trainee beginning, but can also include pauses in his own speech. Measurement necessitates specification of the distinction.

Rating is usually on the basis of quantity but in some studies includes concepts of acceptability (e.g. was voice volume 'appropriate'?), which removes the skill from the low- to the high-inference category.

(2) High-inference Generic Skills. Despite their uniformly high-inferential status these include skills which are variously attributed in the literature to the molar or to the molecular. They feature widely in group studies of assertiveness and have been used with a variety of patients using role-plays of wide situational reference.

Skill	*Focus for Ratings*
Facial expression	Change and variety in expression; suitability in the situation and in respect of the verbal content of the interaction
Questioning	Type and variety of questions asked; modification in response to the other interactor
Expression of affect	Intensity and variety; appropriateness in the situation and in respect of verbal content
Giving and responding to praise	Quantity and appropriateness
Giving and responding to criticism	Quantity and appropriateness
Asking others to change their behaviour	Timing of request; arguments put forward; firmness of manner

Sharing positive thoughts and feelings	Quantity and appropriateness
Negotiation and compromise	Standing up for own rights but recognising the rights of the other
Greetings and farewells	Timing and appropriate content
Friendliness	Non-verbal behaviour; laughter; verbal support of the other

As high-inference skills, these skills are not directly subject to objective measurement and are generally tapped by observer rating (or occasionally by self-report). Acceptability and appropriateness are clearly important – raters are not being asked whether there was any facial expression but whether it was appropriate at various stages in the interaction. Decisions as to what constitutes 'appropriateness' are sometimes left to the rater and sometimes the subject of negotiation between trainers or trainers and trainees. As is immediately apparent from the tentative rating-focuses given beside each of the skills listed above definitions can vary widely. It is argued that so long as trainers and trainees in a particular programme can eventually agree about ratings the process of discussing them is itself a valuable aspect of skill acquisition.

(3) High-inference Situational Skills. Assertiveness training has been applied to many groups and particular skill-focuses derived accordingly. We have noted the specific groups or situations by each skill.

Interacting with authority figures	Women Minority groups Drug addicts Alcoholics
Interacting with females	Minimal daters
Asking for dates	Minimal daters
Refusing dates	Women
Responding to drug or alcohol offers	Alcoholics
Asking others to refrain from verbal abuse and derision	Homosexuals
Using verbal assertion as a substitute for physical aggression	Chronically explosive schizophrenics

As is evident many of these situational skills are highly specific to the needs and circumstances of the trainees concerned. They shade off, however, into skills which are merely situational demonstrations of more frequently-occurring assertiveness skills. We have not, for example, included skills from a number of studies supposedly specific to (for example) marital discord since the actual skills referred to (e.g. giving and responding to criticism, expressing tenderness) also apply in a wide range of situations and for a wide range of trainees.

Lange and Jakubowski (1976) using rating techniques and high-inference skills analysis rely heavily on discussion between the trainer and trainees in isolating skill deficits and improvements. They identify five varieties of assertiveness with which their clients have frequently had difficulty. These five varieties are defined (pp. 14-17) as:

Basic assertion	A simple expression of standing up for personal rights, beliefs, feelings or opinions, e.g. politely stopping someone from interrupting
Empathic assertion	Making a statement that conveys recognition of the other person's situation or feelings and following it by another statement which stands up for the speaker's rights, e.g. making it clear you understand why someone is angry but asking them to stop shouting
Confrontive assertion	Used when the other person's words contradict his deeds. It involves describing objectively what the other person said would be done and what has been done, after which the speaker expresses what he wants, e.g. calmly telling a tradesman he agreed to call on Tuesday; that it is Wednesday and he hasn't called; then asking him to give a firm commitment for some future date
Escalating assertion	Starting with a minimal assertive response and when the other person fails to respond escalating the

	assertion and becoming increasingly firm, e.g. dealing with a sociable drunk by being friendly at first but being increasingly firm when he refuses to go away
I – language assertion	Describing one's own feelings and preferences in an attempt to make clear why the other person should change his behaviour, e.g. explaining that the presence of smoke in a room where you are eating makes you nauseous and suggesting that smokers should consider the rights of non-smokers to unpolluted air; then asking the smoker to put out his cigarette

These varieties of assertiveness differ from the previous list of skills in that they are defined neither in terms of small-scale behaviour units of wide social applicability (smiling, greeting, etc.) or in terms of globally-defined social situations (asking for a date, refusing drugs) but to fairly specific *patterns* of verbal interaction. In each of the skill definitions and exemplars given above the need for performance of the skill concerned is traced to something the other person said or did. Assertiveness is thought necessary because the tradesman didn't call, because the drunk is pushy or because one's rights are in some general way being trampled upon.

As with Hersen and Bellack (1977), 'attention is directed' to components of assertiveness during Lange and Jakubowski's version of assertiveness training, but the precise behavioural emphasis is difficult to discern. Despite their use of assertiveness training jargon, and reliance upon traditional self-report and role-play measures in assessment of clients and evaluation of outcomes, it might therefore be suggested that Lange and Jakubowski's (1976) skills are in fact structured role-plays with emphasis upon scripted verbal response rather than skills as such.

Other Remedial SST

Liberman's (1975) Personal Effectiveness Training employs skills which are heavily reminiscent of assertiveness training. There is more emphasis, however, upon negotiation of the skill programme between trainer and trainee and less emphasis upon psychometric assessment. The skills are:

(1) Low-inference Skills. (Judgements of appropriateness are also made and these skills may, therefore, be categorised as both low- and high-inference.)

eye contact
voice volume
fluency

(2) High-inference Generic Skills.

intonation
pacing of interaction
giving and requesting information
giving and requesting opinions
giving and requesting criticism
giving and requesting praise
approaching strangers

More emphasis is given in this list and in the related training procedures to co-operative and altruistic skills than in some form of assertiveness training and it is assumed that 'personal effectiveness' skills are applicable throughout the spectrum of interactive situations. Training is by means of role-play, but skills are emphasised one by one and role-plays are designed to facilitate their use so that the procedure is more like specialised SST than like assertiveness training.

Liberman's skills are, as noted above, similar to those of assertiveness training and thus at least aspire to the status of behavioural observability. Some SST trainers, however, in wholehearted adoption of the cybernetic paradigm for skill acquisition give training explicitly directed to the development of cognitive skills thought relevant to the production of skilled behaviour. Notable among these is Goldstein whose (1973; Goldstein *et al*., 1976) Structured Learning Therapy skill sequence comprises 59 skills which are presented with suggestions to trainers for vignettes for modelling and role-play and 'learning points' for each skill. These 'learning points' are as much cognitive as behavioural: thus the points for skill number one 'Starting a Conversation' are as follows (our parentheses):

(1) Choose the right place and time (cognitive).
(2) Greet the other person (behavioural).

(3) Make small talk (behavioural).
(4) Judge if the other person is listening and wants to talk to you (cognitive).
(5) Open the main topic you want to talk about (behavioural).

Goldstein *et al*. also give (see below) a series of seven 'Planning Skills' which are entirely cognitive. Their list of 59 skills is divided into five series of basic skills, all of which are assessed by ratings and are, in our terms, high-inference generic skills, and a further series of application skills which are tied to specified situations and are said to be a useful aid to transfer to real life. We refer the reader to Goldstein *et al*. (1976) p. 78ff. for the full list (with exemplars and learning points) but give series titles and selected exemplars here.

Series I *Conversations: beginning skills*: includes starting, stopping carrying on, listening
Series II *Conversations: expressing oneself*: includes expressing praise and encouragement, affection, anger, complaint, asking for help, giving instructions
Series III *Conversations: responding to others*: includes responding to praise, persuasion, complaint, anger, confusion, empathy, apologising, following instructions
Series IV *Planning Skills*: includes setting goals; priorities; gathering information; concentrating on task; evaluating own abilities; preparing for stress; decision-making
Series V *Alternatives to Aggression*: includes identifying emotions, determining responsibility, making requests, relaxation, self-control, negotiation, helping others and assertiveness
Series VI *Application Skills*: these are situational skills and range from job-seeking and moving into an apartment through marital situations to dealing with bereavement (little rationale is given for the selection of these particular situations)

Again little guidance is given beyond the 'learning points' as to the precise behavioural referents of these skills or the way in which trainee attention is to be directed to them. Goldstein's 1973 text however gives a list of cognitive processes said to underlie skilled performance and useful as training focuses. These are:

interpersonal stress rehearsal (i.e. anticipating difficulties and

determining coping strategies)
seeking and clarifying the intentions of others
reduction of information overload by concentrating on relevant aspects of interaction
accurate perception of affect in others
internal control of own affect
self-disclosure decisions
impression management

Role-play and behavioural focus is thus a support to cognitive change as it is in Meichenbaum's (1977) cognitive behaviour therapy where particular emphasis is placed upon problem-solving, coping, and stress inoculation and the trainee is encouraged to change 'the things he says to himself' (p. 47) before, during and after interaction. It is debatable whether these specifically cognitive techniques are really SST, but as the more behaviourally-oriented trainers (Hersen & Bellack, 1976a; Bellack, 1979) have come to recognise the potency of cognitive approaches (at least in training for generalisation and transfer) they have become increasingly influential. Thus a number of programmes have adopted the principle of the 'coping model' in their sensitisation procedures and, indeed, have included specific cognitive training as part of the total SST package. This is apparent in Structured Learning Therapy and some forms of microteaching (e.g. Brown, 1975).

The most comprehensive approach to remedial SST and the clearest application of the cybernetic paradigm is that of Michael Argyle and his colleagues (as presented in Trower *et al.*'s 1978 book *Social Skills and Mental Health*). As might be expected, there is emphasis in this approach upon both high- and low-inference skills and instances occur of direct training of both behavioural and cognitive skill. Trower *et al.* also (p. 174) distinguish between behavioural 'elements' to which attention is drawn throughout training and 'skills' which are specific training focuses and dictate the nature and order of role-plays used. In practice, as will be evident from the lists below, there is some overlap between elements and skills. The precise programme of training for any given trainee is negotiated: Trower *et al.* make specific reference (1978a, p. 176) to 'contracts' between trainer and trainee. This negotiation is on the trainee's responses to the Social Situations Interview and Social Interaction Test which are respectively self-report and role-play measures designed to tap use of the elements in the skill sequences before and after training. The Social Situations Interview also provides evidence on the situations in which the trainee finds interaction particularly difficult and is used in preparing relevant role-plays and, at the end of the programme, specific situation training.

The elements to which Trower *et al.* draw attention (p. 174) are subdivided into verbal and non-verbal and are:

Verbal
asking and answering questions
giving and seeking information
giving instructions
offering and seeking opinions, suggestions
greeting, bidding farewell
apologising, explaining
telling jokes
agreeing, disagreeing
thanking
Non-verbal
gaze, mutual gaze, glance
facial expression
proximity and orientation
voice quality – pitch, loudness, speed, accent
gestures accompanying speech and expressing emotions
posture – relaxed-tense, dominant-submissive
appearance – image conveyed by hair, grooming, clothes

It is clear that some of these elements (e.g. proximity, loudness of voice) are more susceptible to objective low-inference measurement while others (facial expression, telling jokes) are more readily rated with 'appropriateness' as the criterion for inference. In practice in these programmes both objective and rating measures are adopted as trainers judge them useful for assessment and feedback to trainees.

The skills presented in Trower *et al.'s* (1978a) training manual are arranged in eight sets with specific skills and suggestions for training exercises (not always role-plays) given for each. The skills are:

(1) Observation skills: getting information about the situation; getting information about the other's attitudes and feelings; clarifying the causes of the other's behaviour; self-observation;

	recognition of emotions; recognition of attitudes.
(2) Listening skills:	reflection of feelings (and mood-matching); attention feedback (includes nodding, uh-uh, mm . . . etc.); listener commentary (includes verbal and non-verbal response during and after the other's contribution); questioning.
(3) Speaking skills:	disclosure of factual information; disclosure of feelings; fluency of speech and non-verbal characteristics and accompaniments of speech.
(4) Meshing skills.	content and change of content; timing.
(5) Expression of attitudes:	matching the other's style and choosing a different style in order to influence him.
(6) Social routines:	greetings; farewells; requests; gaining access to strangers; offering compliments, praise, encouragement, congratulations, sympathy; explanations; apologies; face-saving; assertion.
(7) Tactics and strategies:	these are revision exercises in which trainees are encouraged to bring together previous skills and to consider alternative ways of 'playing' role-plays. Particular strategies discussed include rewarding and controlling others and presenting self.
(8) Situation training:	situational role-plays in which 1-7 can be used are worked out for each trainee.

The reader is referred to Trower *et al.* (1978a) for greater exemplification of these skills, but it is clear that they vary in observability and behavioural/cognitive emphasis. They also represent the clearest attempt in remedial SST to consider the organisation of skill elements in sequences or other more complex patterns. Specifically, reference is made to skill timing and meshing and more emphasis is placed throughout upon the interactive nature of skilled performance.

The Developmental Setting

SST as a systematic cycle of sensitisation, practice and feedback based upon the empirical analysis of skilled performance occurs relatively infrequently in the developmental setting. The norm in this setting is either an individually-tailored programme of behaviour modification provided for a troublesome or emotionally 'at-risk' child or alternatively a programme of broadly-conceived social education provided for groups of non-referred children. In the former, behavioural targets are very specific but means of modification vary widely and only occasionally parallel the normal SST cycle; in the latter acquisition procedures are similarly varied and, moreover, the behaviours promoted are rarely precisely identified.

Among the more behaviourally-specific programmes are a number of applications of assertiveness training with individual children and groups of children. Interestingly this work reflects more concern with general social skills (such as initiating interaction, participation in play with others) and less with assertiveness *per se* than does the literature on assertiveness training with adults. Drawing upon studies by Bornstein *et al.* (1977), Durlak and Mannarino (1977), Gottman *et al.* (1976), Oden and Asher (1977), Hymel and Asher (1977) and La Greca and Santogrossi (1980) the following skills can be discerned.

Low-inference Skills
eye contact
speech volume
speech duration
smiling/laughing
High-inference Generic Skills
participation with others
communication with others
co-operating with a partner

supporting a partner
working autonomously
friendship-making
distributing reinforcement to peers
greetings
joining ongoing activities
extending invitations
sharing possessions
conversational skills
paying compliments
appearance and grooming

These skills which we have broadly described as high-inference, vary in the amount of inference they necessitate. Successfully joining ongoing activities for example can be fairly readily determined from the length of time taken, the response of other children and the extent to which the activity continues smoothly after the intervention. 'Friendship-making' or 'communication with others' however demands that the observer define friendship and appropriate communication before he can begin to look for behavioural demonstrations. In some cases (e.g. through sociometric measurement) objectively-measurable correlates of the skill are used as well as or instead of ratings. The ages of the children involved in these training programmes vary from pre-school to adolescence and there is reference (Van Hasselt *et al.*, 1979; La Greca & Santogrossi, 1980) to the need for more information on the development of social skill in normal populations. Van Hasselt *et al.* (1979) for example suggests that children's capacity to understand social situations from the viewpoint of others is likely to become increasingly refined in parallel with their capacity to perceive aspects of their physical environment from a variety of viewpoints.

Situational skills in developmental SST are largely confined to individual behaviour-modification programmes and are generally (Cartledge, 1978) classroom skills. They include Hops and Cobb's (1973) 'classroom survival skills' namely:

attending to the lesson
volunteering relevant information
asking and answering questions
working quietly

As noted above the less behaviourally-specific developmental SST programmes frequently fail to record their skills but merely indicate the areas across which role-plays relevant to such situations as job-seeking were devised. One exception to this rule is the Saskatchewan Newstart Life Skills Programme (1972) which lists the following as generic skills applicable across a range of situations in which the young unemployed, delinquents, alienated minority groups (in this case native indians and Esquimaux) and other community 'drop-outs' may find themselves. The skills are:

listening
eliciting information
assumption-spotting
goal setting
questioning
using feedback
deferring judgement
using fantasy
fighting fairly

These clearly vary in the inference needed and since little is given by way of precise behavioural referent it is difficult to know quite what is meant by, for example, 'using fantasy'.

The Specialised Setting

It might be expected that all the skills trained in specialised settings would be specialised skills closely related to the precise professional needs of relevant groups of trainees. In fact, however, as we have argued in this book and elsewhere (Ellis, 1980), there is an initially surprising similarity in the interpersonal skills thought appropriate by various professional groups. Some skills are no doubt the exclusive purlieu of particular groups but as will be evident from what follows there is also a large central core of generic skills.

The specialised areas for which SST has been provided break down (see Chapter 1) into developments of microteaching, developments of micro-counselling, and a few initiatives, e.g. Rackham and Morgan's (1977) behaviour analyses and Melhuish's (1980) skills for doctors, in other areas. We will group skills accordingly.

(1) Microteaching Skills

Microteaching originated in Stanford University (Allen & Ryan, 1969) and although the skills first employed were ostensibly behaviourally-observable they were not derived from empirical analysis. Many of them are only susceptible to rating, as opposed to frequency, measurement. The original Stanford Skills were (Allen & Ryan, 1969, p. 15):

stimulus variation (e.g. varying tone of voice, gesture etc. to give a lively impression)
set induction (i.e. introducing a teaching sequence)
closure (i.e. ending a teaching sequence)
silence and non-verbal cues
reinforcement of student participation
fluency in answering questions
probing questions (e.g. following-up a pupil's previous answer)
higher-order questions (e.g. demanding more than a yes/no answer; stimulating pupil thinking)
recognising attending behaviour
illustrating and use of examples
lecturing
planned repetition
completeness of communication

No guidance is given in the original text as to the relationship of one skill to another ('lecturing' for example includes a good many of the others) or to the optimum order for their presentation.

Since Allen and Ryan's book *Microteaching* was published the technique has flourished and skills (and sequenced skill programmes) have proliferated. Turney *et al.* in 1973, for example, was able to review the skills employed in known programmes and to categorise them as follows. The bracketed number indicates the number of subsets discerned – motivation, for example, includes 'set induction', 'gaining attention' and five others:

motivation	(7)
presentation	(29)
questioning	(9)
groupwork	(8)
developing thinking	(10)
evaluation	(5)
management	(13)

These skills had been partly developed from the Stanford list, but had also been infuenced by other traditional patterns of assessing and training teaching skills (Stones & Morris, 1972) and by the burgeoning in the early 1970s of category systems purporting to account for and measure the totality of classroom interaction (Simon & Bower, 1970; Flanders, 1970). This development of skills from a variety of sources usually took account of the curriculum and staff attitudes prevailing in the institution in which the programme was to be established. It was predictable therefore that the skill sequences would differ. Conversely it is a tribute to the insight of microteaching's originators that so many of their skills have in fact survived.

In 1979, Hargie and Maidment undertook a survey of microteaching in the United Kingdom and derived a rank ordering of the popularity of skills employed in such programmes. The ranking is (from most frequent to least frequent) as follows:

questioning
initiating
reinforcing
closing
stimulus variation
use of aids
communication
pacing
using ideas
demonstrating
cueing
instructing
interacting
self-presentation
explaining
controlling
organising
discussing
liveliness
structuring
rapport

As already noted, microteaching skills vary in their behavioural specificity and in the way in which they are typically assessed. This, as in other areas of SST, is in part a result of ignorance of the precise way in which skills are made up from more elemental units of behaviour and in which they interlock. It is possible, for example, to rate 'appropriate explaining' with reasonable reliability between observers. It is much more difficult (and to date, unaccomplished) to devise an observation system which will reliably and validly express 'appropriate explaining' behaviour as precisely observable units. Attempts have been made (Rosenshine, 1971) to relate precisely counted elements of teaching behaviour to increases in pupil learning with extremely disappointing results. Ratings of skills such as those listed above bear a much closer relationship to such outcomes.

(2) Micro-counselling Skills

Micro-counselling developed alongside microteaching and derived its skills in part from similar traditions of behaviour modification and in part from the distillation of a much more eclectic approach to counselling. Many of Ivey's (1971; Ivey & Authier 1978) skills are, therefore, far from behaviourally specific. Although empirical referents are sought for them in related assessment and evaluation (including attempts to measure counselling outcomes such as client change) their original selection is based on an analysis of counselling rather than field studies of effective counselling. They are also, without exception, high inference and generic across a wide range of counselling situations and clients.

The skills are grouped under three broad headings (see below) and recommendations for training include suggestions for the integration of skills one with another. The skills are:

attending skills	beginning a session
	listening
interpersonal influence	self-expression
	giving directions
	expressing feelings
	expressing information
	summarising
	self-disclosure
	interpretation
	direct mutual communication
empathy	positive regard
	warmth
	concreteness
	immediacy
	confrontation
	genuineness

Ivey (1971) and Ivey and Authier (1978) give ample anecdotal and case material exemplifying the skills and this together with their concordance with traditional approaches in counselling and social work has facilitated their widespread adoption and development. Ivey welcomes the elaboration of his list and suggests that apart from the general skill emphasis and some aspects of the training cycle micro-counselling (or micro-training as he calls it in this context) is (1978, p. 299) 'an open system, an approach to training which allows for alternatives and variations'. These variations include skill variation and Ivey recommends continued research into (p. 38) 'the helping process' in which micro-training can both provide data and use the results of investigation as an aid to skill identification.

Particular developments of micro-counselling worthy of note are its use with lay and volunteer personnel in implementation of Carkhuff's (1971) recommendation that human resources should be trained throughout the community and not merely within restricted professional groups. Carkhuff (1971) does not recommend skill training as such but does offer an analysis of conditions for helping which are similar to Ivey's list. The major features of helping are given as: *empathy, positive regard* and *genuineness*. These are then said to be manifested through the helpers' *discrimination* skills, *responding* skills, *initiation* skills, and *integration* skills.

(3) Other Specialised SST

Many applications of SST for other professional groups are simply collations of skills from microteaching and micro-counselling (see Chapter 6 for the development of such a programme for health visitors at Ulster Polytechnic) and in view of the dearth of empirical study of professional interaction this is perhaps inevitable.

A different response to much the same problem consists of providing trainees with recordings (video or audio) or other feedback about their own interaction (or about the interaction of others working in the same field) and negotiating training focuses in the resulting discussion. Thus Melhuish (1980) provided undergraduate medical students with videotapes of general practitioners conducting consultations along with handouts to be used as a guide for discussion. One such handout (Melhuish, 1980, p. 309) used the following analysis of the consultation:

(1) making a relationship;
(2) gathering information –

relevant techniques include – use of past knowledge
non-verbal communication
physical examination;

(3) defining the patient's problem –
medically
socially
psychologically;

(4) solving the problem;

(5) management.

Precise behavioural referents would be hard to find for several of these headings and the list is in no sense an objective analysis of observed behaviour. Implicitly, however, it provides skill focuses around which role-plays can be derived with (as Melhuish (1980) reports it) benefit to trainees.

Rackham and Morgan (1977) also use discussion of recorded behaviour as an arena for the negotiation of training focuses, but in their case they emphasise the importance of scrupulous objectivity in analysis of the record presented. They, therefore, derive category systems for the observation of behaviour of specific relevance to the job setting of each group of trainees and provide such trainees with a detailed account of their performance. They are encouraged to improve their performance in role-plays and in the real work situation then to undertake further measurement when the hoped-for improvement can be discerned. Such 'on-the-job' training can be undertaken without the active involvement of the original trainers.

Rackham and Morgan (1977) originated this behaviour analysis and feedback system while working with the British Overseas Airways Corporation but have since developed a number of systems for diverse purposes. They continue, however, to use the first instrument they ever designed as a general purpose tool. It has 13 categories grouped (Morgan, 1980) as follows:

initiating skills – proposing
building

reacting skills – supporting
disagreeing
defending/attacking
blocking/difficulty stating
open reacting

clarifying skills – testing understanding

		summarising
		seeking information
		giving information
controlling participation	–	shutting out
		bringing in

Specialised SST thus employs skills which vary in the degree of inference they necessitate and in the extent of their situational specificity. A number of common features can, however, be discerned in programmes under each of the above headings. It would be possible, for example, to divide skills into observational skills, initiating skills and responding skills. Thus Melhuish's 'information gathering', micro-counselling's 'listening' and microteaching's 'recognising attending behaviour' are all aspects of accurately observing the behaviour of others. Likewise 'explaining', 'expressing information', and 'giving information' are selected from different specialised lists but are remarkably alike in notional behavioural reference. Other examples can easily be found.

A further broad division of skills can be discerned in specialised SST, namely the dichotomy between expository skills which, loosely defined, are concerned with the clear transmission of information, and supportive skills where the emphasis is less upon changing the other person's stock of information and more upon changing or consolidating his attitudes and emotional state. Thus expository skills include, for example, explanation, demonstration and lecturing, while supportive skills include reflection of feeling, warmth and positive regard. Some skills such as questioning and reinforcement however are useful whether the broad intention of the interaction is exposition or support and a neat categorisation of specialised SST skills is not, therefore, possible.

Conclusion

In this chapter we aimed to provide a compendium of social skill lists according to settings. We posed questions regarding:

prevalence	–	which skills occur most commonly?
inferential status	–	how can they be recognised?
relationship	–	how does one skill relate to another logically and sequentially?

presentation — how can trainees acquire the skills?

The procedures used to identify skill (see Chapters 2 and3) vary between and indeed within our three major areas. Thus empirical identification combined with rigorous analysis is most common in remedial settings and least common in developmental. In specialised settings microteaching has a strong empirical tradition and micro-counselling a less consistently empirical approach. In general, however, professional groups tend to have an established tradition of experiential or teleological approaches to the acqusition of interpersonal skills and this tends to be matched by an intuitive approach to their identification.

Thus skills may appear in lists because they have been identified through systematic observation, recording and analysis of interaction, because they are demonstrated as a logical requirement of interaction, or because they are felt to be the right way to act.

(1) Skill Prevalence

Given these variations of approach and setting, it is not difficult to explain the differences between lists. However, it is interesting to note that some skills appear frequently in more than one setting. They include greeting, asking questions and giving praise. These are presented as relevant aspects of interaction in a multitude of situations and probably for all interactors. They certainly appear in skill lists in each of our three settings.

We noted in our discussions of specialised SST skills that they could be categorised into observational, initiating and responding skills: such categorisation can profitably be extended across all three settings. Perhaps as a reflection of the behaviourist origins of SST (in assertiveness training and microteaching) observational skills (and, to an even greater degree, other aspects of cognitive processing) have received far less emphasis than initiating and responding skills. Presumably observation of others is implicit in training responses to them but observation is only specified as a skills focus in Trower *et al.* (1978a) and in micro-counselling's 'discrimination skills'. Many programmes use and discuss observation skills during sensitisation but they are not specified as part of the training sequence *per se*.

Initiating skills are much more frequent. They include most forms of verbal content with greatest popularity for the following:

greetings and farewells

questioning
giving factual information
giving praise
giving criticism

These are often expressed in different forms (e.g. giving factual information might be termed lecturing) and there is very considerable variety in the distribution, breakdown and elaboration of such skills across programmes. Understandably, they are at their most elaborated in microteaching.

Responding skills are also more frequent than observation skills and are at their most elaborated in micro-counselling and in some forms of remedial SST. The most popular of these appear to be:

summarising and paraphrasing
clarifying
reflecting feelings
responding to praise
responding to criticism

No doubt elaboration and refinement of the available model of social interaction will alter the balance of skill prevalence. There are indications (see Chapters 5 and 7 for fuller discussion), for example, that training in some currently popular skills does not generalise to real life and it is likely that these skills will be reviewed and elaborated (or discarded) in the light of further empirical data. Similarly, emphasis (Bellack, 1979; Trower, 1980a) upon the perceptual and cognitive components of skilled performance is increasing and it is likely that a compendium of skills produced ten years from now would include more explicitly observational and cognitive skills.

(2) The Inferential Status of Skills

The major distinction between skills which has been discerned is that of degree of inference necessitated. Thus skills vary from the small-scale, behaviourally specific and objectively observable (e.g. loudness of voice) to the large-scale, behaviourally undefined and subjectively judged (e.g. genuineness). Comparing the various settings for SST it is clear that low-inference skills are much more prevalent in the remedial setting than they are elsewhere – indeed although they are acknowledged to be important in the specialised literature they are not to be found as training focuses. The most popular low-inference skills are:

eye contact
speech fluency
response latency
speech duration

These have not, however, emerged from detailed empirical analysis of skilled (or unskilled) interaction, but from intuitive analysis of clinical experience coupled with some reference to the literature of experimental social psychology and backed by rather doubtful (Bellack, 1979) psychometric procedures. The most extensive reference to empirical analysis is to be found in Trower *et al*. (1978a). This may in part be why their list of skills is both the most comprehensive and the one in which greatest reference is made to the more reduced 'elements' (as they term them) of skill.

High-inference skills (as might be expected) vary more across programmes. Some consistency can, however, be observed. There is, for example, particularly frequent use of very high-inference skills in microcounselling and in some remedial SST. This is at least in part a reflection of existing traditions for the adoption of experiential or teleological approaches to skill acquisition in those areas. As we suggested in Chapter 1 the detailed empirical analysis of skills and a focus upon highly-reduced, low-inference skill elements can seem a mechanistic denial of the uniqueness of individuals. Certainly this view has been expressed by social workers or counsellors used to the exercise of intuitive personal judgement. Focus upon relatively high-inference skills on the other hand, if perceived as a simple clarification and analysis of intuition, can be more readily accepted.

(3) The Organisation of Skills

Few trainers give explicit guidance as to the relationship between skills beyond the occasional suggestion that skills might be integrated for revision purposes. This is often related to situational training or to attempts at fostering generalisation. Again, Trower *et al*. (1978a) are the only authors to include specific exercises in the timing and meshing of responses and to give a clear progression from skills to social routines to situations. Interestingly, even Trower *et al*. fail to establish a clear relationship between the elements of interaction and the skill sequences beyond suggesting that elements will be 'drawn attention to'.

It is clear, therefore, that the available knowledge of social interaction is inadequate in so far as it sheds light on the microcosm of interaction. We know something about the articulation of some elements, e.g. gaze (Argyle & Cook, 1976) and facial expression (Ekman & Friesen, 1975) but not nearly enough to provide the detailed analysis upon which a training programme might be based.

(4) The Presentation of Skills

Variation in guidance offered for skill sequencing and presentation varies from Hersen and Bellack's (1977) vague 'attention is directed' through to programmes like Goldstein *et al.*'s (1976) Structured Learning Therapy and to Trower *et al.* (1978a) where a suggested sequence is provided. On the whole, however, guidance is rare and the only principle which emerges is progression from the small-scale, specific and generically applicable to the large-scale, vague and situationally relevant. There does not seem to be any empirical justification for this principle however and it would be interesting to try a programme which reversed the order.

We expressed the hope at the beginning of this chapter that it would be of assistance to people establishing programmes and that it would further illuminate the guidelines for skill selection and arrangement presented in Chapter 2. The skill lists themselves give an indication of possible areas of training and, to a lesser extent, of potential means of skill identification and selection. Regrettably, however, much of this chapter has consisted of critical comment upon identification procedures and lamentation over lack of information in respect of skill organisation and presentation for training. We must, therefore, conclude that further research and development is needed.

Prospective trainers should follow the guidelines of Chapter 2. Obviously they will learn from the skills used by others. In addition we would recommend empiricism, particularly ethnographic studies of relevant encounters, as the best basis for identifying skills. This should be coupled with rigorous analysis of, and deduction from, the agreed purposes of the encounters. Negotiation with informed persons, preferably focussing on publicly observable records of interaction, should be used not only to clarify purposes but to identify skills. The agreed skills should then be subject to continued internal (do they work in the programme?) and external (do they generalise to and work in real life?) monitoring and modification.

4 SST AT ULSTER POLYTECHNIC

It is, we hope, accurate rather than immodest to claim that Ulster Polytechnic occupies a unique position in the United Kingdom with regard to the scope and extent of its social skill training. Ten years ago a microteaching programme was launched for 15 trainee teachers: during the academic year 1979/80 600 students received SST in some form. They included not only trainee teachers but also social workers, community workers, youth leaders, health visitors, counsellors, careers officers, employment advisory officers, speech therapists, physiotherapists, occupational therapists and junior executives.

In this chapter, then, we tell the story of this development, but also try to identify guidelines or principles which may help others who have similar aspirations.

At this point, a brief digression on evaluation is apposite. Microteaching and subsequently social skill training were conceived by us as a form of action research. That is we believed that we had identified a real as opposed to an academically-contrived problem, that we had a solution to implement and that development should be matched by monitoring and evaluation. After a decade we must confess to some imbalance in the accomplishment of this programme. Development has been rapid and extensive, but evaluation has been selective and internal rather than systematic and impartial. Several small-scale research projects have been completed using the activities of the unit to provide data, but these have been far short of the comprehensive evaluation which we would ideally desire.

In a sense, which we would label 'internal', all SST, including ours, is self-monitoring and evaluative. Behaviour change is predicted and the extent of its accomplishment is a measure of the training's success. At this level we have evaluated our SST and found it effective. However, two other forms of evaluation have not been systematically undertaken.

The first involves comparison with other procedures for the accomplishment of similar goals. Thus SST could be compared, using a matched-group design, with other procedures which claim to develop social skills. Our problem here is that few if any other procedures are as explicit in their claims as SST. Furthermore all professional course teams wish to do the best for their students: once convinced of SST they wish all to receive it.

The second would involve a systematic assessment of generalisation from SST to subsequent real-life encounters. There are obvious difficulties of time-scale in such a venture: should generalisation be assessed throughout a career for example? However, studies of generalisation to at least the first year of professional work have begun through studies of teachers of retarded children (Hargie, 1980) and employment advisory officers (Dickson, in preparation).

To return to the story: earlier we pointed out that social skill training may be categorised as falling into one of three areas, the remedial, the developmental and the specialist. Specialist social skill training is provided for persons whose anticipated role will involve a greater than normal degree of social skill. It is for this latter category that our programmes at Ulster Polytechnic have been provided. Thus the professions (or semi-professions) listed above have in common the fact that interpersonal communication is the prime professional activity. Indeed, it might be argued that the principal area of knowledge and skill peculiar to these professions is the exercise of social skill for desirable ends and the ability to reflect upon such skilled operations. Brewer and Lait (1980) argue that most social work has neither purpose nor manifest practical skill. We would argue that SST makes manifest an area of practical skill: the purpose to which these skills are put is, of course, another matter. This common practical purpose has enabled us to develop programmes which have a generic core while including elements, whether of skill, situation or content, which reflect the special needs of the individual groups.

In recounting the history of social skill training at Ulster Polytechnic four main themes emerge. First is the identification of component skills and their development mainly as a general set applicable across professions but also with distinctive emphases for each; second is the refinement of acquisition procedures for these skills; third is the development and refinement of material resources and logistics including audio-visual technology; and the fourth is the deployment of staff with particular reference to the facilitatory and inhibitory attitudes and theoretical positions adopted by participating personnel. We will discuss each of these in the account which follows and will relate them to the larger theme of curriculum integration which will be more fully discussed in Chapter 6. The second section of this chapter comprises case studies of SST in the Diploma Course provided for health visitors, a general social skills course in the BSc in Human Communication and a course devised for SST trainers.

History

SST began at Ulster Polytechnic in the summer of 1972 when the first microteaching courses were set up as part of post-qualification one-year diploma courses for art teachers and craft teachers. The skills employed in these courses were essentially a development of the Stanford package of skills which we had previously devised for use with weak or failing student teachers at Callendar Park College of Education in Scotland. We went to some trouble to define the skills in behavioural terms. However, it will be noted that several definitions move from observable teacher behaviour to intentions regarding pupil cognition (e.g. specified mental set, clarification of substantive meaning) itself less easily operationalised. Our skills and definitions were:

Stimulus variation:	material presented by the teacher which varies both inter- and intra-sensory modality of pupil
Questioning:	teacher verbal behaviour the syntactically or semantically interrogative form of which increases the probability of pupil response
Reinforcement	teacher behaviour which increases the probability of reoccurrence of preceding pupil behaviour
Conceptual variation:	variation of teacher verbal behaviour which clarifies a substantive meaning
Illustration and use of examples:	verbal and non-verbal material presented by the teacher which supports a specified communication
Set induction:	teacher behaviour inducing in pupils a specified mental set
Closure:	teacher behaviour completing and consolidating a specified communication

Each of these diploma courses had been taught elsewhere before moving (with their staff) into the Polytechnic and microteaching was thus grafted on to an existing curriculum. Problems of curriculum integration were compounded by difficulties staff and students experienced in the move from cosy monotechnic familiarity to the perceived soullessness of the larger polytechnic. Microteaching in this scenario, was not on the side of the angels. Interestingly, craft students and tutors found its empirical rigour and analytical approach much more amenable than did their counterparts in the Art Teacher's Diploma. In the latter, teaching methods and principles of education had traditionally emphasised discovery methods and maximum individualisation as stimuli to creativity: apparent curriculum incompatability was thus substantial. It was perhaps exacerbated by the fact that the approach to microteaching adopted in these early months was more strictly behaviourist than it has subsequently become.

Procedurally Stanford again provided the model and students went through a cycle of sensitisation, teach, feedback and reteach. Feedback was given to individual students who viewed the videotape of their performance alone with the tutor. Students and tutors (particularly the professional tutors) had received previous instruction in the observation and analysis of teaching behaviour and used a strict behaviour counting category system (at first the Flanders (1970) Interaction Analysis Category System) during analysis of tapes. Children were brought into college for practice sessions and students taught small groups of about five in the standard Stanford fashion. The children were employed in the art room when not directly involved.

Sensitisation and skill analysis should have provided an opportunity for linking microteaching with the existing curricula but in the event the lack of overall curriculum review and, in particular, inadequate discussion and preparation with professional tutors made matters difficult. Resource and technical problems were also prevalent at this stage. No accommodation was earmarked for microteaching, model tapes were non-existent and recording was by means of a clumsy and potentially intrusive trolley on which cameras and VTRs were mounted and moved from room to room as required. At first only two such trolleys were available and this, coupled with the individual feedback system, made microteaching a lengthy process comprising for individual students short periods of intensive activity alternating with long periods of boredom.

Our first ventures in microteaching were thus less than perfect in respect of curriculum integration, resource deployment and staff and student attitudes. We were sustained, however, by the fact that the skills themselves seemed relevant to students and that they reported having benefitted from (or at least seen the point of) microteaching when they went on subsequent teaching practice.

In September 1972 a further SST course (microteaching) based upon the revised Stanford skills and procedures was run for Home Economics Diploma students. These students had also moved from a small college with an existing curriculum. It contained units of practical teaching and placement, but study of the disciplines of education was confined to history of education, comparative education and a modest element of psychology in the form of child development. Typically empirical studies were focused on the child to the virtual exclusion of the teacher. It was possible therefore to add not only microteaching but related studies in psychology and social psychology. These focused upon the analysis of teacher/pupil interaction and were related to the microteaching skills being practised at the same time. Thus students learning about operant conditioning also learned about the elements of non-verbal communication available as social reinforcers and practised providing them during microteaching. Discussion sessions in micro-teaching and theory classes were mutually enhanced.

Constraints of time and larger student numbers also necessitated the use of group feedback sessions which proved much more successful than at first anticipated and, indeed, fostered the integration of micro-teaching with other elements of the course. Several papers (Brusling, 1972; Young & Young, 1972) given at the International Symposium on Microteaching held in Tübingen that year also bore out the value of group support during feedback.

The first course to be planned from the start using the action focus (see Chapter 6) or skills in context model was the Further Education Teacher's Certificate which was a one-year day-release course for experienced but untrained teachers from further education colleges (including the polytechnic). It began in January 1973.

The curriculum of this course was organised around *five* areas of teaching skill: observation; communication; organisation; planning and evaluation; and research and development. These areas were chosen as an appropriate categorisation of a long list of skilled activities in teaching; as amenable to college and practice-based skill acquisition; and as providing a focus for academic perspectives. Courses in psychology, sociology and philosophy of education were planned to relate specifically to each of these skill elements. As a curriculum feature this was more radical than perhaps it sounds. Traditionally the so-called disciplines of education (psychology, sociology, philosophy and history of education) are taught first to reflect the character of the parent discipline and secondly to analyse these features of education considered appropriate. Practical teaching, or method, conventionally pursues a parallel and non-interacting course.

Of the five areas communication was conceived as the locus for microteaching. Within microteaching material was selected from psychology and social psychology (see Appendix 1) to relate to each skill. Thus students were taught to observe and analyse teaching behaviour as part of the sensitisation phase of each skill cycle and to relate the analysis to 'theoretical' material from psychology and social psychology. We planned that students should acquire teaching skills while observing, analysing, planning and evaluating their own and others' behaviour as a psychologist would.

Model tapes were not yet developed and sensitisation was thus restricted to the description of the skills. Procedurally the course was similar to the home economics course except that for the first time students taught each other, since it was impossible to bring sufficient pupils in to match the students' diverse teaching subject groups (from technical drawing and hairdressing to occupational therapy and geology). Again, by this time there was published evidence to suggest that peer-group microteaching was indeed a viable alternative.

The Further Education Teacher's Certificate was also one of the first courses to be taught in accommodation designated (albeit part-time) as a microteaching unit. Recording and teaching now took place in one room and tape-viewing and feedback in another, with resultant reduction in the obtrusiveness of the equipment.

Since this was the first course to be started from scratch in the faculty, new staff were selected in part on the basis of their commitment to and knowledge of this 'competency-based' approach to teacher training.

In 1973 accommodation was designated for microteaching full-time and further cameras, recorders and microphones were purchased. This allowed the development of a system whereby one student might record a lesson and then proceed directly to feedback while a second student occupied the practice room to record. Logistically this promoted a quicker flow of students through the unit and also allowed for longer practices than previously.

In the first instance practices were strictly the 'scaled-down encounters' of the Stanford original and lasted 5-10 minutes and students were encouraged to choose teaching topics not necessarily from their own subject but appropriate to the 5-10 minute slot. Thus craft students might have taught omelette-making and home economics students how to change a car wheel. It became clear during 1972/3 however that the face validity of the entire exercise improved for students and professional tutors if students taught lessons appropriate to their own teaching subject and that was the procedure adopted from then on. The Physical Education Teacher's Diploma group (which first participated in microteaching in summer 1973) was the first group for whom the skills list was modified to incorporate subject-specific skills. The skill of 'demonstration' was included which involved students in providing a demonstration of some movement or exercise which pupils were to carry out, along with appropriate explanation and questioning to be sure they understood what they were to do. The new skill was clearly an amalgam of other skills (explanation and questioning) already practised and as such was the first explicit venture in skill integration. For this reason (and also because, being physical education, it often involved use of equipment) it took longer than the traditional micro-lesson and was allotted 15-20 minutes.

The major development of 1973 however was the move from micro-teaching to the programme which first incorporated counselling skills: the SST course for health visitors. The detail of this development is presented in the second section of this chapter but, in brief, SST was first proposed for health visitors in 1972 because it was thought that the health education aspects of their work approximated to teaching and that they might therefore benefit from microteaching. In the discussions with health visitor tutors however, it became clear that counselling was a more important aspect of the work and that the health visitor tutors were enthusiastic about the possibility of extending the technique to include micro-counselling skills. Discussions with these tutors had extended over an entire year. Tutors had participated in a short course organised in the autumn of 1972 for professional tutors in all of the areas for which microteaching was provided or intended.

The health visiting course was thus designed with the full participation of professional tutors. Indeed the inclusion and selection of micro-counselling skills was at first more enthusiastically embraced by them than it was by psychology staff who were anxious to preserve the relative behavioural purity of the microteaching system. In the event the course was one of the most successful and the length of time devoted to discussion and preparation with the relevant professional tutors became the model.

Any disagreement between professional tutors and psychology staff regarding SST tends to approximate at any one time towards one of two extremes. First psychology staff may be cast as simplistically behaviourist, while professional tutors are charged with attempting to protect a shaky professionalism through mystique and magic. Secondly professional staff are accused of over-enthusiastically embracing SST as a fashionable panacea, while academics are seen as jealous of irrelevant academic purity and reserve.

Other developments in microteaching itself in 1973 included a course for students on the Teacher's Diploma in the Education of Retarded Children (Hargie, 1977a; 1980) and courses for BEd students majoring in Physical Education. Home Economics and Communication Studies. Microteaching in the BEd courses was one element in a total curriculum (Ellis & Whittington, 1972; Ellis, 1972; Whittington, 1974) designed on the action focus (skills in context) model (see Chapter 6). The skills with which educational studies, teaching practice placements and in-college practical activities were co-ordinated were: observation, communication, organisation for learning, planning and evaluation, research and curriculum development.

As in the previously-designed Further Education Teacher's Certificate curriculum, each of these skill elements was a focus for practical work in school and college and for related theoretical reading and discussion. Thus students working on observation would carry out guided observations of real schools and classrooms. They would undertake detailed analyses of videotaped teaching in college and they would study theoretical material from psychology and sociology selected to exemplify a range of observational methods as applied to children and teaching. Similarly 'organisation for learning' and 'planning and evaluation' were related to material from psychology, sociology and philosophy concerned with aims and objectives in teaching, measurement of teaching outcomes, optimum presentation of material and so on.

The communication units were, of course, microteaching with linked theory and, here again, each skill was related to parallel material from psychology and social psychology. The detailed curriculum is set out in Appendix 3.

A degree curriculum which gave such an emphasis to the development of teaching skills had several radical consequences. It became almost inevitable that teaching performance, as opposed to the ability to write about teaching, should contribute to a student's honours classification. In order that this might be achieved marks had to be available for practical teaching: performance as a teacher had in some way to be assessed in a similar way to assignments or written examinations. Teacher trainers were traditionally reluctant to attempt a precise assessment of a student's teaching. Most courses preferred a global pass/fail categorisation with at most a three- or five-point literal scale. It was, therefore, necessary to initiate a research project whereby a reliable and valid instrument was devised for the assessment of teaching performance. Clearly this project was akin to microteaching in its emphasis on the observation, recording and evaluation of performance. Microteaching and the assessment of teaching performance, therefore, progressed in tandem.

The research project is described by Saunders and Saunders (1977; 1979). It was conducted in four phases. In the first, teachers and polytechnic tutors compiled lists of statements, giving advice to students in a predetermined teaching situation. These lists were then the basis for the development of a rating schedule which the teachers and tutors refined in the observation of videotaped teaching sequences. A questionnaire was also completed in which they commented freely upon the schedule. Finally the rating schedule was tested for reliability.

The competency-based action focus model (see Chapter 6) was thus extended across the entire degree curriculum with the exception of main subject studies (in this case home economics, physical education or communication studies) within which a separate logic obtained. Professional tutors were, however, deployed in practical teaching (including microteaching) and as supervisors of teaching practice placement. Substantial efforts were made to link lesson content back to concurrent main subject teaching.

The BEd curriculum thus developed was a four-year 'concurrent' programme in which teacher training was a component from the first year. Recent cutbacks in teacher employment have rendered such curricula less desirable. We now train a more limited number of teachers in a curriculum with two alternatives. Students may study the main subject for itself until graduation at the end of three years or may take a teaching option which lasts for four years and in which the study and practice of teaching occurs halfway through the third year. The focus of this last 18 months is thus entirely upon teaching: the action focus curriculum designed originally for the concurrent degrees is again used.

By now the unit had been retitled, following Flanders (1970) as the 'Simulated Social Skill Training Unit' reflecting the significant generalisation of approach from teacher training to the education and training of other interpersonal professions. The academic year 1973/4 saw the addition of courses for diploma students of social work, youth and community work within which the micro-counselling skills employed with health visiting students (paraphrasing, reflection of feeling, sustaining) were used. As with health visitors, students counselled each other in specially-designed role-plays the elaboration and grading of which has remained a central concern of both courses. These role-plays were also used for integration of skills and were longer than the standard 5-10 minutes if appropriate. Sample role-plays from the Diploma in Health Visiting are included in Appendix 4.

Model tapes for both micro-counselling and microteaching skills were now used and the present system of cued sensitisation through the use of observation exercises was initiated. In these exercises and in the development of observation schedules for use during feedback it became increasingly clear that the high-inference skills of micro-counselling (e.g. sustaining) were less immediately susceptible to behaviour counts than the lower-inference skills of microteaching (e.g. questioning). This brought to a head the difficulties which had been experienced with behaviour counts in feedback since the first courses in 1972. It therefore became general practice to restrict behaviour counting to use for demonstration of skill elements during sensitisation and occasional use for specified low-inference skills in feedback. All other skills were rates (see Appendix 4 for examples of rating focuses in the health visiting skills).

A short course for playgroup leaders was developed in 1973/4 in which students practised reinforcement and questioning skills and made extensive use of their tapes (recorded using portable equipment *in vivo* in the playgroups) for analysis of interaction between children and between children and leaders. The course unfortunately lapsed after two years, but the commentaries students prepared on their tapes seemed valuable and it may be that discrimination training of this kind would be a useful addition to other courses.

In 1974/5 the major additions to the now substantial list of courses including SST were the Music Teacher's Diploma Course, the BA course in Social Work (using skills and procedures akin to those of the Diploma in Social Work) and the first course in the area of vocational guidance, namely the Diploma in Careers Guidance.

The Diploma in Careers Guidance is a course of professional training for careers officers (in Northern Ireland employees of the Department of Manpower Services) and its curriculum is, therefore, constrained by the requirements of the professional validation body. None the less, the action focus model was employed and SST with linked psychology was an integral part of the principles and practice course unit. Within the SST programme itself students practised teaching and counselling skills. More attention was paid to the integration of skills than in previous courses and the SST programme culminated in a series of interviewing exercises using traditional vocational guidance approaches such as the seven-point plan (Rodgers, 1974). Subsequent vocational guidance courses have used a similar format.

One other development in 1974/5 was a Careers Teacher's Course which used similar skills to the Diploma in Careers Guidance, but also included the first of the group discussion exercises (see p. 135 for a fuller description) which have now become a feature of other vocational guidance courses and of health visiting, social work and youth and community work.

Accommodation and resources until 1975/6 were limited to three recording and feedback units and pressure towards expansion was thus considerable. In 1975/6 partitions were constructed in a large room adjacent to the unit and three additional recording/feedback units were created. Among other things this allowed the organisation of a number of short courses for (for example) volunteer personnel and business studies students about to go on sandwich placement. In a new polytechnic where several existing colleges had been federated on a new site, pressure for accommodation was acute. This extension of SST facilities had to be justified with a closely-argued case in which existing and proposed SST was compared with conventional professional practice for economy and effectiveness.

The major programme developments of 1976/7 were the Employment Advisory Officers Course (using the vocational guidance format) and the special programmes devised for the BSc Speech Therapy and the BSc Physiotherapy.

The speech therapy course placed greater emphasis upon the micro-analysis of interaction than had previous courses and students were encouraged to relate the behaviour analyses they conducted in SST to other analyses of interaction undertaken in linguistics. The skills practised were based upon Oratio's (1977) analysis of skills in speech therapeutics but, interestingly, turned out to be a selection from the existing repertoire of teaching and counselling skills.

SST for physiotherapists similarly exploited other areas of their curriculum. In this case there were similiarities between the kind of micro-analysis undertaken of patients' movements and therapists' manipulations and the analysis of interaction undertaken in SST

In 1977 and 1978 the major developments were programmes in the full and part-time advanced diplomas for teachers of guidance and counselling, in the BSc Psychology and in the BSc Human Communication (see the second section of this chapter). The BSc Psychology curriculum is unusual in including placement in settings where psychology is applied. Students take SST before the placement period. It is thus a preparation for potential interaction with patients or clients and also a first exemplification of psychology applied to real problems. In all of the courses established in 1977 and 1978 the linked theory was based on students' particular commitment to the analysis and development skills and was thus more critically oriented.

In September 1979 the unit moved into the custom-built accommodation described in detail in Appendix 5. It has eight recording/feedback units, full colour and a number of other technical refinements. Recent developments have included programmes for sports studies, occupational therapy and health education students and, significantly, the first courses for trainers other than our professional tutors.

Unit staffing has, of course, expanded in parallel with the expansion of courses and has grown from the involvement of two psychologists (the authors) during approximately one-eighth of their committed hours to a full-time unit staff of three working together with professional tutors and research students.

Training of professional staff has also been a very important feature of the expansion. As discussed later in this chapter this has included short courses but has largely been *ad hoc* discussion and guided reading taking place during the negotiation of skill sequences and related curricula for specific groups of students. A particularly valuable feature has been the small but growing number of professional tutors who have themselves participated in SST in either their initial qualifying course or in a subsequent course of teacher training such as the Further Education Teacher's Certificate (now the Certificate in Education (Further Education)). This course has been approved by the professional bodies for health visiting, occupational therapy and physiotherapy as a course leading to tutorship qualification.

We referred earlier to shortfalls in the evaluation of the unit's work. However, each course has been subject to continuous monitoring using formal and informal assessment of student performance and of staff and student attitudes. The increasing acceptability of the technique in new areas of the faculty's work is some measure of the positive outcomes of such monitoring. The assertion that SST and its variants are now established and acceptable features of professional education and training at Ulster Polytechnic and elsewhere is not, however, sufficient proof. We would like to be able to refer to a comprehensive evaluation programme comparing SST with other procedures and following up trainees into their professional careers. Lacking a comprehensive evaluation, however, we have tried to walk the tightrope of action research steering a course between the evaluation of practice and the investigation of matters of theoretical interest. This has included work on: (1) behavioural outcomes (Hargie, 1977b); (2) attitudinal change (Tittmar *et al*., 1978; Hargie, 1978a; Hargie *et al*., 1979); (3) review of literature on specific component skills (Hargie, 1978b; Hargie & Dwyer, 1979); (4) relationships between SST outcomes and student personality

(Hargie *et al*., 1978a, b); (5) developments in the procedural model (Hargie & Maidment, 1979; Hargie *et al*., 1977); (6) refinement of the total professional curriculum to include a social skills course (Ellis & Whittington, 1972; Ellis, 1972; Ellis, 1974; Whittington, 1974; Ellis, 1977; Whittington, 1977).

Work is presently in progress investigating further manipulations of procedural variables, exploring further personality and intellectual correlates and pursuing follow-up investigations of counselling skills in employment guidance personnel.

It is to be hoped that this and subsequent research will contribute not only to the evaluation and refinement of our SST procedures but to the derivation of a model of the cognitive processes underlying social interaction as such. This in its turn should contribute to the continuing elucidation of an appropriate heuristic for the promotion of effective interaction in novitiates to the interpersonal professions.

We began this section by identifying skill selection, procedural refinement, resource development, staff involvement and curriculum integration as themes emerging from our historical account. As must be evident from the above they are interwoven and interdependent, but separate summaries may help to make them more explicit.

(1) Skill Selection

Skills have always been selected at Ulster Polytechnic on a mixed empirical/analytical basis with heavy emphasis placed upon the participation of relevant professional staff. It might have been thought that this would result in the derivation of very idiosyncratic specialist skill sequences but this has not proved to be the case. No doubt the continued presence of a nucleus of unit staff explains this in part as does the probable reluctance of professional staff new to the field to move from established practice.

Differences between professions have been evinced more in the emphasis given to particular skills and in the content chosen for the exercise of skills than in the derivation of skills specific to an individual profession.

A broad distinction between information gathering, expository, and supportive skill sets has proved to be the most useful model in our initial categorisation of professional activity. Thus in social work there is *some* use of exposition (e.g. explaining points of benefits legislation to clients), but the major emphases are upon supportive and information-gathering skills, whereas in teaching the emphasis is reversed with exposition, information gathering and support being the order of importance and skill priority. Within these broad divisions some skills are more frequently selected than others and indeed some are used in all of our programmes – although particular emphases and content may vary *within* the skill practice. Thus questioning for students of teaching would usually have a different emphasis from questioning for social workers.

We have termed these frequently selected skills 'generic'. They are:

exposition	–	explaining
		set induction
		closure
information gathering	–	questioning
support	–	reinforcement
		paraphrasing
		reflection of feeling

The list could be extended since many other skills (e.g. demonstration, sustaining, self-disclosure) are common across several courses and indeed many courses are artificially curtailed by the constraint of available time.

Our total skill-list continues to expand. Recent developments include group discussion skills. Skills appropriate to occupational therapists working with patients involved in therapeutic activities are at present under discussion. Interestingly, despite the continuing diversification of professional groups, the skills first identified for teachers and health visitors have proved extremely robust. With a few additions (such as self-disclosure) skills at Ulster Polytechnic now comprise the following:

Stimulus variation:	behaviour which through its variety has a high probability of increasing fellow interactors' interest and arousal
*Questioning:	behaviour, the interrogative form of which increases the probability of response
*Reinforcement:	behaviour which increases the probability of reoccurrence of preceding behaviour
Illustration and use of examples:	presentation of verbal and non-verbal material which supports a specified communication

*Explanation:	verbal behaviour which clarifies a substantive meaning
*Set induction:	beginning a specified communication so that fellow interactors anticipate its development in predetermined directions
*Closure:	completing and consolidating a specified communication
Demonstration:	verbal and non-verbal behaviour aimed at increasing the probability of its accurate imitation
*Paraphrasing:	responding to the contributions of fellow interactors by restating them in a more concise form
Summarising:	interrupting the flow of a dialogue by concisely restating its previous content
*Reflection of feeling:	responding to the emotional tone of fellow interactors' contributions with verbal and non-verbal behaviour from which the same emotional tone might be inferred
Sustaining:	responding neutrally to emotionally charged communication from fellow interactors; increasing the probability of further display of the behaviour
Self-disclosure:	verbal reference to personal experience likely to facilitate similar disclosure in fellow interactors

Each addition and modification to the skills-list has been the result of lengthy debate and negotiation with professional tutors supplemented by empirical analysis of relevant videotape skill. Integration is also a current concern and several course teams are reconsidering the order of presentation of skills. Rating focuses (and in some cases observation schedules for behaviour counting) have been developed for each of our skills. Those asterisked are described in detail in Hargie *et al.* (1981), the companion volume to this book.

(2) Procedural Refinement

All of our programmes continue to use the classic sensitisation, practice, feedback cycle. Within each of these headings, however, substantial modifications have taken place. Sensitisation, for example, now takes much longer than previously and is supplemented by log-book preparation and other homeworks. Within the college-based sensitisation work the availability of demonstrative model tapes continues to improve as 'simulated' exemplars become easier to prepare and as we gain increasing access to real professional interaction. Our descriptive model material has also developed over the years: the Hargie *et al.* volume referred to above is based upon such descriptive material.

Refinement of our approach to skill practice has largely consisted of increased flexibility to meet the needs of diverse courses. Students practise with school pupils, real clients, peers or special confederates as seems appropriate and it is our impression that there are advantages and disadvantages to each variant. Likewise the length of skill practice varies with the skill in question. Broadly speaking, integrated skills take longer than single skills although again there are variations for particular courses.

Initially skill practice was 'content neutral' but we very quickly realised that this reduced the face-validity of the skill considerably. Skill content (e.g. lesson-plan, role-play, discussion topic) now varies in both type and specific content and indeed is the most idiosyncratic aspect of the practice phase.

Feedback is now given exclusively in groups and in the presence of the tutor since we have found that group support is an advantage and that students prefer to have the tutor present. Tutor style in these feedback sessions is facilitative rather than directive, although students are pressed to make as much use of the taped evidence as possible and to relate it where possible to the sensitisation phase. Supplements to videotape feedback in the form of observation schedules were initially exclusively behaviour category systems. Recently we have tended to make more use of rating focuses although systematic investigation of the relative merits of two forms of behaviour counting (sign and category systems) and of rating continues.

(3) Resource Development

We started SST (microteaching) at Ulster Polytechnic with two CCTV trolleys and no designated accommodation.

The trolleys were planned as self-contained audio-visual recording and playback units. Each contained a video-camera, video-tape recorder (reel-to-reel ½"), 9" monitor and microphone mixer. Microphones were separate from the trolley to be placed strategically with regard to teachers and those being taught: we experimented with a radio microphone for the teacher but it proved most unreliable and thus intrusive.

The idea was that the trolley should be trundled from room to room allowing microteaching to occur where appropriate. In the event the trolley proved transportable rather than portable. Lengthy readjustment seemed necessary after every trip: clearly movement did not suit the CCTV technology of the time. Wires seemed to sprout everywhere and, left to their own devices, were prone to mingle in a tangled embrace.

The trolley was certainly perceived as conspicuous. Its technicalities, while simple in principle, proved unduly challenging to many staff in practice, and the frequent interventions of a technician were an added distraction. It was a significant advance, then, when several small rooms were acquired and the present system of separate recording and playback was initiated. In essence, the system consists of a basic two-room unit. In one room – the recording room – are microphones and a remote-controlled camera; in the other – the playback room – are controls for the camera, microphone mixer, videotape recorder and monitor. This system has survived, in essence, in our latest accommodation.

The recording room is furnished with basic chairs, tables and easy chairs which are arranged to simulate classroom, clinic, office or home. The remote-controlled camera, which has zoom lens and pan/tilt facilities, is inconspicuously located above head-height in a room corner. Microphones are suspended from the ceiling, again well above head-height, as inconspicuously as possible.

The playback room has VCR, microphone mixer, remote controls and monitor on a stout bench at one side of the room with all wires neatly 'plumbed-in'. Sufficient seats are provided for group viewing and analysis. There are cupboards for videotapes, observation schedules and handouts.

Subsequent developments involved the creation of additional two-room units, as specified above, until six units were available. Three units had recording rooms of small size, 200 square feet, while three were of classroom proportions, 600 square feet. The latter were useful for certain microteaching ventures but generally inappropriately large necessitating screens for counselling and similar activities.

In 1979 the unit moved to new custom-built accommodation. Here eight units (16 rooms) of suitable proportions (recording room 300 ft^2, playback room 150 ft^2) are available. A further large room acts as a studio for the preparation of model tapes. There are rooms for unit staff (academics and technicians) and a store.

Communication between recording and playback rooms is effected by means of a telephone intercom system. A visual display of red, amber and green lights also allows unobtrusive signalling from control room to recording room so that participants know when to begin and end interaction. These systems replaced a buzzer system which trainees had found intrusive.

Until 1979 the unit had worked with reel-to-reel black-and-white CCTV equipment. The move to new accommodation coincided with an upgrading of CCTV equipment. The camera was relocated in the playback room and now records events in the recording room through a small glass screen located above head-height. Reel-to-reel recording tape was replaced by cassette, a distinct improvement in convenience and ease of handling. Black-and-white yielded to colour. When properly adjusted this is, of course, strikingly more realistic. However, no systematic comparison has been made of the value of black-and-white compared with colour for feedback. A full specification of the present equipment of the unit is given in Appendix 5.

(4) Staff

The most significant resource in the enterprise, and the most expensive, is staff. It would be neither appropriate nor particularly helpful, in a book of this kind to catalogue the virtues of the individuals who have contributed to SST at Ulster Polytechnic. However, certain general trends may be discerned.

It has been most valuable to have first one and now three members of staff whose sole workload is SST. The logistics of SST, where a large number of students receive tuition over short time-spans and where clients must be organised to coincide with trainees, are complex and time consuming. The development and refinement of model tapes, role-plays, observation schedules and general handouts is a major task. Tuition for trainees is intensive and requires sensitivity, tact and sustained concentration. We have no doubt that these tasks require a full-time commitment. The background of our SST staff is in psychology and this seems to us essential in view of the theoretical provenance of the activity. Previous experience in SST would obviously be desirable but is not easy to come by!

Equally important to the central nucleus of staff is the contribution of professional tutors, i.e. qualified social workers, health visitors etc. As we have stressed throughout this book, we see the skills and procedures of a particular programme emerging from negotiation between professional tutors and unit tutors. The teaching of the programme with regard to both practical work and theory is then shared between unit and professional tutors. We have been fortunate in the commitment and capabilities of our professional tutors; over the years some 40 tutors from the various interpersonal professions have shared in the development and teaching of the SST programmes for their students.

One of the most interesting features of these negotiations has been the relationship between the theoretical background and practical experience of the participants and their acceptance or rejection of SST. At one end of a continuum, psychologists with a behavioural orientation and an applied commitment have moved into SST fairly naturally: conversely tutors in English Literature with no background in empirical investigation and an intuitive approach to interaction have found SST uncongenial or even abhorrent.

The likely initial (and sometimes sustained) response of participating staff seems to be related to the values characteristic of their academic discipline or profession. It is no doubt also related to personality, ability, and attitudinal factors but we have no data on these. The following are our observations on the academic and professional groups with whom we have been involved.

Social skill training has a clear academic provenance in the observation and analysis of social interaction and in cybernetic models of skilled performance. Psychologists with these interests, and indeed most psychology graduates, find SST a readily intelligible and congenial activity. Psychologists of a more humanistic persuasion tend to characterise SST as over-mechanistic and positivistic. A similar stance to the latter is frequently adopted by sociologists who subscribe to the anti-empirical, anti-positivist position characteristic of many practitioners of the discipline. Linguistics, conversely, has swung in recent years from predominantly theoretical preoccupations to an enthusiastic commitment to empiricism in the form of psycholinguistics and sociolinguistics. We have found linguists, particularly those interested in discourse analysis, keen to contribute to SST. The important characteristic here seems to be a methodological commitment to the empirical investigation of social interaction with its acceptance of publicly observable behaviour as a significant feature of this interaction.

Differences have also emerged between our interpersonal professions with regard to their acceptance of SST. Some professions have a ready acceptance of the observable as significant material and of controlled experience as a legitimate feature of professional education and training. Others couple a dismissal of behaviour as legitimate subject matter with a rejection of controlled behaviour change as a training goal. A related dimension concerns the willingness of the profession concerned to focus on tactics as well as broad strategies. Thus social workers are frequently more at ease in the discussion of social change at a societal level than in the analysis of behavioural change in their clients. Conversely physiotherapists readily accept a most refined description of their clients' movements and the therapists' intervention while eschewing critical discussion of medicine and paramedicine as aspects of social policy. Professionally then, SST chimes with a willingness to focus on the micro-features of professional-client interaction and to make explicit the objectives of professional action and the goals of professional training.

For those who intend to mount social skill training programmes it is as well to anticipate those academic and professional values which might facilitate or inhibit the process. It is a tribute to the robustness of SST that in our experience initial antipathies can be overcome and, indeed, many of the most initially resistant participants have become the most fervent converts. We would emphasise again however that it is better for the conversion process to take place before training itself begins and a preparation period for new tutors (including if need be a formal course) is vital.

(5) Curriculum Integration

We will return to this theme more fully in Chapter 6, but we will here summarise our approach to SST in the curriculum: we have over 10 years become increasingly committed to SST as a microcosm of a total approach which addresses skills in context and which applies across a wide spectrum of higher education. We have also become increasingly aware that SST is not in itself and by itself a panacea for whatever ills beset professional training. Without adequate integration and without adoption of the larger model it is a transplant prone to rejection outside the intensive care available within the training unit.

Case Studies

SST at Ulster Polytechnic began as microteaching, extended to SST as an element in courses of professional education, generalised from this to constitute a generic course in social skills, and now includes a course for SST trainers. The second part of this chapter presents three case studies chosen to exemplify the significant steps in this development.

Microteaching is sufficiently well-documented elsewhere so our first case study is of a professional course which includes SST: the Health

Visitor's Diploma. The SST part of this course is a blend of two traditions: microteaching and micro-counselling modified to suit the needs of this unique profession which includes elements of nursing, social work and teaching.

The second course chosen as a case study is that provided for undergraduates studying for a BSc in Human Communication. Here social skills are presented at the most generic level compatible with maintaining a practical focus.

The increasing popularity of SST has created a demand for persons who are able to plan and implement SST programmes. Our final case study, therefore, is of a course for such would-be trainers – 'training the trainers'.

In the case of health visiting and human communication the SST course will be considered as an exemplification of the decision-making process for course designers which we outlined in Chapter 2. The integration of each course with the rest of the diploma or degree curriculum will be treated in outline only as the issue concerned will be fully discussed in Chapter 6.

(1) A Professional Course: SST for Health Visitors

Background. The Diploma in Health Visiting has been sited in Ulster Polytechnic since September 1972 when it moved from the Royal College of Nursing, Belfast, and six intakes of approximately 40 students have since completed the 51-week course. All but the first group of students have undertaken SST as part of the course.

Health visitors are qualified nurses and midwives who, after training, work as community nurses in a specified geographical area or attached to a specified doctor's practice, which is usually a group practice and which can, of course, overlap geographically with other practices. They are conceived as members of a primary health care team and have a particular responsibility for preventive medicine, giving a wide range of advice and guidance on health and social problems and acting as case-finders for other more specialised health or social work agencies. They usually have a defined role to visit all mothers of children under five years of age to give advice on childhood problems and are thus the only welfare agency with responsibility to visit all families whether the family requests a visit or not.

Originally most of the health visitor's work was closely related to health problems, but this has gradually expanded into general areas of counselling and support for parents so that pre-school education, behaviour problems, family readjustment following the birth of a child and other 'social' problems are commonly dealt with. A similar expansion has taken place in the range of clients dealt with and health visitors can be found giving antenatal advice, working in family planning clinics, as contact tracers in VD clinics, or liaising with a particular hospital unit which provides a community service (e.g. psychiatric, renal dialysis or coronary care departments). They also play a large part in formal health education taking a teaching role in schools and community groups. In the specifically domiciliary context an increasing proportion of the health visitor's time is now spent in routine visiting of the elderly where counselling on social as well as health problems is again given. As a professional activity health visiting represents an interesting interface between conventional models of teaching, group work, counselling and nursing.

Embarkation upon the Diploma in Health Visiting is thus in several respects a watershed in the career pattern of its students. It represents a change from a clear primary focus on patients' health and physical well-being to a more diffuse concern for their social and psychological welfare; from curative to preventive and educational measures; from hospital ward to community; and from action within the framework to shared responsibility offered by hospital work to the relatively autonomous action expected of the community worker. Students are thus required to develop new knowledge, attitudes and skills. In particular, compared with their role as nurses, they are required to develop interpersonal skills appropriate to interaction with a wider range of people in a wider range of settings and in pursuit of more varied outcomes.

The curriculum which they follow during 51 very intensive weeks of study is as recommended by the Central Council for the Education and Training of Health Visitors who oversee the courses provided by the various educational institutions, who approve external examiners to the courses and who make the award of qualification as a health visitor. The CETHV's recommended syllabus (1979) has a section entitled 'Theories and Methods of Health Visiting Practice' within which it is suggested students will develop 'the art of looking and listening' and 'the use of understanding and empathy'. It is within that rubric that SST was introduced into the Diploma course at Ulster Polytechnic.

Curriculum Innovation. It is rare for SST to be planned as an aspect of a coherent curriculum design. More usually it is added to an existing curriculum as an experimental novelty. In this case SST was introduced as a partial solution to the well-known problem of how to bridge the gap between college work and placement: to find a middle ground between contemplation and theorising on the one hand and everyday activity on the other. Health visitor tutors charged with the paradoxical injunction to teach practice recognised that the microteaching being provided to link educational studies and teaching practice for teacher trainees might similarly link principles of health visiting and fieldwork practice for their students.

The Planning Team. Planning was undertaken by health visitor tutors and psychology tutors, the latter being more or less entirely employed in the provision of microteaching and associated studies. Hardly surprisingly this team tended to emphasise initially the teaching aspects of health visiting and relied heavily on the Stanford package of skills and procedures. Gradually the programme introduced more profession-specific skills and broadened to include counselling skills adapted in the first instance from Ivey (1971). Health visitor tutors varied in their initial reactions to the proposed programme but quickly became enthused by its possibilities. It may be that the empiricism of their medical and scientific background coupled with the heightened consciousness of interactive skills induced by the transition from hospital to community nursing engendered a complex of attitudes and awareness in which SST was readily acceptable.

The Trainees. Admission to a course of health visitor training is contingent upon possession of general and obstetric nursing qualifications and students are, therefore, by definition more mature than the average undergraduate student. Additionally, most health visitor students spend some years in general hospital nursing before making the move towards the community and many use the health visitor course as an appropriate preparation for the return to work after years of raising their own families.

Thus health visitor students manifest characteristics typical of mature students, including anxiety about standards of work, difficulty in unaccustomed 'academic' tasks such as essay writing, examination answering etc. These particular mature students also suffer from the contrast between their past educational and work experience and the notionally freer and more questioning ambience of a polytechnic. Dingwall (1977) for example, suggests that health visitor students come to the course imbued with commonsense prescriptive notions about individual and social problems and that while they can accept their replacement by other prescriptions presented by authority figures (e.g.

tutors) 'teaching which directly questions this (prescriptive) style of teaching is quite unintelligible to the health visitor students' (p. 212).

The influence of these student characteristics upon the effectiveness of the SST programme is difficult to assess precisely but it is our impression that anxiety levels are somewhat higher with this group than with younger students and that the so-called 'cosmetic effect' (a preoccupation with how one looks on TV) takes somewhat longer to wear off. It has also been the case that while almost all health visitor students have been overwhelmingly enthusiastic (after the event) about their experience a small number have maintained a vocal antagonism throughout. Such persistent disapproval is unusual (or at least unexpressed) in other groups. It could be argued that health visitor students respond well to the apparent prescriptiveness of the technique but find it less easy to work their way through the analysis and questioning of empirical evidence which afford an arena for more rational debate.

The Context. Given the limitations of CETHV guidelines it has not been possible to integrate SST as fully as will be recommended in Chapter 6. None the less steps have been taken to ensure the maximum possible exploitation of the 'action focus' model (see Chapter 6). Thus the total curriculum is conceived and taught as comprising three major elements namely practical skills, knowledge directly related to such skills and knowledge which provides a context for the operation of the skills. SST is, therefore, closely linked not only to the directly-relevant theory presented in the sensitisation and feedback phases of the training programme but also to contextual theory from psychology and sociology taught in concurrent courses in 'The Development of the Individual' and 'The Individual and the Group' both of which are curriculum blocks prescribed by CETHV.

More obviously, perhaps, links are fostered between SST and other practical skill areas of the course, particularly fieldwork practice. Students do five weeks of block practice and 20 single days of practice during the first two semesters of the course and it culminates in a ten-week supervised practice. The SST course takes place during the first two semesters in parallel with the one-day-per-week concurrent practice. Students are encouraged to relate their SST experiences to fieldwork and vice versa and are given exercises for inclusion in the SST log-book which they can only complete successfully by reference to their fieldwork practice. The health visitor tutors who are responsible for preparing students for fieldwork are also involved as members of the SST team and can thus discuss both fieldwork and SST with students with similar emphases upon skill practice and can pick up the strengths and weaknesses which students displayed in SST for further work on placement. These tutors also visit students on practice, but close day-to-day supervision of students is provided by fieldwork supervisors who are health visitors practising in the unit or area to which the student is attached. To some extent, therefore, the exploitation and transfer of SST skills stands or falls by the extent to which these supervisors understand and concur with its objectives. The potential difficulty is exacerbated by the fact that while SST itself is not assessed, fieldwork supervisors' assessments have a substantial weighting in the final judgement upon students. Thus students who find it difficult to relate SST to the circumstances of their practice might be encouraged to abandon the specificity and rigour of the skills approach for a more diffuse attempt to model themselves upon the 'master practitioner' – in this case the fieldwork supervisor.

All supervisors undergo periodic training courses and a gradual attempt is being made to foster understanding of SST and its relationship to fieldwork practice. It is hoped that supervisors will also be involved in the skill-analysis exercises which are described below. One further long-term source of influence upon supervisors is the relative geographical isolation of Northern Ireland which engenders a fairly stable professional group within which an increasing number of practising health visitors and hence of supervisors will have experienced SST in their own training courses.

Logistics. SST for health visitors has, of course, benefitted from the gradual expansion of equipment, staff support and accommodation for SST which has taken place between 1973 and 1980. None the less logistic constraints remain since demand for SST has tended to increase rather faster than facilities for it. Furthermore the intensity of the health visitor curriculum as a whole has limited the extent to which SST could expand within it.

Five hours per week during 23 weeks of the course are now designated as SST time. This represents a substantial investment from a total weekly contact time of some 25 hours. The five hours includes all teaching which takes place in the unit, but does not include the time which students spend in related private study or in relevant learning in psychology, principles of health visiting or elsewhere. The sessions can include periods in which the whole group gather together (e.g. for sensitisation lecture/discussions) and periods in which students work in small groups (e.g. for skill practice and feedback). In the first few years of the health visitor course only four recording and playback units were available and students therefore worked in groups of ten. This was less than satisfactory and groups of six to seven now occupy each of six units of the new suite. Even so, it is sometimes difficult within the available five hours to ensure that all students have sufficient time for practice and feedback.

As in all professional courses the staff working as SST tutors are a combination of professional tutors and tutors on the permanent staff of the unit. Responsibility for sensitisation sessions and other work with the whole group of 40 students is shared between both groups of staff. One tutor, who can be professional or SST, is assigned to each small group. In the initial stages of SST for health visitors professional tutors spent a considerable time in formal and informal discussion with SST staff, both to determine the best skills and procedures for students and to extend their awareness of the objectives and principles of SST. Naturally, health visitor staff differed in their response to the initiative and although all eventually agreed to the inclusion of SST in the course, variations in enthusiasm and approach to the work with students remained. Enthusiasm apart, individual tutors inevitably adopt slightly different styles and emphases in the feedback and guidance which they offer. This is likely to be particularly marked between tutors with and without a professional background. Students perceive this difference but when invited to state a preference for one kind of tutor or the other are reluctant to do so; those who have been tutored by a professional see the advantages but wish they had been able to focus more on the rigorous analysis of their interaction while those who have been tutored by unit staff also see the advantages but wish they had been able to explore the health visitor context further. This observation has a parallel in Griffiths *et al.'s* (1977) finding that students who had experienced different tutor 'styles' all 'wanted more of what they did not receive and less of what they did receive. That is they were declaring that more effective supervisory sessions depend upon various strategies and that they could make use of the information which such variety would provide'. It seems clear, therefore, that students benefit from the variety of tutors provided in the health visitor course, but that there is merit in encouraging them to compare notes and share experiences. It is important, however, that all tutors appear to students as committed to the general objectives of SST, and general discussion sessions with all staff and students are, therefore, used to foster a spirit of exploration and critical debate within the agreed consensus.

The Skills. SST with any professional group is premised upon preliminary analysis of relevant interaction and, ideally, such analysis is derived from extensive empirical study. Unfortunately such empirical enquiry remains rare. When SST for health visitors was first proposed in 1973 the available data (Nuffield Provincial Hospitals Trust, 1950; Morris, 1971; Clark, 1973) provided useful information on the day-to-day activities of health visitors, but employed a global level of analysis (e.g. method of communication viz. letter, telephone, face-to-face, other (Clark, 1973)) or failed to focus upon interpersonal communication at any level. Skills for the SST programme could not, therefore, be derived direct from empirical data. Health visitors were, however, being trained and it seemed likely, therefore, that health visitor tutors and other experienced practitioners had arrived at some implicit consensus as to the relevant interpersonal skills of health visiting.

In the first instance the emphasis of the skill sequence was upon the teaching role of the health visitor (in health education activities in schools and clinics) since it was possible to adapt the microteaching skill sequence. These skills at least had some valid relationship to positive outcomes and, indeed, could be included in programmes of skill training with some hope of acceptability to trainees. The skills first used were the Stanford skills of questioning, reinforcement, set induction, closure, explaining and demonstration.

Health visitor staff and students recognised that SST could have a utility beyond the strict confines of health education and teaching. Since SST staff at that time had become aware of Ivey's (1971) work on micro-counselling, it was entirely predictable that the interviewing and counselling aspects of health visiting should present themselves as likely arenas for the extension of microteaching into 'miniteaching' as it was first called and, eventually, social skills training. Sustaining, reflection of feeling and paraphrasing (as defined above) were the skills adapted from Ivey (1971) for incorporation in the health visitor sequence.

As already noted there is a dearth of appropriate empirical evidence for the prevalence or significance of specific interpersonal skills in professional interaction and health visiting is no exception to this general rule. The criteria for skill selection were, therefore, analytical and their validity was limited in the first instance to face validity. Skills were included if they could be demonstrated as a logical consequence of health visiting aims and were at the same time intuitively 'right' for professional health visitor tutors.

The generic applicability of questioning, reinforcement, paraphrasing and reflection of feeling has already been discussed in Chapter 3. But as included in the health visitor sequence they are applied in situations relevant to health visitor practice and some subsets of the skills become more important than they might be in other professional areas. The subsets given particular emphasis are those included as rating focuses in the schedules (see Appendix 4). Thus questioning skill is rated for wording, variety, sequence and structure, appropriate use of probing and prompting, and attending to responses. As indicated in the brief discussion of questioning in Chapter 3 and as elaborated in Hargie *et al.* (1981) these focuses are useful in many contexts, but in health visiting SST rating is carried out with regard to appropriate health visitor practice in a one-to-one interview. For example, matching the wording of questions to the comprehension skills of a range of clients and the avoidance of unnecessary medical jargon is more important to health visitors than might be the case in teaching where it would be appropriate to incorporate technicalities so as to extend and test pupils' knowledge. Similarly probing and prompting in a supportive framework of explanation and approval may be more important than prompting to facilitate problem-solving achievements. The technique of prompting by restating or exemplifying a previous question ('Yes, you're not remembering things so well – do you sometimes have to go back to the shops for things you've forgotten'?) is identical to that used in teaching (Yes, it's a kind of fossil – can you remember the ones we saw at the beach last week?), but the context in which it is set and the content upon which it is focused are very different and behaviour rated highly on probing and prompting in microteaching might be regarded as unduly assertive (or even aggressive) in one-to-one interviewing or counselling. It is, incidentally, apparent that the non-verbal accompaniments of verbal questioning make a considerable difference to interactional style – a measure of briskness as expressed through posture, facial expression, tone of voice etc. is more likely to be rated highly in teaching and less likely to be so rated in counselling.

Similar variations between specific professional groups occur in the rating focuses and patterns of tutor scoring for the other skills in the health visitor sequence but, as discussed in Chapter 3, the skills themselves and to a large extent their subsets, have been remarkably recurrent across different professions and groups. Indeed, it has been at times a disappointment to SST tutors to discover that the professional specificity of interpersonal behaviour is something of a chimera and that broad categories of expository, information gathering and supportive behaviour may provide sufficient differentiation between groups to allow for the design of appropriate SST programmes built around skills and subsets of skills already in use with other groups.

During the seven years of SST with health visitors which have now passed, modification and development of the skills-list has continued in the light of feedback from students, tutors and fieldwork staff, developments in other areas of SST and further observation and analysis of the professional activities of health visitors. Regrettably, the systematic investigation of health visitor interaction on a large enough scale for generalisation beyond our own student groups has proved difficult to find although CETHV has encouraged small-scale initiatives and a good deal of preliminary work has gone on.

The skill sequence now used is as indicated in Table 4.1.

Table 4.1: Skill Sequence for Health Visitor Students

Week (5 hrs per week)	Skill	Practice Mode*
1	Introduction to unit; explication of skills model; first self-observation	
2	Principles of behaviour analysis; video-recording of conversation (no skill focus) with subsequent analysis	
3	Reinforcement	One-to-one
4	Questioning	One-to-one
5	Integration of reinforcement and questioning	One-to-one
6	Group problem-solving exercise	
7	Group leadership skills	Group
8	Set induction	Group
9	Closure	Group
10	Integration of set induction and closure	Group
11	Integration of reinforcement, questioning, set induction and closure	Group
12	Sustaining	One-to-one
13	Reflection of feeling	One-to-one
14	Paraphrasing	One-to-one
15	Integration of reflection of feeling and paraphrasing	One-to-one
16	Explaining	Group
17	Demonstration	Group
18/19	Integration of all expository skills	Group (longer practice)
20/21	Integration of interview skills	One-to-one
22/23	Review and evaluation	

*All practices are with fellow students and, except where indicated, last for 5-10 minutes. Practice group size is 6-7.

The major recent additions are the weeks devoted to the integration of skills and the small sequence on group discussion. The group discussions have been included on the observation that health visitors working in schools, antenatal clinics and day-centres for the handicapped or elderly spend a good deal of time in such discussion. In group discussions facilitative leadership skills are at a premium. It has also been suggested by tutors that such skills might transfer to case conferences with other professionals (e.g. in a group practice) or to general committee work.

The order in which the skills are presented and the length of time devoted to each of them has been arrived at by gradual negotiation and feedback, but it retains some of the characteristics of the classic micro-teaching and micro-counselling lists in that the more elemental skills (see Chapter 3) occur first (i.e. questioning and reinforcement) so that they can be exploited within the 'larger' (see Chapter 3) skills such as closure or explaining which follow. A further advantage of this ordering is that objective observation of skill frequency and spread is easier to achieve with the more reduced skills. Students can thus be led into analysis techniques during feedback which they might find both more difficult and less acceptable if they were working on a less specific skill like paraphrasing or explaining which demands a higher level of inference (Rosenshine, 1971) in identification and rating. Other aspects of the skill-order have been influenced by the special needs of health visitor students. The sequence progresses for example from 'teaching' or expository skills through supportive 'counselling' skills and back to teaching skills and from one-to-one to group interaction. This progression is in part designed to mesh with concurrent (one day per week) fieldwork activities and in part to facilitate the teaching of linked theory in a coherent fashion.

Similar evolution has led to the significant extension of the introductory or 'cosmetic' period. This now occupies up to two weeks or ten hours in which students learn about the social skill model upon which SST is based, observe, discuss and try to analyse videotapes of relevant interaction and have their first experience of 'seeing themselves on television'. As already indicated these students are often very anxious and log-book entries from the first two weeks reflect their early preoccupation with superficial appearances. The period also gives tutors an opportunity for individual counselling. Health visitor tutors report that every year so far one student at least has come privately to enquire whether she 'really had to do it'!

The Procedures. At the beginning of SST with health visitors a standard procedure for sensitisation, practice and feedback was followed, but as the skills list developed some flexibility became necessary and slightly different procedures are now followed at different stages in the sequence. This is particularly so with group discussion skills.

In each typical week approximately two hours are devoted to lecture discussion with the entire group and three hours are spent in small-group practice and feedback. Each session begins with a sensitisation period. Students are given handouts outlining the justification for the skill's inclusion, identifying and describing it and exemplifying its use in health visitor practice. These are then discussed and clarified with tutors and exemplar videotapes are shown. Further discussion takes place based on the tapes and students are given observation schedules which they will later use in the analysis of their own practice tapes.

These schedules were initially category schedules and students were required to score the frequency and spread of skill elements, but these proved difficult for students to use and also difficult to design for high-inference skills. Little is known, for example, of the precise role of gaze in appropriate reflection of feeling or of the precise syntactic forms which engender 'clarity' in an explanation. These features can, however, be reliably rated and students are, therefore, taught to use rating schedules (see Appendix 4) for each skill in the sequence and are encouraged in feedback discussion with tutors and fellow students to justify their ratings by reference to behaviours observable on their tapes.

The model tapes currently used with health visitor students are 'mock-up' tapes devised by unit and professional tutors rather than tapes of real *in vivo* health visitor interactions. They have proved satisfactory in so far as they exemplify skills and facilitate imitation by students. Face validity can be lost, however, when students recognise a simulated client as 'one of last year's students' or 'that other psychology tutor' and recognition of the simulated professional (often a professional tutor) can provoke other biases towards tact and social desirability in the comments offered. Alternative model tapes from 'real life' are presently being collected, but it will be some time before a complete set is available since access with video equipment can only be gradually obtained as confidence is built up and problems of confidentiality and professional ethics are resolved.

In the typical skill students move (after sensitisation) into small-group practice using role-plays. Two students are cast respectively as client and health visitor in each role-play. After some time for thought they act it out in the recording room while the other four to five members of the group and the tutor observe them through the monitor in the playback room. Real clients may in future be brought into the unit for some skills (e.g. teaching skills), but it will always be difficult, and probably unethical, to use real clients for the more supportive skill areas where appropriate role-plays might deal with personal problems of a confidential nature. Fortunately it can also be argued that knowledge that problems are simulated encourages students to experiment with their own interactional style whereas real problems might encourage undue caution. Similar support for the use of peers rather than real clients derives from the well-established finding that perceptions of clients are elaborated if students are encouraged to take their part in role-plays. Thus although the focus in SST is upon the student role-playing the health visitor, benefit also accrues for the student playing the client.

The role-plays used by health visitors are devised by professional tutors in consultation with unit tutors and are all health visitor-related. In the first year of SST the health visitor role-plays were deliberately 'content neutral' in an attempt to increase focus on the skill rather than upon loose health visitor prescriptiveness. The loss of face-validity was such, however, that role-plays of health visiting were rapidly substituted and have been used ever since.

Skill focus has become increasingly easy to ensure as professional tutors have increased in experience. The role-plays now used (see Appendix 4) are presented in brief outline with an integral prompt as to intended action. Previous role-plays were presented in much more detail, but students reported that they spent a great deal of time memorising the role rather than exploring its implications and having memorised it often reproduced it verbatim in acting it out. Tutors report that feedback discussions are both more likely and more skill-focused since the change to briefer role-plays. The content of role-plays covers a range of settings and client types and varies according to the skill to be practised. No attempt is made to increase the 'difficulty' of the problems encountered and within each small group students choose which role-plays they will act out. Each student role-plays a client and a health visitor during each skill practice session.

The major departure from this practice scheme takes place in the weeks devoted to group discussion skills. In these weeks students are first given a problem to discuss in a leaderless group. They then view the taped discussion using a variant of Bales Interaction Analysis (Bales, 1950) and discuss their performance. This entire exercise is effectively a sensitisation phase for group discussion skills. In the second week attention is focused upon leadership tasks and styles and each student then leads a brief discussion on a specified topic. The discussion is taped.

In these and other weeks once each student has completed the role-plays the entire small group moves into the playback room for analysis and feedback. Tutor and fellow students alike comment upon the performances and tutors endeavour to be facilitative rather than directive in their supervisory style. Typically the entire group will review the tape with the 'performer', adding to their rating schedules as appropriate. The 'performer' is invited to comment upon the tape and to give her own ratings which then form the basis of discussion. Willingness to comment adversely or even accurately upon colleagues' performance varies as the group becomes accustomed to the procedure and each other, but frankness is customary and the presence of the tape encourages justification of comments by reference to observable evidence. These sessions also stimulate reference back to general points of theory and forward to potential fieldwork and post-qualification experience.

Relevance to health visiting is fostered throughout sensitisation, practice and feedback and it is hoped that this in itself will promote transfer and generalisation of skills learned and developed in the unit. Further steps towards the optimisation of transfer are taken by asking students to keep a log-book in which they collate all relevant lecture notes, observation schedules etc. (guidelines for the log-book are reproduced in Appendix 4). They are also asked to comment upon the implications of each skill for health visitor practice, to evaluate the skills in the light of SST, relevant theory and fieldwork experience and to take the log-book with them for regular discussion with the fieldwork supervisor. Thus SST is integrated as far as possible with the rest of their course experience and in particular with fieldwork.

Monitoring and Evaluation. SST for health visitors has been informally monitored throughout its operation by means of discussion between staff and students, between unit and professional tutors and between practising professionals and tutors. Student log-books and tapes have provided bases for these discussions which have led to significant modifications in the skill sequence. Face-validity at least has thus been ensured but predictive validity as measured against post-qualification performance has yet to be systematically evaluated. Informally, fieldwork supervisors' increasing enthusiasm for SST and qualified students' reports (as gathered at occasional in-service courses and meetings) lend support to the hypothesis that the technique is successful. Systematic research on the usefulness of specific aspects of the health visitor programme, on individual skills, on skill order and on feedback and sensitisation techniques remains desirable as does analysis of the relationship between interpersonal skill and the outcomes in real health visitor practice.

(2) A Generic Course: SST for Undergraduate Students of Human Communication

Background. Generic SST courses are a relatively recent development in SST at Ulster Polytechnic and, indeed, elsewhere since almost all SST in tertiary education takes place within a context of professional education. We have justified SST in non-professional courses such as the BSc in Human Communication and BSc Psychology on educational and vocational grounds. The arguments for the inclusion of SST in the school curriculum have already been rehearsed. Its extension into higher education involves a change in emphasis from the simple transmission of skills to the analysis and understanding of the skilled behaviour as a whole and to the methodology underpinning the acquisition and organisation of knowledge about such behaviour. Thus SST in the undergraduate curriculum is not just a technique for training students to do certain things (however skilfully), but is one among several opportunities for them to encounter a particular tradition within the social sciences – in this case the micro-analysis of interpersonal interaction which has been fostered within the skills model. It might, of course, be argued that such an encounter could be contrived without students undergoing training themselves (by, for example, having them read this book) but, in our experience, involving students in practical problem-solving through training itself is both highly-motivating and a useful exercise in the clarification of concepts.

SST (in the non-professional undergraduate curriculum) can thus be justified on educational grounds. Vocationally its justification is not as direct as it might be in a professional curriculum but none the less, all undergraduates will eventually seek employment, if only after a period of postgraduate training and, arguably, the areas of their employment will bear some relationship to their undergraduate studies. Thus social science or communication studies graduates are likely to move into employment areas where understanding and skill in dealing with people are the major emphasis. The generic SST course is a first step towards the range of postgraduate training experiences which will eventually lead to the acquisition of such understanding and skill. Its inclusion in the non-professional undergraduate curriculum is thus vocationally justified.

The objectives set out for the SST unit in the BSc Human Communication reflect this balance between educational and vocational emphases. They are as follows.

(1) To enable the student to identify, discriminate, and analyse specified social skills.
(2) To encourage the student to relate his study of social skills to a theoretical framework derived from a range of perspectives on group and dyadic interaction.
(3) To provide the student with a comprehensive training paradigm which will enable him to develop and refine his own repertoire of social skills, in diverse social contexts.
(4) To develop in the student a sense of critical awareness, both of self and of others, in interpersonal encounters.

The Planning Team. As a late development in SST at Ulster Polytechnic this course was designed by staff who have a broad experience of SST, particularly in its specialised setting. It thus draws from the start upon wider frameworks both theoretically and practically than did earlier professional courses such as health visiting.

The Trainees. Students embarking upom this course are as diverse as any other group of undergraduates in age, background and level of social skill. They do, however, share a concern for and, by the time they take the SST unit (in their second year), experience of the study of communication within the social sciences. This seems to foster a spirit of enthusiasm tempered with some degree of academic caution. In particular they find it easier to focus upon skill analysis than do professional students and are somewhat less likely to demand instant prescriptions. They also find the techniques of observation and analysis easier to grasp, having already acquired some familiarity with research methods and statistics in their first-year studies.

The Context. The BSc Human Communication approaches the study of communication through major discipline studies in psychology and linguistics with ancillary studies in biology and physics. The integration of these disciplines in the exploration of applied topics is a major emphasis and the SST course is thus one of several in which theory and practice are closely aligned. Students are encouraged to develop links with all other curriculum areas but particularly potent connections exist with courses in social psychology and discourse analysis.

The 'real' context of interaction provided by fieldwork in professional courses cannot be exploited for these students since any such experience is for them both postgraduate and unpredictable. None the less students' experience in summer work or as members of families, leisure groups or, indeed, the student group does involve them in the exercise of social skills. It is to these contexts that this SST course looks in developing practical exercises and assignments.

Logistics. There are normally around 20 students per annum on the course and they are divided for small-group practice into four groups of five. They spend three hours per week on SST for 30 weeks and the typical session includes 1.5 hours of large group work and 1.5 hours of practice and feedback.

So far staffing on this course has been exclusively drawn from SST staff since there is no professional group analogous to the health visitor group. It is hoped, however, that staff from linguistics with an interest in discourse, who are already involved in discussions of skill identification and analysis, may also become involved as tutors to the course.

The Skills. The skills for this programme are chosen according to two basic criteria. First, they must be skills of proven applicability across a wide variety of settings (i.e. they must be among the more generic skills of Chapter 3). Secondly, they must facilitate students' further exploration of the theoretical and methodological context.

In practice the skills included are as set out in Table 4.2. Each skill has also been trained in a number of professional contexts and the complete list contains within it significant skills for expository, persuasive or supportive interaction. It is thus an indirect preparation for a range of employment including teaching, management, salesmanship and the various forms of social work and counselling. A more even balance of time is maintained between skills than in professional courses since no one particular emphasis would be appropriate and the order of skills is determined according to their place on the continuum which extends from elements through sequences of elements to sequences of elements in situations.

The Procedures. Practice as such occupies less time in this course than on professional courses, thus accommodating an increase in the time available for the more theoretical activities derived from the sensitisation and feedback phases. Put crudely, these students spend more time reflecting upon SST than actually doing it and, indeed, in about one-quarter of the course weeks no practice takes place. In these weeks (at the beginning and end of the course) students are helped to relate SST to their other studies and undertake a number of practical exercises in the observation and analysis of interaction which are not only useful in subsequent feedback but are also appropriate to their developing repertoire of research techniques.

Table 4.2: Skill Sequence for Undergraduate Students of Human Communication

Week* (3 hrs per week)	Skill	Practice mode**
1	Introduction to unit; review of social skills model; first self-observation	
2	Reinforcement	One-to-one
3	Questioning	One-to-one
4	Integration of reinforcement and questioning	One-to-one
5	Reflection of feeling	One-to-one
6	Paraphrasing	One-to-one
7	Integration of reflection of feeling and paraphrasing	One-to-one
8	Sustaining	One-to-one
9	Listening	One-to-one
10	Integration of sustaining and listening	One-to-one
11	Self-disclosure	One-to-one
12	Integration of sustaining, listening and self-disclosure	One-to-one
13	Integration of all interview skills	One-to-one (longer practice)
14	Set induction	Group
15	Closure	Group
16	Integration of set induction and closure	Group
17	Explaining	Group
18	Integration of all expository skills	Group (longer practice)
19	Group problem-solving exercise	
20/21	Group leadership skills	Group
22	Review	

* The course lasts 30 weeks in 8 of which lecture/discussion of relevant theory takes place without related skill practice; 5 of these precede the skill sequence and 3 succeed it.
** All practices are with fellow students and, except where indicated last 5-10 minutes. Practice group size is 5.

In weeks in which skill practice as such is to take place a sensitisation session akin to that provided for health visitors precedes it. The tapes used as models are selected from the stock of professional and other interaction sequences so as to exemplify best the skill and so as to provide a range of settings across the total programme. Where a particular type of role-play is to be used in practice the sensitisation tape is matched to it. Inevitably these students are less likely to identify with the models to which they are exposed since they do not share a common professional concern with them. Tutors try to turn this potential problem to advantage, however, by encouraging students to look for skill exemplars and to undertake practical assignments in skill identification and categorisation in a wide range of contexts. They might, for example, be asked to complete observation exercises while watching television 'chat-shows' or elsewhere in their own daily life.

As in health visiting, sensitisation takes place in discussion with the large group and handouts and observation schedules are distributed and discussed. In this case observation schedules are more sophisticated and by the end of the programme have included examples of category and rating forms. Problems of schedule design and validation are more extensively discussed than they are with professional groups and, indeed, discussion throughout the sensitisation phase is placed in a broader evaluative context.

Practice sessions include role-plays of selection interviews, survey interviews and helping interviews, but the total list is more flexible than with professional groups and students are encouraged to participate (a week or so in advance) in devising an appropriate sequence. Role-plays are exclusively with peers and include dyadic and group work in a similar pattern to that for health visitors, although analysis of group interaction is rather more sophisticated since human communication students can draw upon a wider knowledge of the social psychology of small groups.

Feedback is again very similar to that for health visitors although much more attention is paid to the rigorous analysis of tapes using a variety of schedules. These schedules and their discussion are an important element in the log-book compiled throughout the course, the objective of which is to foster transfer not only to potential employment but also to knowledge and skills acquired elsewhere in the curriculum. For students on this generic course the acquisition and refinement of cognitions about social skill is an end in itself as well as an adjunct to behaviour change. Thus traditional academic exercises in essay writing, critical discussion etc. have, legitimately, a central place.

Monitoring and Evaluation. Generic SST has been provided for only two years and monitoring and evaluation are thus in their early stages. Student feedback so far has, however, been positive and traditional academic measures (e.g. examinations) have shown that students can indeed relate their SST experience to other curriculum areas and to hypothesised 'real' interactions.

(3) Trainers' Courses

It is paradoxical that the training of practitioners of systematic interaction training should in itself be unsystematic, but none the less few if any systematic training courses have been organised for social skill trainers and, to our knowledge, none have been subject to empirical validation or indeed to public scrutiny through journal or other publication. Typical trainers have, therefore, developed such skills as they possess by variously reading about SST, observing and discussing it with more experienced trainers or by engaging in it on a trial-and-error basis. The selection of SST trainers is likewise *ad hoc* and formal qualifications range from PhDs and masters degrees in psychology through to 'O' levels and 'some experience' as a supervisor of salesmen. Information qualifications such as previous experience of interpersonal training or enthusiasm for SST also vary widely – the latter from the extremes of proselytising zeal to downright antagonism (cf. Macleod and McIntyre's (1977) comments on teaching practice supervisors' reactions to becoming involved as microteaching tutors).

Despite such variation there is a relationship between degree of qualification and skill and the degree of responsibility taken for the SST programme. The initial design and establishment of a programme is unlikely to be undertaken by an inexperienced opponent of the technique and, typically, programmes have been initiated by individuals with knowledge of (and usually qualification in) psychology and some previous experience of other forms of interpersonal training. These individuals have usually also been responsible for the subsequent induction of trainers with fewer initial qualifications.

The design of effective training programmes (for SST trainers or otherwise) must take account of the objectives of training and of the entry characteristics of trainees. As a first step towards the systematisation of training the trainers it is useful to categorise training objectives. The likely degree of responsibility as trainers provides a rubric for so doing.

Potentially trainers may be involved in SST at the following levels:

(1) Assisting in skill acquisition: in the preliminary assessment of trainees;
as a supervisor of practice and provider of feedback;
as an aide in generalisation procedures.
(2) Implementing pre-existing programmes with minimal modification for specific groups.
(3) Designing and evaluating innovative programmes.
(4) Carrying out basic research on skill identification and acquisition.

The objectives of training and selection criteria for participants in courses vary between each of these levels and we have found it convenient to divide trainer training into tutor training, advanced tutor training and research training.

Tutor Training. Tutor training is essentially the induction of SST staff as programme assistants – levels one and two above.

It might be argued that SST is a potent and even potentially dangerous technique only to be employed by individuals with the highest qualifications and training, but it is clear from the literature that the most successful programmes frequently employ a very wide range of helpers and, indeed, that trainee involvement in the programme may increase if tutors can be readily identified with. We would argue that with training and access after training to more experienced trainers, assistance in the implementation of SST can be readily effected by nurses, social workers, occupational therapists, speech therapists and other paramedicals in the remedial context, by teachers and youth leaders in the developmental context and by a wide range of professional tutors, personnel officers and others responsible for training in specialised contexts. Indeed, if assistance in the generalisation of SST to real-life settings is included it becomes clear that spouses, parents, colleagues at work and, indeed, anyone in the community may provide assistance.

Given this breadth of potential entry to 'training for trainers' it is clear that the training provided must be simple, practical and clearly related to the specific programmes in which participants are to become involved. It should also be fairly brief. None the less it should in our experience, provide the following.

(1) Appreciation of the basic skills model, with emphasis upon the

fact that skills are learned, that trainees can improve and that inadequate social performance is not blameworthy.
(2) Acceptance of the potential effectiveness of the technique.
(3) Skill in objective observation and understanding of the difference between observable events and justified (or unjustified) inference and of the difference between description and prescription.
(4) Understanding of the techniques of reinforcement and feedback to be incorporated in the programme and skill in the use of relevant observation schedules.
(5) Understanding of the specifics of the programme viz. skill sequence, sensitisation procedures etc.

As previously indicated the routes towards the achievement of such objectives are many and various, but we would recommend that minimum tutor training should include discussion and exemplification (preferably with video-tapes) of SST in action, observation practice using appropriate schedules and, preferably, some degree of personal participation as a trainee. The length and degree of difficulty of such tutor training depends upon whether tutors are to be involved in all or part of the acquisition procedure and upon the previous experience and knowledge of the trainee tutors, but the main emphasis at this level should be upon 'how it is done' rather than 'why it is done'. If trainee tutors need or demand a greater critical perspective then it is likely that they would be better accommodated in advanced tutor training.

Advanced Tutor Training. Advanced tutor training is necessary for individuals at level (3) above whose commitment to SST is likely to be greater than occasional participation under the supervision of more experienced tutors. It is particularly important where new SST programmes are to be developed or where the tutor trainee is to have a co-ordinating role in a series of programmes. Likely candidates for such training would include tutors in charge of professional training courses, school teachers with responsibility for careers or pastoral guidance, senior personnel officers, senior paramedical staff etc. Most of these people would have previous experience of training and probably some acquaintance with psychology. A few might have formal qualifications in the subject.

Advanced courses should, of course, achieve the objectives of the basic course outlined above but additionally they should promote:

(1) Appreciation of the methodological context of SST.
(2) Skill in the assessment of individual skill deficit including use of appropriate inventories.
(3) Skill in the design and use of observation schedules for skill identification.
(4) Understanding of the principles of demonstration, practice and feedback underlying acquisition and skill in implementing appropriate procedures for promoting it.
(5) Appreciation of the need for monitoring and evaluation and skill in undertaking appropriate measurement.
(6) Understanding of the principles of programme design.

As should be clear from the above the basic difference between the two forms of training is that advanced tutor training seeks to place SST in a wider critical context. It is assumed that tutor trainees successfully completing such a course would be capable of developing and refining SST procedures to fit the demands of their own trainees and situations and would also be able to participate in basic research in the area.

Research Training. Understanding of the need for research and willingness to participate in it is a desirable outcome of training at all levels but, of course, the design and carrying through of worthwhile research demands special skills.

Typically research in SST has been carried out by practitioners whose research expertise is a function of previous training in psychology or other social science. As has been frequently noted in this book such researchers are often limited by the particular tradition of clinical, educational or social research from which they come and few, if any, SST researchers make cross-reference between remedial, developmental and specialised contexts. Thus behavioural clinicians use psychometric assessment and single-subject methodologies and educationists use classroom observation schedules and attitude scales, while practitioners of specialised SST use research methodologies more obviously derived from their specialism (e.g. intuitive assessment in social work training, emphasis on client acceptability in management training) than from the provenance of SST.

Choice of methodology should be determined by the nature of the problem investigated rather than by the restricted skills of the researcher. Training for SST researchers should, therefore, provide an overview of the entire field. Candidates for such courses would include post-graduates with first degrees in social science and experienced SST practitioners who wanted to develop their evaluative skills.

Each of the levels of training described above is necessary for the development and evaluation of SST. As previously noted, however, systematic courses are rare. We at Ulster Polytechnic provide basic tutor training on a fairly *ad hoc* basis as new groups of professional tutors or fieldwork supervisors become involved with our students. We are also involved in occasional research training for small groups of (or individual) research students. Our first systematic trainers course, however, is an advanced tutor training course and will be provided in 1981/2 as a final-year option for undergraduate students of human communication. These students will have studied psychology as a major subject for two years and will have themselves undergone SST in the programme described above (p. 137). They will thus have a reasonable basis upon which to develop the contextual and critical study of SST. The course will lay particular emphasis upon programme design since it is assumed that many graduates in human communication will find employment in settings where SST might be a useful innovation.

Conclusion

This chapter has consisted, mainly, of case-study material from the SST Unit at Ulster Polytechnic.

We hope that we have provided sufficient material to allow replication of our programmes in whole or part. It is, perhaps, more important that the material should illustrate principles of approach, planning and procedure.

Those visiting the unit tend to be impressed by the CCTV equipment and accommodation. We try to point out that these are accidents rather than essence. Central to the work of the unit are the views that:

(1) professional education and training should focus on informed practice;
(2) social skill constitutes a key element in this practice;
(3) the understanding of social skill, and its development for training purposes, is best approached scientifically and empirically.

Thus commitments, on the one hand, to the integration of theory and practice in professional training and, on the other, to the empirical investigation of social skills have combined to produce the unit and its programmes. These commitments, we believe, must be shared by social skill specialists, professional tutors and students for the work to succeed. It is these principles we would commend for emulation rather than, necessarily, any particular skill, resource, or procedure.

5 TRANSFER OF TRAINING

Social skill training programmes do not operate in isolation. In an obvious sense we all undergo a somewhat haphazard life-long social skill training. Any specially devised programme will interact with preceding, concurrent and successive features of this *éducation sociale pérmanente*. A more specialised context is provided by the curriculum or training programme of which social skill training may constitute a part. Thus, for example, social workers who experience social skill training will also encounter a range of other theoretical and practical exercises similarly aimed to develop professional competence.

In this chapter we will consider the relationship between social skill training and subsequent transfer to real life. In Chapter 6 we will consider the various ways in which social skill training might relate to the curriculum of which it forms a part.

All trainers face the problem 'what happens after training stops?' or, more subtly 'what am I to do to ensure that the effects of training are maintained over time and, probably, in novel situations?' It may be relatively simple to show that trainees have changed immediately after the programme but what will happen after months or years in the absence of specific assistance?

In the study of motor skill training, generalisation or transfer of learning from the controlled conditions of training to the less predictable conditions of the real world has been shown to be more likely under some circumstances than others. Annett *et al.* (1974), for example, suggest that transfer is most likely if the following obtain.

(1) Learners have understood the principles for action rather than responding by rote.
(2) The conditions of training have been designed to closely resemble the conditions under which it will be applied.
(3) Learners have continued in training to consistently high levels of success.
(4) Learners have been given information (feedback) about their own performance.

Implicit in this list is the notion that training has an influence not only upon behaviour itself but also upon the cognitive processes upon which (in the cybernetic models of skill acquisition discussed in Chapter 1) behavioural change is contingent. Thus if social skills training follows a similar pattern it will be important that, for example, trainees understand why eye contact is important and do not merely produce more of it because the trainer says so.

In recent discussion of the application of the skills model to social performance Welford (1980) suggests that performance 'was determined by three types of factor: the capacities possessed by the performers of a task; the demands of the task and the . . . strategies the performer uses to relate demands to capacities. What we term skill seems to be the use of efficient strategies'. Welford thus makes it clear that the skilled performer is differentiated from the unskilled not only in terms of his performance but also in terms of the strategies, plans and tactics which underly it. Training therefore should be addressed not only to the improvement of performance but also to the acquisition of such strategies. Such an emphasis might also be hypothesised to promote generalisation.

That hypothesis has not, however, been systematically investigated and, indeed, the whole issue of generalisation has been paid surprisingly little attention in the development of SST. Some studies have, however, been undertaken and the remainder of this section will first review them and secondly offer guidelines for optimising transfer through programme design.

What is Known about the Generalisation of SST?

Few studies specifically addressed to issues of generalisation have been undertaken. Those which have, tend to idiosyncrasy in the definitions of generalisation employed and, indeed, vary widely in the procedures adopted for skill identification and acquisition. It is thus singularly difficult to make comparisons between studies or to draw general conclusions. The difficulty is particularly marked if comparisons between settings are attempted since the criteria for adequate generalisation accepted in remedial SST vary somewhat from those accepted in specialised SST. Studies of generalisation in developmental SST are very rare indeed. We will, therefore, make separate reviews of the evidence for generalisation in remedial and specialised SST.

In assertiveness training it is traditional to train single subjects in very specific aspects of behaviour and to undertake pre- and post-training measures specially tailored to that particular subject. Such studies (Goldsmith & McFall, 1975; McFall & Lillesand, 1971; Hersen *et al*., 1974) generally show that trainees who have been trained to increase the frequency of some aspect of assertive behaviour (e.g. number of requests made) in specific role-play scenes also demonstrate increased frequency of the behaviour in other role-plays for which they have not been trained. The measure is almost always undertaken in the laboratory or clinic and immediately after training. It is thus a very limited measure of generalisation. Indeed, Hersen and Bellack (1976a), Van Hasselt *et al*. (1978, 1979) and Lange and Jakubowski (1976) all lament the lack of real investigations of generalisation and suggest that studies of *in vivo* generalisation where subjects are pursued from the laboratory into the real-life situations in which they were previously perceived as incompetent are essential for the evaluation of training. The need for such studies is made more pressing by the fact that several which have been undertaken (McFall & Marston, 1970; McFall & Lillesand, 1971; Shepherd, 1977) have shown that generalisation did not take place.

Trower *et al*. (1978a) summarise the wider remedial social skill training literature and conclude that while there is 'encouraging evidence' for short-term gains with psychiatric in-patients 'there is no evidence that these changes either lasted or helped patients to cope with real-life situations'. Their conclusions regarding SST with out-patients (Argyle *et al*., 1974; Trower *et al*., 1978b; Marzillier *et al*., 1976) however, are more optimistic and they report positive results from self-report and clinical measures up to six months after training.

In summary, generalisation and transfer in remedial SST are inadequately investigated and judgement must, therefore, be suspended until additional data become available. All that can safely be concluded at present is that the closer the measure of generalisation is to the time and circumstances of training (Shepherd, 1977, 1978; Gutride *et al*., 1973) the more likely it is that generalisation will be demonstrated.

While generalisation and transfer are equally important in specialised SST the problems they present are somewhat different. In this setting trainees may be entering professional agencies after SST and thus may have little experience or understanding of relevant interaction strategies to bring to training. They have been selected as 'good potential' teachers, social workers or what have you and, it may be surmised, are normally competent interactors who may resent the implication behind training that their approach to clients or pupils needs improvement. A further difference between remedial and specialised SST which may be relevant to transfer and generalisation lies in the frequency with which specialised SST is accompanied by some other form of interaction training such as teaching practice or fieldwork placement. These *may* operate as a bridge between SST and real-life interaction but may also act as a barrier between them.

Studies of generalisation which have been undertaken in specialised SST tend to be relatively short-term and are more likely to follow students into subsequent placement activity than into post-qualification employment. They are largely correlational in design since control-group studies (see Chapter 7) would deprive part of the training group of what is seen as a useful part of professional induction. Brown (1975) cogently points out that such studies may be demonstrating that students who are good at SST are also good at placement work – implying that they would have been equally good without the SST. None the less such studies (Brown, 1975) in microteaching at least, do generally show a carry-over of students' improved performance and positive attitudes during and after subsequent teaching practice. The evidence remains relatively scant, however, and Turney *et al.*'s (1973) comment that 'little is known about transfer' (p. 86) remains appropriate if transfer is taken to mean long-term transfer to real classrooms.

The micro-counselling literature is similarly patchy although some control-group studies (Guttman & Haase, 1972) have been carried out and do show a maintained superiority for the trained group. A number of studies cited by Ivey and Authier (1978) suggest that generalisation may depend on the extent to which the real situation affords opportunity for the practice of micro-counselling skills.

It is difficult, therefore, to judge from either remedial or specialised SST literatures the extent to which training effects are maintained over time or generalised to situations outside the training unit. The question has not been adequately put.

A number of authors have, however, discussed possible reasons for the failure to generalise. The following are among the reasons put forward.

(1) Inadequate Skill Identification/Patient Assessment. It is clear from the considerations discussed in Chapters 2 and 3 that skill identification is both difficult and crucial. It is only logical to conclude that where the skills identified are not in fact salient in the real-life situation the trainees' improvement as a result of training will equally lack salience

and will, therefore, be fairly useless in real life. Assertiveness training in particular has been widely criticised for its narrow approach to the identification of skill deficit and it is perhaps not surprising, to find that there is little evidence for its generalisation.

(2) Artificiality of Training Situation and Procedures. While some artificiality is inevitable as a result of the very act of setting up a training programme it is clear that programmes vary in the degree to which trainees are isolated from the concerns of real life. This may account in part for the disparity between in-patient and out-patient studies in remedial SST.

(3) Lack of Specific Attention to Transfer and of 'Bridging' Experiences. Again it is easier to provide such experiences with out-patients and studies of programmes in remedial SST where patients' training exercises included work outside the training unit have shown more generalisation (Trower *et al*., 1978b; Shepherd, 1978; Eisler *et al*., 1974). Similar emphasis is placed upon such 'bridging' experiences in specialised SST (Ivey & Authier, 1978) and particular stress is placed upon the role of professional tutors and placement supervisors in effecting these.

These three types of argument are at best tentative. Advice to ensure the maximum long-term effectiveness of training must, in the absence of anything more relevant, turn to the basic studies of transfer of motor performance. The point was made earlier in this chapter that transfer is most easily effected when concepts or principles capable of application in new situations have been internalised or when learning (Ausubel, 1968) is meaningful rather than rote. Given the proposition that social events may be more persistently novel or at least, a good deal less predictable than events generated by objects, it can be argued that the human capacity for concept learning is particularly vital for interpersonal behaviour. It may therefore, be the focus provided by SST for the development of appropriate concepts and plans rather than any mechanical reproduction of specific behaviours which is the 'active ingredient' of the process. Probably SST draws attention to social interaction and allows a whole set of perceptual, cognitive and performance factors to come into play at a far more complex and effective level than mere imitation of behaviour. There are a number of pointers to this conclusion in the literature.

Hersen and Bellack (1976a, p. 575) for example suggest that 'an intriguing possibility for promoting the generalisation of social skills involves the use of self-monitoring, self-reinforcement and other self-regulation procedures'. The procedures to which they refer (Kanfer, 1975; Kazdin, 1975; Meichenbaum, 1977) all involve training subjects to modify their own behaviour by means of previously-modified thought processes. Put crudely, subjects are taught to control 'what they say to themselves' before, during and after producing a response. The theoretical models underpinning these procedures (Kanfer, 1975) allow for the mediation of internal events between stimulus and response and in their strongest form (Meichenbaum, 1977; Mahoney, 1974) represent a clear shift from behaviourist to cognitive (or cybernetic) models of interpersonal behaviour and social skills training. It is interesting to note in this context that Hersen and Bellack (1976a) cite no less an authority than Skinner (1953) in support of their contention (p. 575) that 'internal events can be examined objectively and are subject to the same principles of behaviour as are external events'.

This self-regulatory approach has been used successfully in changing a very wide variety of behaviours (Meichenbaum, 1977; Kanfer, 1975; Goldfried & Goldfried, 1975) and gains have been shown to last over time and to generalise to new situations. In many cases the techniques have been used in conjunction with others – notably those involving some form of behaviour rehearsal or role-play and including assertiveness training (Kazdin, 1974; Lange & Jakubowski, 1976) and SST (Zielinski & Williams, 1979). Zielinski and Williams (1979) explicitly compared the traditional overt behaviour rehearsal technique of SST with a covert or imagined behaviour rehearsal within a similar SST procedure and found that the covert rehearsal group showed superior gains immediately after treatment. Jackson and Oei (1978) however (in a less elegant study) showed that an SST group were superior to a group who have received a form of 'cognitive restructuring', but that the superiority was not maintained in a follow-up investigation. They concluded that cognitive restructuring was more likely to be maintained over time.

The relationships between specifically cognitive techniques, behavioural rehearsal techniques and SST (and indeed between behavioural and cognitive components of SST) are clearly complex but important in the promotion of generalisation and transfer. Mahoney (1974) gives a 'cognitive theory of behaviour change' which may help to account for the findings. In this theory the process of behaviour change occurs as a result of changes in each of three elements namely

(Meichenbaum, 1977, p. 218):

(1) the clients' behaviours and the reactions they elicit in the environment;
(2) the clients' interpersonal dialogue or what he says to himself before, accompanying and after this behaviour;
(3) the clients' cognitive structures that give rise to the specific internal dialogue.

Meichenbaum suggests that the optimum strategy for changing a particular maladaptive behaviour will vary across individuals, behaviours and situations, but makes clear that it is the relationship between cognitive and behavioural change which is crucial in all cases. Thus behavioural rehearsal and the exploration of alternative responses is integral to the restructuring of cognitions which are in turn integral to the maintenance of behavioural change. In the context of SST the conclusion might be reached that generalisation is facilitated by the development of efficient strategies (see Welford's definition of skill above) which is facilitated by cognitive change which is in turn facilitated by behavioural rehearsal.

The specialised SST literature also reflects increasing concern with the relationship between behavioural and cognitive change. In microteaching, for example, Macleod and McIntyre (1977) review a series of studies analysing students' written comments on microteaching and, in particular, their comments upon various supervisory styles. They are impressed by the flexibility with which students make use of different forms and sources of information about their performance and by their desire for more of it. They conclude from these and other studies that the most important feature of microteaching is the development of cognitive structures which in Bartlett's (1932, p. 501) words 'allow escape from the complete sway of immediate circumstances' and provide ways of 'matching infinite diversity by increasing delicacy of response'. Thus they define microteaching as

> a means of producing changes in one's cognitive activities while teaching, changes in the ways one construes the courses of action open to one and the effects of one's actions . . . the value of a skills approach . . . would depend on the extent to which the disparate discrete events of the classroom came to be perceived as exemplars of a more general skill concept, rather than as unrelated events each

requiring an entirely new decision.

By implication, therefore, generalisation can only take place where it has been preceded by cognitive change.

How Can Transfer and Generalisation of SST Skills be Optimised?

It is clear from the previous section that not enough is known about the generalisation of SST skills to ensure its occurrence. It is also clear, however, that a number of theoretically fairly obvious procedures have not been adequately explored. Guidelines for the optimisation of transfer and generalisation can, therefore, be offered in the hope that outcomes might be monitored and results in turn contribute to the literature on the subject.

All generalisation procedures link the artificiality of training to the uncontrolled circumstances of real life. Some do so by making training more realistic and others by extending control and training beyond the programme itself. The brief guidelines for generalisation presented in Chapter 2 (p. 74) can be reviewed in that light.

(1) Making Training More Realistic

As has been frequently argued, some artificiality is inevitable in SST. No matter how carefully skills are identified or how important they are for the individual trainee before and after training, once they are isolated, ordered and enshrined in a programme they have suffered a change and may no longer be perceived by the trainee as significant.

A number of authors (Hersen *et al.*, 1974; McFall & Twentyman, 1973; Swenson *et al.*, 1978; Higgins *et al.*, 1979) have commented on the invalidity of role-played behaviour as an analogue of natural behaviour. Higgins *et al.* (1979), for example, show that students told that a role-play was as a real situation were less assertive and more compliant than students who knew it was role-play and point out that this invalidates the use of role-plays for the assessment of assertiveness before and after training. This and similar studies might, however, be reinterpreted as showing that role-plays offer trainees an opportunity to display more extreme behaviour when the 'real-life' consequences of such behaviour have been removed. Allen and Ryan (1969) offered just such a rationale for microteaching as a 'safe encounter' with pupils. For generalisation, however, it is important that the 'safe' environment retain sufficient similarity to real life to allow the exploration of relevant levels of skill. It is also important that trainees perceive the tasks undertaken as similar to those they will undertake in real life.

Morgan (1980), describing training for salesmen, presents an extreme solution to the dilemma in suggesting that training should take place in the real situation and similar attempts at field training (Borg, 1971) have been made in microteaching. Given, however, that field training is often impossible (as with psychiatric in-patients) and that the disadvantages of artificiality are usually outweighed by advantages of greater control over events and greater freedom for the trainee to make 'safe' mistakes, most SST will continue to use simulation and role-play.

Such artificiality is, therefore, best combatted by ensuring that links with 'real-life' interaction are underlined wherever possible. Thus, models, sensitisation sessions and practice tasks should resemble outside events and relate to trainees' perceptions of themselves in real life wherever possible. Whatever the setting – remedial, developmental or specialised – this necessitates discussion and negotiation with the trainee. One of the virtues of covert behaviour rehearsal lies in the fact that by definition the trainee believes in the relevance of the situation – he dreamt it up. Using overt techniques, however, the onus is upon the trainer to make sure that trainees can discriminate the skill from other behaviour and relate it not only to the role-played task but also to other tasks and situations which they can imagine in their own out-of-training interaction. This is thus a topic for discussion and exploration in both sensitisation and feedback sessions.

A further potential source of artificiality and, thus, impediment to generalisation, resides in the specificity of the skills practised in SST. It is not 'natural' to think about eye contact when meeting a stranger or to monitor pauses carefully when trying to reassure a social work client. 'Naturally' trainees might think in more global terms – 'making a good impression' or 'being friendly'. SST in other words deliberately promotes a closer focus upon the minutiae of interaction. The rationale for this lies in the cybernetic skills model itself. Discrete elements of behaviour are put together to form coherent displays. Strings of behaviours are in turn put together in higher-order units which are at first consciously controlled but ultimately become automated. Skill consists of specific short-term tactics generated from more general long-term strategies. That being so the training programme which focuses exclusively upon specific behavioural tactics is unlikely to generalise to the real world where the unpredictability of events necessitates broader strategic planning and capacity to deal with novel problems. The trainee needs help in putting things together.

Surprisingly little practical attention has been paid to the integration of skills although a number of authors (Turney *et al.*, 1973; Macleod & McIntyre, 1977; Shepherd, 1978; Goldstein *et al.*, 1976) suggest that the problem may exist. Specific procedures for skill integration in microteaching are described by Hargie *et al.* (1978) and in remedial SST by Trower *et al.* (1978). In the former case previously-practised skills are grouped together (and the length of the practice session is gradually extended until it approximates a 'normal' 20-minute classroom lesson). Questioning and reinforcement, for example, are practised first separately then together and ultimately in a final teach in which seven skills are practised. Trower *et al.* (1978a) similarly group previously-practised elements of behaviour under more general headings (e.g. controlling others, presenting self). Situations are described and trainees are encouraged to explore alternative strategies for action before and after the actual role-play which is longer in duration than previous exercises. In both cases the integrated practice is seen as a specific aid to the generalisation of training.

Integrating the skill elements in this fashion involves the trainer in deciding which elements go together to form coherent units useful for training. Ideally such decisions would be informed by a theoretical model of interaction. We discuss the inadequacies of existing models at length in Chapter 7, but would agree with Trower's (1980) comments that SST 'has laboured under simplistic conceptions of social behaviour, a legacy which probably comes from the behaviour therapy tradition'. Trower (1980a) also suggests that an adequate model will recognise the complexity of interaction and will adopt concepts from psychology, sociology, anthropology and sociolinguistics. Much, however, remains to be done in establishing such a more comprehensive model while preserving the advantages of rigour and explicitness afforded by the conceivably 'simplistic' behaviourist tradition. Meanwhile the pragmatics of practice suggest that SST trainers give due consideration to skill integration as an aid to generalisation. The results of such attempts may even contribute to the development of the comprehensive model.

(2) Extending Training Beyond the Programme

SST differs from other forms of skill training in that the skills being promoted (or skills closely related to them) will inevitably be practised between formal training sessions. The golfing tyro may slump into sedentary habits between Saturdays, but the social skills trainee would be hard pressed to avoid some form of interaction between sessions. Accounts of remedial, developmental and specialised SST all suggest that even where trainees are not specifically encouraged to do so, their return to each training session is likely to be marked by discussion with fellow trainees of the relevance of 'last week's skill' in their intervening home, work or ward experience. Indeed some trainees (Hargie, 1980) report an excessive self-consciousness in respect of specific skills immediately after training sessions.

This constant availability of practice opportunities has obvious advantages and disadvantages. The pattern of feedback and reward carefully established in the training programme is unlikely to obtain in the outside world and the carefully-graded progression through increasingly complex skills and increasingly difficult situations is even less likely. Indeed, if the trainee is not helped to cope with (and, if possible, exploit) his between-training interactions, their effect may be that of interference rather than transfer. He may return to training having suffered a setback in previous learning or having divorced his SST from real-life concerns and thus having created a barrier to generalisation. Such negative outcomes are particularly likely if the individuals with whom the trainee interacts between sessions are ignorant of or antipathetic to the programme.

Macleod and McIntyre (1977), discussing individual differences in performance after microteaching, acknowledge that while differences between groups of students preparing to teach different subjects may be interpreted 'in terms of the different demands and opportunities involved in teaching different subjects, it should also be noted that different subject specialists (tutors) in the Stirling department vary in their enthusiasm for microteaching'. Similarly, Ivey and Authier (1978) stress the need to involve supervisors and employers outside the microcounselling clinic so that newly-acquired skills can be used and integrated into the 'real' counselling work pattern and Goldstein *et al.* (1976) suggest that 'relatives, friends, parents and other real-life reinforcement distributors' be taught 'procedures for providing the patient or ex-patient with continued feedback'. Van Hasselt *et al.* (1979) make a particular point of the importance of obtaining the co-operation of authority figures such as parents and teachers in undertaking SST with children.

It seems clear, therefore, that wherever possible other individuals who are likely to interact significantly with the trainee between training sessions or after them should at least understand what is going on and, ideally, share the trainees' commitment to learning. As will be made clear later in this section such involvement is probably most effective when the 'surrogate trainer' has specific tasks to undertake.

Random informal interaction between or after training sessions may influence training. Some forms of interaction are specifically designed to influence the trainee in aspects of his cognitions and behaviour closely related to those being trained in SST. Thus remedial SST is often provided as part of a larger 'package' of therapeutic procedures. Students and schoolchildren are exposed to a wider curriculum which may well have implications for social learning and interpersonal behaviour.

The next chapter will focus particularly on problems of curriculum design in specialised SST within professional education, but the basic problem of potential contradiction and conflict between trainings, advice or guidance with an interpersonal focus obtains in all settings. It is, in fact, a tribute to the resilience of SST that short-term results do not seem to be afflicted by such interference. Thus in remedial SST such results as can be found for SST used in parallel with other therapies (Hersen & Bellack, 1976a; Trower *et al.*, 1978a; Phillips, 1980) show it to be successful. Likewise in specialised settings SST is very rarely integrated with the rest of the curriculum but none the less produces positive short-term outcomes.

Despite these successes it seems likely that benefits will be increased and generalisation promoted if trainees are helped to cope with the resolve potential contradictions and, indeed, to exploit potential consolidation and support for their SST. Turney (1973), for example, recommends that teaching practice tutors should structure teaching practice tasks to mesh with microteaching and stresses that students are helped if microteaching and teaching-practice tutors use the same 'language' in analysing and assessing teaching whether it be in the limited micro-class or in the larger world of the teaching-practice classroom. Similarly it might be suggested that the therapist offering traditional supportive therapy alongside SST might profitably use the patients' SST experience as a topic for discussion and exploration. It is important, however, that all parties know that such links are being established and trainees should have ample opportunity to explore and clarify developing ideas about their social behaviour in both arenas.

Morgan (1980) combines the principles of making training realistic with that of relating it to concurrent training. He suggests that it be carried out in the trainees' normal place of work and that it be supervised by the person who would normally oversee the work done and who is responsible for other forms of training. Few trainers would go as far as this in releasing training from their control, but many do suggest that trainees carry out autonomous activities between and after sessions. In specialised SST this is most often a reflective exercise such as essay writing or log-book keeping (often related to other areas of the curriculum), although practical discrimination exercises (usually viewing and analysing videotapes) and work on particular observation systems also occur. Specifically interactional homework exercises are more often a feature of remedial SST where Trower *et al.* (1978a), Falloon *et al.* (1977) and Goldstein *et al.* (1976) all suggest that patients be given specific tasks to carry out and comment upon at the next training session. Lange and Jakubowski (1976) suggest that trainees should help to determine the homework tasks and recommend that they be taught the basic principles of self-monitoring and self-reinforcement to help them in their homeworks. Thus (Lange & Jakubowski, 1976, p. 773) 'planning in small segments, rewarding one-self for each small improvement, being behaviourally specific, and recognising competing short and long-term rewards . . . can be invaluable'. All advocates of homeworks stress that the tasks given should be well within the trainees' capacities (i.e. easier than those undertaken in the unit) and Lange and Jakubowski (1976) make the point that trainees who have failed in a homework task will need to discuss and explore their failure in the unit if they are to continue with high motivation for generalising and applying trained skills. Additional support for homework activities can be obtained by involving significant others in the trainees' environment. Thus Falloon *et al.* (1977) and Goldstein *et al.* (1976) recommend that trainees keep records of progress for discussion with a named friend who is (1) more readily available than trainers and (2) primed as to the aims and procedures of training. Confederates of this kind have also been involved (Callner & Ross, 1978; Shepherd, 1978) in role-playing exercises taking place between sessions in the unit.

Conclusion

We have argued that the evidence for generalisation of SST outcomes to situations outside training and for their maintenance over time is incomplete. The guidelines which we have put forward for making training more realistic and for extending it beyond the formal programme are, therefore, tentative. None the less we suggest that they are founded in principles derived from a sound model of motor skill learning and are thus at least worth trying within a framework of careful monitoring and comparative investigation.

The integration of SST with other concurrent learning was given the briefest consideration above. We believe, however, that in specialised SST at least, the relationship between SST and the curriculum of which it forms a part is complex, interactive and potentially profitable not only for SST but for the entire pattern of professional education and training. We, therefore, devote the following chapter to the curriculum context.

6 THE CURRICULUM CONTEXT

Social skill training may be provided for an individual who has problems in interaction. He is diagnosed as socially deficient and a programme of treatment is prescribed for him. Alternatively a group of persons may be identified for whom social skill training is considered useful. The individual programme may be characterised as clinical, while the second where the needs of a group are identified might be characterised as a curriculum. The label 'curriculum' is particularly appropriate when successive cohorts of individuals are subjected to a similar training programme. This distinction between clinical and curriculum applications of social skill training provides an alternative dimension for the matrix which we have divided into remedial, developmental and specialist. As might be expected clinical applications of social skill training most frequently occur in the remedial setting. Developmental SST is more likely to be presented to successive groups of adolescents as a curriculum element and similarly specialist social skill training is usually encountered by, for example, teachers, social workers and counsellors as an element in their curricula.

It is our intention in this section to consider how a social skill training programme might be part of a complete curriculum. In particular we are concerned with social skill training as part of the education and training for one of the interpersonal professions. These professions we have defined as those which rely on dyadic or small-group interaction as the prime means for achieving their objectives. Professionals in these areas spend the majority of their working day exercising their social skills whether consciously or unconsciously. It might, therefore, be expected that whatever course of training they undertake it should address both practically and theoretically the acquisition and development of social skills.

Our own thoughts on an appropriate curriculum for the interpersonal professions have developed in close relation to our thinking about SST. Like many working in this area we have addressed a set of problems which are usually collectively described as requiring the integration of theory and practice.

The injunction to integrate theory and practice has become a slogan for teaching, and indeed research, in higher education. The injunction takes various forms: epistemologically, the flights of reasons should regularly touch down on empiricism; economically, imagination and speculation must be harnessed to produce more wealth; educationally, degree courses should become more vocational. Those who seek knowledge should relate more evidently to those who do, who make, who change and who destroy.

Slogans are known for their capacity to enthuse but obscure; they may be stimulating to live by but unsatisfactory to live with. We will, therefore, have to set the scene for this section by giving some consideration to the notions inherent in the so-called integration of theory and practice.

We are interested in courses of education and training for the interpersonal professions. Specifically our experience has been with such courses for teachers, social workers, youth leaders, community workers, counsellors, health visitors, speech therapists, occupational therapists and physiotherapists. These professions range across the education, health and personal social services. They have in common, to labour the point, a working life which consists primarily and in many cases, almost exclusively of interacting with persons variously described as pupils, patients or clients. Interactions with these persons may be on a one-to-one basis or with the professional interacting in a more complex way with groups of up to 50. In the case of these professions, practice, in its observable form at least, consists largely of verbal and non-verbal sequences of behaviour which are integrated in some way with the verbal and non-verbal behaviour of the pupils, clients or patients.

At a more general level 'practice' might be conceived as the set of observable behaviours and inferred attitudes, deliberations and decisions which constitute legitimate action to achieve agreed professional goals: it is the things professionals do and think; it is their job. What then is the theory which is to be integrated with this practice?

An adequate definition of theory is more elusive. It is trite to point out that man thinks as he acts. If thinking, however defined, always constitutes a form of theory then clearly all practice, however apparently mindless, has a theoretical component. Following this analysis, the problem of integration would disappear since it would be unavoidable! However, the problem does exist and requires a different approach for its identification.

If we accept that there is this grey area of internal processes where theory and practice are inextricably intermingled, then the distinction might be clearer if we address extremes. Thus we might readily accept that a trainee teacher writing an essay on the concept of justice in education is engaged in theorising while the same person attempting to quell an unruly class of infants is engaged in practice.

Theory then perhaps refers to propositions which are more or less related to a particular set of actions but which are one or more removes from the essential practising moment. In one sense to say that I will teach an infant class at 9.00 a.m. or have taught an infant class last week is theoretical: only the teaching itself is practice. Usually, to talk of the theory of teaching is to imply a more ambitious set of propositions concerned with and including abstraction and generalisation from a number of teaching moments and the attempted establishment of laws of teaching and learning. This suggests a distinction between everyday and higher-order, legitimised theory. But in the sense that we are using theory, it is taken to include propositions at all levels from the most minutely specific to the grandly universal. The determining feature of theory is that it is at the level of proposition rather than action.

For courses of professional education and training these propositions may be conceived as existing at (at least) three levels. First, and usually pre-eminent, is the implicit and occasionally, explicit, set of assumptions regarding purpose and practice which the student brings to the course: for this analysis this could be labelled *personal theory*. Second is the explicit theory associated with professional practice and expounded by professional tutors and fieldwork supervisors – this may be labelled *professional theory*. Third is the set of propositions contributed by certain academic disciplines deemed, for various reasons, to be relevant to the profession concerned. This may be labelled *academic theory*.

The integration of theory and practice, therefore, now requires relationships and reciprocal influence to be established between four levels. They are professional practice, personal theory, professional theory and academic theory.

Thus it is the case that interpersonal professionals must interact with their clients. These moments and sequences of interaction constitute practice in this case. Professionals and trainee professionals will bring to this practice their own views, assumptions and values regarding personal interaction. They will also be exposed, through explicit exposition and discussion and by subtler influences, to the body of knowledge and values held by qualified professionals. Finally they will be exposed to knowledge, models and standards of evidence regarding interaction from, for example, psychology, social psychology and sociology. Thus a conventional training in social work includes: periods of practice in social work agencies and associated advice on the job from fieldwork supervisors and college staff; lectures, seminars and tutorials which, at times, address interaction with clients, provided by professional tutors, and courses in psychology, social psychology and sociology which again will sometimes address issues related to social interaction.

A further complication concerns the important distinction which can be made between the descriptive and the prescriptive as forms of theory. Descriptive theory is concerned with what is the case while prescriptive theory is concerned with what ought to be. Thus, for example, we can describe the relationship between schedules of reinforcement and the behaviour which is likely to be emitted, but we would be prescribing if we suggested that a teacher should use such schedules to achieve behaviour change in the classroom. Put another way, it is one thing to say what is or might be or probably is, on the basis of personal reminiscences, public evidence or indeed rigorous analysis: it is quite a different thing to say what ought to be and to tell people what they ought to do. A source of great contention in many course teams is based on this imperfectly understood distinction. Thus in a course of teacher training lecturers might be criticised for presenting current evidence on a particular topic without being prepared to commit themselves as to how the student teacher should behave in the classroom. Conversely other lecturers may be seen as over-eager to tell the student what to do without having any basis other than assertion to justify these injunctions.

It is well to remind ourselves that so-called scientific disciplines including psychology and sociology, as much as anatomy, physiology and physics are, by definition, descriptive only, whereas professional training must be prescriptive otherwise it is failing in its job.

This has introduced a further complication into the problem of integrating theory and practice. There is no logical justification for the step from the descriptive to the prescriptive. It is salutary to remind ourselves of the so-called naturalistic fallacy identified so cogently by David Hume which warns that we cannot logically proceed from what is to what ought to be.

Our analysis has now yielded a 3 x 2 matrix of theory, with perhaps descriptive and prescriptive forms of personal, professional and academic theory. In practice personal theory, which is frequently not made explicit anyway, probably crosses the boundary between the prescriptive and the descriptive without too much difficulty. Professional theory likewise often tends to be unselfconsciously prescriptive. Academic theory, however, should be descriptive only, on principle. These often hidden tensions lie behind the problems inherent in devising courses of professional training and education and it is in working out their implications and attempting some form of integration that we have developed social skill training.

Phenomenologically the student might express the problem as 'what should I do given conflicting advice, no advice or advice which doesn't make sense'? Even assuming a conformity of advice, i.e. prescriptive theory, which correlates with his own explicit prescriptive theory, how should this be translated into action, into practice and into performance?

The initial problem, therefore, may be rephrased as encompassing the integration of descriptive theory, prescriptive theory and practical performance. Within the SST programme itself and in its curriculum context it is necessary to integrate descriptive theory, i.e. the evidence and models concerning social interaction drawn from psychology, social psychology and sociology, with prescriptive theory, i.e. advice as to how the student might use social skills in practical work whether in college or out on placement.

In our experience most designers of professional training courses avoid the problem of integration by selecting material for inclusion in the obviously theoretical or academic part of the courses by a process which seems to be based on an extraordinary act of faith or perhaps a false syllogism which runs as follows.

> All psychologists/sociologists know about people.
> All occupational therapists, physiotherapists, social workers, teachers, etc. need to know about people.
> All occupational therapists, physiotherapists, social workers, teachers must study psychology/sociology.

Put more seriously, it is not unreasonable for professions whose area of work is unequivocally psychosocial in nature and whose stated and agreed purpose is attitude and behaviour change to expect guidance, advice and illumination from the disciplines of psychology and sociology. It is a source of great perplexity to these professions to find, first, that psychologists and sociologists seem hardly able to communicate across disciplines and secondly that the desire to know does not in any sense logically or psychologically connect with the desire to help. There is an extraordinary lacuna in social science between the scientist and (for lack of a better word) the technician: there is little or no technology. To paraphrase Lord Calder, the technician desires to do, the technologist to help and the scientist to know: there is a gap between college work and placement: to find a middle ground between contemplation and theorising on the one hand and everyday activity on the other. Health visitor tutors charged with the paradoxical injunction to teach practice recognised that the microteaching being provided to link educational studies and teaching practice for teacher trainees might similarly link principles of health visiting and fieldwork practice for their students.

The Planning Team. Planning was undertaken by health visitor tutors and psychology tutors, the latter being more or less entirely employed in the provision of microteaching and associated studies. Hardly surprisingly this team tended to emphasise initially the teaching aspects of health visiting and relied heavily on the Stanford package of skills and procedures. Gradually the programme introduced more profession-specific skills and broadened to include counselling skills adapted in the first instance from Ivey (1971). Health visitor tutors varied in their initial reactions to the proposed programme but quickly became enthused by its possibilities. It may be that the empiricism of their medical and scientific background coupled with the heightened consciousness of interactive skills induced by the transition from hospital to community nursing engendered a complex of attitudes and awareness in which SST was readily acceptable.

The Trainees. Admission to a course of health visitor training is contingent upon possession of general and obstetric nursing qualifications and students are, therefore, by definition more mature than the average undergraduate student. Additionally, most health visitor students spend some years in general hospital nursing before making the move towards the community and many use the health visitor course as an appropriate preparation for the return to work after years of raising their own families.

Thus health visitor students manifest characteristics typical of mature students, including anxiety about standards of work, difficulty in unaccustomed 'academic' tasks such as essay writing, examination answering etc. These particular mature students also suffer from the contrast between their past educational and work experience and the notionally freer and more questioning ambience of a polytechnic. Dingwall (1977) for example, suggests that health visitor students come to the course imbued with commonsense prescriptive notions about individual and social problems and that while they can accept their replacement by other prescriptions presented by authority figures (e.g.

and other 'social' problems are commonly dealt with. A similar expansion has taken place in the range of clients dealt with and health visitors can be found giving antenatal advice, working in family planning clinics, as contact tracers in VD clinics, or liaising with a particular hospital unit which provides a community service (e.g. psychiatric, renal dialysis or coronary care departments). They also play a large part in formal health education taking a teaching role in schools and community groups. In the specifically domiciliary context an increasing proportion of the health visitor's time is now spent in routine visiting of the elderly where counselling on social as well as health problems is again given. As a professional activity health visiting represents an interesting interface between conventional models of teaching, group work, counselling and nursing.

Embarkation upon the Diploma in Health Visiting is thus in several respects a watershed in the career pattern of its students. It represents a change from a clear primary focus on patients' health and physical well-being to a more diffuse concern for their social and psychological welfare; from curative to preventive and educational measures; from hospital ward to community; and from action within the framework to shared responsibility offered by hospital work to the relatively autonomous action expected of the community worker. Students are thus required to develop new knowledge, attitudes and skills. In particular, compared with their role as nurses, they are required to develop interpersonal skills appropriate to interaction with a wider range of people in a wider range of settings and in pursuit of more varied outcomes.

The curriculum which they follow during 51 very intensive weeks of study is as recommended by the Central Council for the Education and Training of Health Visitors who oversee the courses provided by the various educational institutions, who approve external examiners to the courses and who make the award of qualification as a health visitor. The CETHV's recommended syllabus (1979) has a section entitled 'Theories and Methods of Health Visiting Practice' within which it is suggested students will develop 'the art of looking and listening' and 'the use of understanding and empathy'. It is within that rubric that SST was introduced into the Diploma course at Ulster Polytechnic.

Curriculum Innovation. It is rare for SST to be planned as an aspect of a coherent curriculum design. More usually it is added to an existing curriculum as an experimental novelty. In this case SST was introduced as a partial solution to the well-known problem of how to bridge the group dynamics is taught to social workers since they must interact with their clients. Much worthy and conscientious teaching has followed this model, but all too often it fails. As an attempt to link theory to practice it is fraught with problems.

There is a marked discrepancy between scientific enquiry surrounding a topic and the practical decisions and actions which a professional must take in the area described by that topic. Prospective physiotherapists interested in learning are unlikely to find the legitimate scientific investigation of avoidance learning in the woodlouse of compelling interest and the investigation of perceptions of fullness as a ratio is not of immediate relevance to a health visitor despite its crucial significance in differentiating the developmental theories of Piaget and Bruner. Thus the drives towards understanding on the one hand and action on the other, while related in principle, are often widely divergent in practice.

Even when the time-scale and focus of scientific investigation and professional action are similar, there is still a disjunction between the descriptive objectivity of the academic and the need for prescriptive advice felt by the professional. It is not unknown for an academic enquiry into a topic on which policy-makers are required to take decisions to conclude with a greater aura of uncertainty than that with which it commenced. The academic has explored in far greater depth than was initially possible alternative courses of action and their possible consequences; with appropriate reserve he is unwilling to commit himself to one solution. Those who make and implement policy, however, have to make up their minds and in so doing might prefer a simpler set of possibilities and a less complex analysis of consequences. Logically, as pointed out above, there remains the problem of the step from description to prescription, from what is to what ought to be.

When asked to define knowledge Wittgenstein said that it was 'all that is the case'. However, knowing what is the case is not the same as doing. I may understand the principles of biomechanics but be unable to ride a bicycle; have mastered the collected works of Nicklaus, Jacklin and Player but be unable to hit a golf ball; have accompanied Slocum, Chichester and Francis round the world in print but be unable to sail a dinghy across a gravel-pit lake. Put more technically, propositional knowledge does not translate easily or necessarily into skilled performance. Even the most relevant and prescriptive set of propositions do not ensure effective professional action. No matter how much advice we might give to the prospective professional about social skills we cannot guarantee that this will translate into skilled social performance with clients.

Thus the semantic conjunction model may founder: through the divergence between scientific enquiry and practical decisions; through the disjunction between the descriptive objectivity of the academic and the need for prescriptive advice felt by the professional; and through the problem of translating propositional knowledge, however relevant and prescriptive, into professional action.

Finally the semantic conjunction solution is inherently prone to fragmentation. It usually involves a parallel and unrelated presentation of carefully-chosen topics by several academic disciplines and by those who are responsible for professional theory. The course team piously expects the student to integrate these parallel strands and to translate them into action.

Sometimes the team ambitiously attempts to tackle the problem of fragmentation by extending semantic conjunction across academic disciplines. Again topics are identified which appear to be studied, perhaps with some difference in emphasis, by several academic disciplines and these topics are chosen as similar to those which concern performance. Such ambitions are laudable and may involve the student in valuable comparison and contrast, but they still fall far short of bridging academic and professional concerns, of crossing successfully from the descriptive to the prescriptive, and, most fundamentally, of translating proposition into practice.

As we welcome refuge from the problems of devising any kind of syllabus, it has become fashionable to allow the curriculum to 'emerge' from problems raised by students who undertake a concurrent practical placement. This approach which we have called the *emergent* model is based on the no-doubt sound pedagogical principle that one should begin from what students are interested in before one encourages them to learn what is in their interest. It has the advantage that students might reveal to their teachers those problems, albeit in propositional rather than exemplary form, which they have encountered on their practice. However, once these topics are raised, academic staff must still say more about them than the exchange of commonsense, general encouragement and homely advice which will probably accrue. They must in fact plan a course of study focusing upon these anticipated topics. This approach, in our view, confuses a legitimate pedagogical technique with a curriculum plan and is fundamentally contradictory to the notion that a course of professional education and training should be an introduction into an established body of practical and theoretical knowledge.

The *action focus* model, which we are advocating in this book, and which we believe is best exemplified through our approach to social skill training, attempts to make professional action the central focus of the curriculum. Professional action is conceived as involving planning, performance and evaluation. The professional must identify the tasks which he must undertake as appropriate parts of his professional role, plan how he will undertake them, undertake them and reflect on this undertaking. This planning and evaluation is, in the sense we identified earlier, a form of theorising. Plans and evaluations are expressed in propositional form, but they relate in the clearest possible way to the central core of professional action.

The Action Focus Curriculum

In this curriculum model, propositional knowledge, whether derived from professional or academic theory, must be interwoven with the predictions and descriptions of professional action which the student undertakes.

This implies and necessitates close analysis of professional practice and skills, including, in the interpersonal professions, interpersonal skills. Learning experiences are then devised so that a student can integrate his developing capacity to articulate and comprehend propositions with his selection, implementation and evaluation of courses of professional action.

The first thought may be to use the real professional situation as a source of such learning; but this is fraught with ethical, logistic and, indeed, economic difficulties. It is here that social skill training with its element of simulation and its college base can serve as a logical and coherent substitute.

Two significant shifts of emphasis led to us moving from the semantic conjunction model to this action focus curriculum. The first came, as described in Ellis (1974) from the framing of objectives for psychology courses for the interpersonal professions. At that point we addressed the distinction between the descriptive and the prescriptive. We believed psychology to be a descriptive discipline in some way separate from the set of prescriptions which characterised professional theorising. We realised, however, that while psychology might be in principle and practice descriptive, it also contains prescriptions as to how one should approach knowledge, evidence, problem-solving, evaluation and development. These standards, ultimately prescriptions as to how the psychologist ought to behave, are more fundamental to the discipline, we believe, than any particular substantive material generated by these approaches. It, therefore, seemed to us that the objectives for a psychology course should be concerned with communicating to students the standards which characterised psychology and that these standards would be best communicated if the student could learn to approach problems and evidence 'as a psychologist should'. Thus in a scaled-down way we would be trying to educate and train the student to become a psychological researcher into his own work situation.

Our second move concerned the integration of theory with practical performance. We became convinced that theory from any quarter would be best integrated with practical performance if the theory was used by the student to illuminate his work situation: first, in conceiving the nature of that situation; then in identifying problems within it; then in proposing solutions to these problems and finally in evaluating attempts to implement those solutions. Thus a student undertaking a psychology course should learn to identify psychological variables within his work situation, should learn to propose psychological solutions to the problems of the work situation, should practise implementing these solutions and should evaluate objectively, as a psychologist, his own actions and the effect of these actions on others. In particular we chose to make interpersonal interaction the central focus of the course and conceived the prime contribution of psychology as a particular approach to the observation, recording, analysis, planning, implementing and evaluation of action.

In this way we believe we have chosen the best features of the preceding models. In identifying that which is fundamental to psychology, essential rather than accidental, we have tried to promote the educational values of the personal education model. In relating this psychological approach to planning, action and evaluation we believe we have gone deeper than mere semantic conjunction and that we have tapped the same personal potency claimed for the emergent curriculum. How then does one go about devising this so-called action focus curriculum? The action which is focused upon is that of the competent professional. It may seem a relatively simple matter to describe competent professional action, to encourage novitiates to develop this competence and to evaluate critically this competence using perspectives from various academic disciplines.

Unfortunately this simplicity falls at the first fence. For most if not all interpersonal professions there is a dramatic lack of adequate literature describing those activities which constitute professional competence. In part this is a problem of access. Even teaching which has the most substantial literature based upon the observation, recording and analysis of teachers in classrooms, is racked with debate concerning the relevance of this material to the central purpose of education, pupil learning. In the other interpersonal professions the material scarcely exists.

Thus in the various forms which social work and the professions supplementary to medicine take there is a striking lack of ethnographic studies of professional-client interaction. Ideally the action focus curriculum should be based upon such studies. In its absence we have to work from hints, traces, recollections and deductions from first principles.

In practice, therefore, while using all studies which do exist of professional-client interaction, we have based our model of professional competence in part on second-hand empiricism and in part on deduction and argument by analogy. Thus professionals, particularly those involved in training and education, have to reflect on their own experience to identify skills and groupings of skills. In this they are helped greatly by practising professionals, such as fieldwork teachers whose recollections are likely to be based on more recent experience. Various devices can be employed to stimulate these recollections. We have found it particularly helpful for professional tutors and fieldworkers to examine together tapes of professional-client interaction so that they might identify first independently, then collectively, the skills which they think are operating. The focus of such sessions is to identify 'what makes a good . . .'. The spin-off from this activity is first to provide material for the curriculum and secondly to suggest categories and criteria for the assessment of the students' practical performance. A detailed description of such an exercise is provided by Saunders and Saunders' (1977, 1979) study of teachers' analyses of student teaching performance.

In addition to this approach curriculum planners must try to deduce skills from first principles. Thus shared and explicit professional values, agreed aims, guidelines from professional associations and similar material may be used as a basis from which skills may be inferred or deduced. If such statements bear some resemblance to other professions where skills have been identified, then it may be appropriate to transfer skills across.

The identification of skills must be, as the computer scientists put it, iterative. Thus those who plan the curriculum must constantly refer their plans to practising professionals to check whether their notion of professional competence bears some resemblance to the view of professional practice held by practitioners.

One problem in identifying skills concerns the level of analysis and detail. Thus skills may be described at the level of minute-by-minute observations and an enormous list of specifics will emerge. Conversely grand higher-order statements of skill may emerge which are difficult to translate into particular actions. We have found the concept of a skill area to be useful in this respect, the area being an intermediate statement which subsumes a whole set of individual actions. This intermediate level is occupied by descriptions which have a clear behavioural referent but which subsume numerous molecules of behaviour. They must be amenable to the devising of systematic skill acquisition procedures and must present an appropriate focus for the presentation of analytical perspectives from academic disciplines.

The skill areas we have found most useful for the interpersonal professions have been: observation; communication; planning and evaluation; and organisation.

Observation includes all those activities which enable the student to identify significant features of the behaviour of clients and professionals.

Communication includes all those social skills which constitute professional-client interaction.

Planning involves all those processes whereby the professional makes his intentions explicit and *evaluation* all those activities whereby he ascertains whether his intentions have been realised.

Organisation includes all those activities whereby the professional arranges materials or the actions of others to achieve his intentions.

We have found these skill areas to be remarkably robust across interpersonal professions, although their origin was in the curriculum of one particular profession, teaching.

Social skill training is, of course, the college-based practical activity aimed at developing communication skills. One purpose of this book has been to demonstrate its effectiveness in developing these skills. It is, however, exemplary in another sense in that it shows how a practical activity can make an excellent focus for the introduction at the planning, implementation and evaluation stages of material from psychology and social psychology.

The action focus curriculum then begins with the identification of skill areas for the professions concerned. For each of these skill areas, acquisition procedures must be developed, first in the controlled environment of the college, subsequently in the real-life professional situation. Linked studies must then be provided from appropriate academic disciplines to illuminate this skill acquisition.

The danger of such a model is, of course, that it may become static in that it merely reflects present professional competence. Put another way, it implies epistemological and ethical stability and fails to address fundamental critical questions regarding the legitimacy of professional action.

We have tried to address these deficiencies by conceiving the curriculum as a series of concentric circles. Central is the process of skill acquisition. Surrounding it is theory which informs and critically evaluates professional competence: this we have called related theory. At a further remove are theoretical perspectives which are aimed at addressing the wider context of existing and possible professional activity: this level of theory we have described as contextual theory.

A curriculum devised along these lines has a central strand of practical activities where students develop the skills which characterise professional competence. This practical strand begins in the controlled environment of the college and shades into a period of supervised internship.

Clearly related to this practical work are sequences of so-called competency-based theory. The material presented in this part is intended to have a real impact on the students' practical work:

(1) by increasing his capacity to identify significant features of this practical work;
(2) by helping him to identify problems in his practical work;
(3) by suggesting solutions to these problems;
(4) by encouraging critical evaluation of the implementation of these solutions.

Social skill training is, of course, the prime example of this approach. As shown in Appendix 3, a typical social skill training curriculum presents linked theory from psychology and social psychology which helps the student to perceive and conceptualise social interaction more precisely and sensitively, highlights functional and dysfunctional aspects of social interaction and presents alternative ways of behaving for the student to practise.

This sequence of practical work and related theory is complemented by contextual studies which, in a course of professional training, address fundamental issues regarding the role, purpose and legitimacy of professional action. Typically contextual studies are drawn, in courses for the interpersonal professions, from sociology, social policy and social philosophy, although there are many alternatives. The point is that these disciplines are freed from unrealistic demands for immediate and situational relevance whereas the competency-based theory must have clear impact on professional action.

It is beyond the scope of this book to consider in detail the development of an entire curriculum for professional education and training. However, in this section we have tried to elaborate on the problems which we believe social skill training goes some way towards solving. We have proposed social skill training as the most thoroughly worked-through example of a curriculum unit which makes professional action its focus. This focus is expressed not only through practical work but also through the application of the substance, theory and approaches of selected academic disciplines to the identification of problems, generation of solutions and evaluation of results.

We would argue for SST as an integral part of a competency-based curriculum which is characterised by a focus on skills in context. However, it is obvious that much SST will exist as an element in a curriculum which has been devised along quite different lines. Each of the professional courses into which SST has been introduced at Ulster Polytechnic had its own traditions; sometimes the course was established prior to the introduction of SST; in all cases courses of professional training were well-established elsewhere and provided a tradition to which we were bound to relate. Usually the preferred practices in the area were institutionalised through a professional validating body whose approval was necessary; in most cases professional staff brought to the course a commitment to practices experienced elsewhere (and usually and understandably conceived such commitment as a requirement for the job!).

The position of SST within the curriculum may be illuminated through a medical metaphor. At best SST is an integral part of an organism of which it is a microcosm: at worst it is a cosmetic graft soon rejected or isolated by the host. At intermediate points SST may constitute an effective substitute for a malfunctioning organ; or less economically, may operate redundantly in tandem with an organ devoted to similar functions.

In conclusion we would like to tie together certain features of our SST programmes at Ulster Polytechnic with the increasing attention being paid to cognitive factors in promoting effective social skill acquisition and generalisation.

We have argued that social skill training may be at its most effective when it acts as a focus for the elaboration of the trainees' perceptions, cognitions and plans regarding his social interaction and not merely as an opportunity for the reproduction of specified behaviours. This process of cognitive elaboration we believe to be greatly enhanced by the provision of linked theory courses from psychology and social psychology. In a sense these theory courses are an extension of the sensitisation and cognitive preparation elements found in many social skill training programmes. In another sense they represent the most appropriate use which may be made of the educational components of professional courses which become not only a desirable thing in themselves but also functional in the preparation of an effective and creative professional.

7 EFFECTIVENESS AND EVIDENCE

But does it work? Is this particular emperor really wearing clothes? In previous chapters we have discussed the strengths and weaknesses of SST and have made some reference to research and evaluation studies. We have also made the point that systematic, objective and, if possible, quantitative evaluation is an essential rather than accidental part of SST. The process involves setting behavioural goals and measuring their achievement to show that training has taken place. We have also admitted shortcomings in our evaluation at Ulster Polytechnic since there are few comparisons with alternative procedures or follow-up studies of generalisation. In this chapter we will summarise evidence regarding SST.

In large part this evidence will be presented as it addresses the following questions.

(1) Does SST change the behaviour of trainees?
(2) Are these changes indicative of increased social skill and how is this defined?
(3) How do the elements of training contribute to these changes?
(4) In what circumstances and for whom can SST be recommended?

In each case we will consider the evidence from remedial, developmental and specialise settings.

(1) Does SST Effect Changes in Trainees?

The evaluation of any form of training is essentially measurement of the extent to which objectives have been achieved. It is not surprising, therefore, to find that the outcomes selected for measurement and adduced as evidence in evaluation are closely related to the objectives set out prior to training. Thus SST trainers working within a behaviourist tradition and emphasising increased frequency of specific units of behaviour as objectives of training are likely to regard such an increase as evidence that training 'works'. Similarly trainers in specialised areas, whose ultimate concern is with the effect that trainees have upon others, are likely to consider the measurement of pupil learning or client satisfaction in groups taught or counselled the most appropriate source of evaluative evidence.

Thus the range of changes measured in assessment of the success of SST is wide. Comparison of studies across and, indeed, within settings is extremely difficult. Frequently programmes vary not only in their objectives, but also in trainees, situations, skills and procedures. Nonetheless, some consistencies can be reported.

It is clear, for example, from an abundance of studies across settings and procedures that SST effects short-term changes in behaviour. Trainees are able to do things at the end of training which they could not, or did not, do at the beginning.

Thus in remedial SST McFall and Marston (1970) using the Behavioural Assertiveness Test (Eisler *et al.*, 1973a) on a group of unassertive college students immediately before and after a four-session programme found that there was a significant change in their performance on the role-play items of the test and that their improvement was significantly greater than changes in a comparable group of college students who had not undergone SST. In related studies McFall and Lillesand (1971), McFall and Twentyman (1973) and Kazdin (1976) varied the procedures of training but continued to find significant differences between the BAT performances of students who had undergone training and the performances of those who had not.

These studies were the first of many which have used student volunteers as analogues of trainees who would normally be psychiatric patients or at least social work clients. Such analogue studies also shorten the period of training and modify the circumstances in which it takes place and are therefore open to the criticism that results might not be similar in a population of real trainees. Studies have, however, been undertaken in genuine clinical settings comparing groups of patients who (like the students) did and did not undergo training. Alternatively, single subject methodologies have been used. In these the performance of individual patients is measured on repeated occasions before, during, between and after treatment periods and variations in performance are compared with the schedule of training sessions.

Group studies were undertaken (again using BAT and employing varied procedures) by Eisler *et al.* (1973b), Hersen *et al.* (1973b, 1974) and Goldsmith and McFall (1975), which showed the performance of psychiatric patients who had received SST to be superior immediately after training to the performance of those who had not. Similar studies using other role-play measures are reported by Goldstein *et al.* (1973), Gutride *et al.* (1973) and Finch and Wallace (1977) and again short-term behaviour change is demonstrated in patients who have undergone SST.

Single-subject studies allow for detailed observation of behavioural changes in one patient over a period of time and although they might be challenged on the grounds of lack of general applicability to other patients they make up for that deficiency by the specificity of the data which can be collected. Thus Hersen *et al* . (1975) used role-play scenes from the BAT not only as bases for overall ratings of the behaviour of a chronically-withdrawn schizophrenic but also as opportunities for measuring the frequency of specific behaviours including eye contact, requests and speech disruptions. These measured behaviours then became target behaviours during training and were reassessed at the points indicated by the research design. Improvements were found in eye contact and in requests, in other measured but non-targetted behaviours and in overall ratings of skill after training. Similar single-subject clinical studies have been undertaken by Eisler (1976; Eisler *et al*., 1974); Foy *et al*. (1975), Edelstein and Eisler (1976) and Hersen and Bellack (1976b) targetting a variety of specific behaviours and using subjects of varied clinical diagnosis. In each instance changes in behaviour were demonstrated subsequent to training. Analysis of the timing of specific targetted changes showed a close relationship with the application of the relevant training measures.

In summary both analogue and clinical, and group and individual studies of remedial SST have shown that behavioural changes can be detected in trainees subsequent to training. Latterly, simple assessment of the behavioural outcomes of remedial SST has given way to subtler analysis of the relative efficacy of various manipulations of the training procedure. There has also been recent critical discussion (Bellack, 1979) of the validity and application of the skills and the measures employed for their assessment, so that the positive outcomes detailed above should perhaps be viewed with caution.

Investigation of SST outcomes in developmental SST is less extensive than in either remedial or specialised settings. It is particularly lacking where training has been undertaken as part of the general social education curriculum for normal children. 'Abnormal' in this case refers to those who have been specially selected by teachers as troublesome or by researchers looking for subjects whose performance is sufficiently deficient to be picked up by measuring techniques derived from remedial/clinical work. As discussed in Chapter 2 the bulk of developmental SST is in fact with individual children either judged as failing to achieve normal levels of social skill or, more often, diagnosed in the first instance as withdrawn or disturbed and, subsequently, judged to be candidates for SST.

Van Hasselt *et al*. (1979), reviewing the literature on SST with children, make it clear that much of this single-subject work (they record 17 such studies) is systematic and behavioural in orientation and aimed at improvement of social skill, but that it varies so widely in the techniques used for skill acquisition that it can only in the loosest sense be termed SST. A few studies however (Bornstein *et al*., 1977; Whitehill, 1978; Beck *et al*., 1978) have used the classic sensitisation, practice, feedback cycle and have worked within the traditions of remedial SST. Specifically both Bornstein *et al*. (1977) and Whitehill (1978) made use among other measures of the BAT-C – a specially derived children's version of the BAT. In both of these studies and in those of Beck *et al*. (1978) and Panepinto (1976) training was effective in improving performance on role-play items. Bornstein (1977) used the multiple-baseline technique and showed that improvements in performance were related to the sequence of training.

Group comparison studies are few in this setting although a number of applications (Raushbaum-Selig, 1976; Bower *et al*., 1976) are reported at case-study level. Several better controlled studies (O'Connor, 1969, 1972) exist showing effects for partial applications of SST such as modelling. Comparisons of groups of third to fifth grade children who underwent instructions and coaching in social skills with matched control-group children were undertaken by Oden and Asher (1977) and Hymel and Asher (1977) with mixed results. In the 1976 study, trained children were superior on a sociometric measure of their acceptability as friends for other children but were no different from untrained children on behavioural measures. In the 1977 study, trained children were no different on either measure. Recently, however, La Greca and Santogrossi (1980) used a fuller training cycle (modelling, coaching and practice) with similarly selected children and found that trained children were superior to untrained on a role-play measure and in initiations of interaction with schoolmates.

Evidence for short-term behaviour change in developmental SST is thus not conclusive but it is certainly encouraging. Much more research, however, is needed on both outcomes and procedures.

Evaluative methodology in specialised SST differs somewhat from that employed in remedial and developmental contexts in that single-subject studies are virtually non-existent and even analogue studies are a good deal less frequent. The typical design is one in which outcomes (or potential outcomes) are measured before and after training for a specific group of genuine trainees who (unlike many analogue remedial groups) have undergone an entire training programme. These measures may or may not then be compared with a matched control group who have not undergone training. Such control-group studies are particularly difficult to achieve since professionals in training are likely to demand some substitute form of interpersonal practice. Indeed, if, as we have argued in Chapter 6, one of the useful outcomes of SST is its influence upon the rest of the curriculum then students who receive that curriculum but not SST are in fact a contaminated control. To select controls receiving a totally separate curriculum on the other hand would be to fail to match groups and to introduce further uncontrolled variables. Solutions to the dilemma involving correlations between SST scores and subsequent practice (Brown, 1975) have been proposed. Brown also suggests that single-subject methods should be applied to single training groups so that the timing of improvements might be related to the timing of training.

There are, therefore, difficulties of controlled comparison which have led to many writers eschewing the classic experimental paradigm and proposing some form of illuminative case study. Brown is relatively unusual in linking this with sophisticated statistical techniques. This kind of design is being followed by Dickson (in preparation) in his evaluation of SST for employment advisory officers. This study exemplifies a development away from simple outcome studies towards more subtle analysis of the effects of training components and in particular of the generalisation and transfer of training to placement or post-qualification practice.

Internal evaluative studies measuring the short-term outcomes of specialised SST programmes have, of course, taken place. Indeed, short-term behavioural outcome has been the most common criterion employed in evluation whether that outcome has been recorded by rating or by actual counting of behaviours. Representative studies can, therefore, be quoted demonstrating the short-term effectiveness of training.

Thus Moreland *et al*. (1970) trained ten graduate psychology students in six micro-counselling skills and rated their use of the skills and general interview effectiveness in interviews with the same clients before and after training. Post-training ratings showed an improvement. Group comparison studies of micro-counselling undertaken by Scroggins and Ivey (1976) and by Kerrebrock (1971) show similar improvements and indicate significant differences between the trained and untrained groups in paraphrasing, reflection of feeling, reinforcement and summarisation as measured immediately after training.

Probably the major area of specialised SST is microteaching and here also studies have been undertaken demonstrating behaviour changes after training. Thus Fortune *et al*. (1967) and Cooper and Stroud (1966) report studies undertaken at Stanford University (where microteaching originated) showing improvements in over 200 students in planning, clarity of explanation, use of pupil ideas and positive reinforcement as rated by pupils, supervisors and independent observers. Similar results were obtained: by Kremer and Perlberg (1971) who found that students improved questioning behaviour as rated by two independent raters; by Kieviet (1972) who found that trained teachers improved on five out of seven selected variables related to the Flanders' (1970) interaction analysis category system; and by Perrott *et al*. (1975) who found significant changes in eight out of 14 aspects of questioning being trained through use of a standardised self-instructional course focused upon 'Effective Questioning'.

Among the many group comparison studies of microteaching Allen and Fortune's (1966) study (again at Stanford) was the first to compare students who had undergone an intensive (one hour per day for 15 days) microteaching course with students who had experienced normal teaching practice (three weeks). Results favoured the microteaching group and it was argued that they were achieved for much less effort. In 1970 Davis and Smoot compared 85 secondary teacher trainees who had taken microteaching courses with 55 who had undergone traditional training experiences on 22 behaviour counted scores and found significant differences in favour of the microteaching group on 17 of the 22 scores. Similarly favourable results are reported by Davis (1970), Kissock (1971), Allen (1972), Jensen and Young (1972) and many others and it seems clear that although some varieties of microteaching and some combinations of microteaching with other aspects of training may be more successful than others, in general microteaching produces short-term behavioural change and does so to a greater degree than other forms of teaching practice.

In each of remedial, developmental and specialised SST, therefore, short-term behaviour change is reported in trainees subsequent to training. As discussed in previous chapters, however, assessment strategies in SST are by no means limited to behavioural measurement. Indeed, self-report measures derived in part from Wolpe and Lazarus' (1966) inventory are particularly common in remedial SST. Typically (see Chapters 1 and 2) these measures are used to assist clinicians in designing SST programmes to fit individual patients' needs, but they have also been used before and after training as a possible measure of its effect. Many of these measures are of doubtful validity and as Hersen and Bellack comment (1977, p. 549) 'Self-report and behavioural measures have had consistently low relationships with one another'. None the less it should be noted that several early analogue studies in remedial SST undertaken by McFall and colleagues (McFall & Marston, 1970; McFall & Lillesand, 1971; McFall & Twentyman, 1973; Goldsmith & McFall, 1975) and by Kazdin (1976) do show improved self-report scores after training.

Such self-report measures are less common in specialised SST although the Minnesota Teacher Attitude Inventory has occasionally been used (e.g. Goldman, 1969), and students have been shown to have more favourable scores after training. Measurement of students' attitudes to training, however, has frequently been made in specialised SST (Ivey & Authier, 1978; Hargie & Maidment, 1979; Rackham & Morgan, 1977). Particular aspects of training may be approved or criticised in particular programmes, but in general results are favourable.

Attempts have also been made in specialised SST to relate training to trainees' capacity to influence clients. Thus in microteaching pupil learning has been assessed for groups of novice teachers who have and have not experienced training. Studies have been few and results have been far from clear however and as Hargie (1980) suggests, differences in pupils, school settings etc. may prove uncontrollable obstacles to clearer investigation. Results from client outcome studies in microcounselling are clearer. Kelley (1971) found that the clients of counsellors who had undergone training talked more and Welch (1976) found that they talked about themselves more as did Gluckstern (1973). Such studies remain rare in the literature. This is unfortunate since change in the trainee's effect upon others is probably more relevant to the purpose of the training than a narrow focus on the trainee's behaviour. Most studies seem (if we might pursue the golfing analogy) overly concerned with the swing of the club to the exclusion of the flight of the ball.

All of the studies discussed above offer general support for the notion that SST changes trainees in the short-term. People can be induced to nod more, talk less, ask more questions: there is some limited evidence that they may appraise themselves more positively after the experience. As discussed in Chapter 5 evidence for the application of these changes to related situations outside of the training unit or, indeed, for their maintenance over time is less positive. Some suggestions were made in Chapter 6 for the explanation of this failure to generalise, but we would now like to return to the question in the more general evaluative context and to relate it to the issue of skill validity. Are these demonstrable increases in nods, questions and silences and so on in fact increases in some general facility termed social skill or are they merely increases in nods, questions and silences?

(2) Are Such Changes Indicative of Increased Social Skill?

Definitions of social skill vary considerably, not only in the general confusion (see Chapter 1) between assertiveness and social skill, but also in their behavioural reference. Wolpe and Lazarus (1966) for example defined social skill as 'all socially acceptable expressions of rights and feelings' (p. 39) which begs any number of questions about the nature of 'rights' and 'acceptability'. Similar criticisms apply to Alberti and Emmons' (1974) definition of assertiveness as (p. 2) 'behaviour which enables a person to act in his own best interests, stand up for himself without undue anxiety, to express his rights without destroying the rights of others'. Libet and Lewinsohn (1973) avoid such value judgements in their definition of social skill as 'the complex ability both to emit behaviours which are positively or negatively reinforced and not to emit behaviours which are punished or extinguished by others' but, of course, leave undetermined the nature and assessability of reinforcement as does Hersen and Bellack's (1977, p. 145) 'ability to express both positive and negative feelings in the interpersonal context without suffering consequent loss of social reinforcement'.

As suggested in previous chapters we prefer a more cybernetic definition such as Welford's (1980, p. 11) 'social skill is conceived as the use of efficient strategies to relate the demands of tasks or situations to the performers' capacities' or our own (Ellis, 1980; Ellis & Whittington, 1979) 'Sequences of individual behaviour which are integrated in some way with the behaviour of others and which measure up to some predetermined criterion'. This definition, however, still requires that the behaviours chosen and the criterion levels set should be related to a more general model of social effectiveness in a chosen range of situations. Thus specific behaviours and general descriptions must be related and must satisfy some test of validity.

In social skill training two extremes of error are possible. Specific behaviours may be chosen as a focus for training but lack any higher-order integrative notion of competence. Conversely a general aim may be set which lacks specific behavioural referents. In either case the targets set may not relate, either analytically or empirically, to everyday life.

These two forms of error may be characterised respectively as 'specific irrelevance' and 'vague significance'. In the first case training may grind exceeding small with no integrating purpose. Validity beyond the level of short-term behavioural changes is difficult, if not impossible. In the second case training may be ill-specified, haphazard and intuitive with consequent problems for description, replication and evaluation.

In practice, although not in such extreme forms, such difficulties have been manifest and as previous chapters have noted the majority of SST programmes proceed (and claim success) despite what Bellack (1979, p. 158) refers to as the 'uncertain reliability, validity and utility' of their assessment measures and resulting skill focuses. In remedial SST in particular, considerable concern has recently been expressed: over self-report measures (Arkowitz, 1977; Hersen & Bellack, 1977) of doubtful psychometric sophistication; over role-play tests (e.g. BAT) which have been shown to bear limited relationship to *in vivo* observations or self-reports from the same patients (Higgins *et al.*, 1979; Van Hasselt *et al.*, 1978; Westefeld *et al.*, 1980; Bellack *et al.*, 1978); and over the scarcity (and technical inadequacy) of such naturalistic observation as has been undertaken (Van Hasselt *et al.*, 1978; Hersen & Bellack, 1977; Bellack, 1979). For example, while groups 'known' as lacking social skill perform differently on role-plays from groups 'known' as normally skilled the instruction to role-play consistently changes behaviour. Correlations (for known or unknown groups) between behaviour observed in role-play and behaviour observed *in vivo* are low. In specialised SST similar debate is centred upon whether behaviour change is best measured by rating or by category system and upon low correlations between skill increment as measured in the unit at the end of training and as measured *in vivo* in real practice (Turney *et al.*, 1973).

The problem may be characterised as (Bellack, 1979, p. 167) 'the central question: what should be assessed?' or (Trower, 1978, p. 327) 'the . . . requirement is a body of scientifically validated knowledge of normal social behaviour to provide training targets and assessment criteria'. In other words, while we have a more or less adequate procedure for skill acquisition, we lack an adequate model of skill use and may, therefore, be wasting our training effort upon inappropriate targets.

Interestingly, there is a body of evidence (Rosenshine, 1971; Bellack *et al.*, 1978) which suggests that ratings of social skill by experienced observers are much better predictors of such future outcomes as ability to increase pupil learning than are the more straightforward measures of increased frequency of observable units of skill. Somehow, it seems, experienced individuals observe, record, process and judge subtleties of interaction which as yet escape our explicit attempts at modelling.

As noted in Chapter 3, the skills used in SST vary in what might loosely be described as 'size' or 'grain of analysis'. Hersen and Bellack (1976a) discern somewhat crudely two categories of behavioural unit which have been profitably employed in training. These they term the 'molar' and the 'molecular' – the one being larger than the other. They do not indicate how a boundary might be established between the molar and the molecular but give examples which suggest that the dimension along which they are in fact arranging skill units is Rosenshine's (1971) low-inference/high-inference dimension. Thus, their examples of the molar include 'assertiveness', 'heterosexual dating skill', 'appropriate interview behaviour', all of which might be evinced in a variety of ways combining different notionally 'smaller' behavioural units. They exemplify the molecular as 'eye contact', 'voice volume', etc. and Bellack (1979) contrasts the 'highly objective' manner in which these can be observed with the fact that the more 'molar categories have defied operational definition and cannot be measured in a purely objective fashion' (p. 168).

Other authors make similar distinctions about levels of skill analysis and it is clear that a refined model would have to take account both of the high/low inference dimension and of the disappointingly negative relationship between low-inference objectivity and the validity and general application of skill units.

It has been suggested (Bellack, 1979; Trower, 1980a) that one reason for this lack of validity and general application of skills derived from rigorously objective observation is that they fail to take account of the sequencing and organisation of units in smooth skilled performance. Such a technique applied to the measurement of physical skills might, for example, produce assessments of car driving in terms of the number of occasions on which the indicators were used – a relevant measure no doubt, but highly misleading unless related to other skill units and, indeed, to the intended destination and surrounding road and traffic circumstances.

Trower (1980b, p. 328) refers to the distinction as being between 'skill components' and 'skill processes' in which components are taken to be single 'elements' or routinely organised 'sequences' of elements' such as 'looks, nods, lexical clauses' etc. which individuals normally 'run off automatically' whereas 'processes' refer to the individual's ability to generate skilled behaviour 'according to rules and goals and in response to social feedback'. These processes are exemplified by timing, sequencing and monitoring. Bellack (1979) makes a similar distinction in suggesting that it will be important to examine (p. 170) 'the flow of behaviour . . . to identify instances in which changes in the nature of various responses are more significant than their static occurrence or non-occurrence'.

This distinction between static and dynamic analysis is clearly important and, as Duncan and Fiske (1977) have demonstrated, hypotheses as to the regularities of interactional dynamics can be derived from intensive observation of small numbers of interactors and recording of the occasions in which events of type A are followed or accompanied by events of type B, C, D, etc. Thus in their study of 'turn taking' in conversation, Duncan and Fiske (1977) were able to determine from computerised analysis of such detailed data that change from one speaker to another is determined by a complex process of decision-making in both participants. It is influenced by variations in present state of interaction (i.e. who is speaking), in gestural and other signals displayed by the non-speaking partner and by the speaking partner, in the 'moves' recently undertaken by each partner, and in tacit 'rules' for interaction accepted by both partners.

It will be noted from this that Duncan and Fiske (1977), who are exemplary in their empirical rigour, do not argue against all reference to unobservables. Intervening variables or hypothetical constructs 'have their proper place as postulated or hypothesised entities in the description of the organisation of interaction' (p. 327). Thus in the study of 'turn taking' they argue that interactors operate according to *internalised conventions* (our italics) which are chosen according to a prior strategy which is applied within the situation as the interactor perceives it. The precise way in which a 'convention' is performed is also, in their analysis, 'subject to both strategy and perceived situation'. In both cases unobservable processes of analysis and decision-making are postulated. The implicit model is highly reminiscent of Welford's (1980) definition of skill as the possession of efficient strategies for the accomplishment of goals. Both Welford (1980) and Duncan and Fiske (1977) suggest that investigation of the rules by which such flexible goal-seeking behaviour is organised is central to the development of an adequate model of interaction.

However such rules are acquired and applied they must account for decisions relating behaviour to situations. Duncan and Fiske (1977,

p. 328) acknowledge that 'the greatest single omission of the turn system study was the failure to specify the situational requirements of conventions represented by the turn system'. Pursuing the earlier car-driving analogy this is akin to describing rules for driving in a car with no windows. Unfortunately the models of interaction implicit in most SST not only ignore skill sequencing and the rules which govern it but also ignore, except in the most limited sense, the situations within which skilled behaviour is to be displayed.

Attempts at specific training for generalisation have, to some extent, recognised that skills may be differently deployed in different settings. But the rules governing such differentiation are far from clear. Generalisation training (see Chapter 5) therefore tends to rely on the intuitions of trainers rather than upon an explicit model of situational variables and socially-skilled behaviour. Recent empirical investigation (Argyle *et al.*, 1979; Argyle & Furnham, 1980; Morton, 1978; Trower, 1980b) has suggested not only that situations are significant determiners of behaviour in normal populations, but also that being unable to tailor one's behaviour to meet situational requirements may be a significant element in deficient social behaviour. These, however, are mere preliminary indicators and much work remains to be done in the analysis of situational rules and their relationship to skilled social interaction.

It is clear that social skill is much more complex than might be surmised from superficial scrutiny of the SST literature and that evaluation of training exclusively in terms of changes in behaviour at the end of programmes is at best partial and at worst highly misleading. As we have noted, however, many recent commentators have expressed dissatisfaction with this state of affairs and as Trower (1980b) puts it 'after a period of euphoric expectations SST and the attendant research have entered a more healthy period of critical evaluation'.

Within that evaluation much attention must surely be paid to refinement of the underlying model of social skill and to the derivation of indices of skill which can be incorporated in adequate assessment and evaluation procedures. Such indices will certainly include regularities in the occurrence of observed behaviours but they may also include other measures of perceptual and cognitive processing capacity in an attempt to measure, in Welford's (1980) characterisation, 'efficient strategies' from all possible angles.

An adequate model of skilled social performance must, in summary, take full account of the cognitions and perceptions of the participants, the settings in which the exchanges occur and the temporal organisation of situational, behavioural and cognitive events.

(3) How do the Elements of Training Contribute to the Changes it Effects?

The overall evaluation of SST is made difficult not only by variations of definitions, models and chosen skills, but also by variations in procedures. As was illustrated in Chapters 1 and 2 programmes vary extensively: in the detail of their sensitisation and modelling procedures; in the tasks they set for practice; in the people with whom trainees are asked to interact in practice; in the circumstances and physical settings of practice and in the nature, timing and source of feedback, coaching and general supervision.

Without knowing which are the most effective elements of training it is particularly difficult to compare outcomes. Thus if study A reports success for a programme using cued sensitisation, role-play and feedback through discussion with fellow trainees and study B reports failure for a programme using instructions, role-play and individual feedback through detailed behavioural analysis, it is difficult to know whether differences are due to the explicit differences in sensitisation or in feedback. Alternatively they may be due to some other unnamed and uncontrolled variable such as tutor-role during feedback. There is a particular need for studies recognising this problem and explicitly controlling as many potentially confounding variables as possible. Many studies have been conducted which manipulate the elements of SST in order to determine which of them are most effective, but only rarely do they give sufficient detail of other aspects of their procedures to allow collation of results with those of other studies. Some cautious conclusions may, however, be reached.

In remedial SST, for example, McFall and Twentyman (1973) compared student groups who each received short-term treatment in which various combinations of behavioural rehearsal, modelling and coaching were employed. They concluded (1) that behaviour rehearsal and coaching accounted for most of the treatment effects, (2) that the addition of modelling made no difference and (3) that the type of behaviour rehearsal used (covert or overt or a combination) made no difference. Feedback was not considered as a separate variable and it is difficult to determine in this study exactly what was meant by coaching. Friedman (1971), Kazdin (1976) and Young *et al.* (1973) however showed that modelling did affect behaviour change when undertaken in isolation (Kazdin, 1976) or when combined with various forms of behaviour rehearsal and reinforcement. Hersen and Bellack (1976a) reviewing these and other analogue studies conclude that although inter-study comparisons are difficult, modelling might not be an important component of programmes for undergraduates where (p. 566) 'it would seem that . . . instructional control coupled with guided practice (i.e. coaching and behaviour rehearsal) may be sufficient to facilitate appropriate . . . responding'. This ran counter to an interrelated group of studies which they and their colleagues carried out with psychiatric patients (Eisler *et al.*, 1973b; Hersen *et al.*, 1973b, 1974) which showed that modelling and instructions were the most important components of training and that (Hersen & Bellack, 1976a, p. 569) 'Mere practice is ineffective in bringing about behavioural change. In contrast to college student populations, modelling or modelling plus interactions is required for effecting change in the more complicated components of assertiveness'.

Early studies of microteaching (McDonald & Allen, 1967; Koran, J., 1969; Higgins *et al.*, 1970) established a clear case for the importance of modelling as a component of training and subsequent studies (Berliner, 1969; Borg, 1970; Gilmore, 1977) compared various types of model with results which showed an effect for modelling of any kind but (possibly as a result of other programme variations) failed to show a clear result in favour of positive, negative, video, audio or other variety of model. As noted in Chapter 2 there is some evidence (Borg, 1970; Ebert, 1970) for the importance of 'cued models' in which the trainer stops to discuss significant aspects of the model and for the importance (Koran, M., 1969) of models with which the trainee can identify and who may even be observed (Meichenbaum, 1977) coping with mistakes.

Wagner (1973) demonstrated (as did Kazdin (1976) in the remedial setting) that modelling and related discrimination training was a more effective way of training teaching skills than was practice with feedback. A number of other studies (Goldthwaite, 1969; Kallenbach & Gall, 1969) which failed to show differences between microteaching and non-microteaching groups can be reinterpreted to show that they were in fact comparing modelling alone with modelling plus practice so that their results might be taken to indicate the potency of modelling.

This stress upon the importance of modelling in some areas (notably psychiatric remedial SST and microteaching) and not in others is difficult to interpret and becomes more so if it is accepted, as Borg (1970) suggested, that modelling continues throughout practice and feedback since the trainee is using the model as a comparison for his own performance and thus sharpening his awareness.

Ivey and Authier (1978), reviewing studies of components of micro-counselling procedures, concur that both modelling and instructions are important, but develop the argument by suggesting that instructions alone may be efficacious where so-called 'simple' skills are being promoted (re-statement is given as an example), whereas modelling is said to be important for 'more complex' skills such as reflection of feeling. This distinction between 'simple' and 'complex' is analogous to Rosenshine's (1971) high- and low-inference distinction and indeed it may be the case that the only way to recognise, understand (and produce) a high-inference skill is to see it thereby being exposed to just the subtle visual cues and complex sequences of behaviours which sophisticated raters pick up but no one seems yet able to render explicit. The analogy might be with an instrumental master class, where detailed and specific technical advice eventually yields to the master pianist producing a passage and suggesting 'do it like this'. Psychiatric trainees it might be argued are even *less* able to pick out regularities in interaction and to render them in an explicit verbal form and thus need to see even the so-called low-inference skills in ostensive demonstration and what is more then need to practise them to be sure the developing concept is 'right'.

The practice element of SST has also been extensively explored (see Chapter 2). Some studies (e.g. Wagner, 1973) seem to indicate that it is less important than sensitisation or (Kazdin, 1976; Flowers, 1975; Zielinski & Williams, 1979) that covert practice is as good as overt practice. Yet programmes which have abandoned overt behaviour practice are very few indeed. This may be explained by the fact that trainees (Borg, 1970; McIntyre, 1977; Zielinski & Williams, 1979) prefer overt practice despite the fact that covert produces equally good results.

Variation of feedback procedures (see Chapter 2) has received less attention in remedial SST than it has in the specialised literature although the conclusion is generally reached that (Bellack & Hersen, 1977, p. 154) 'simple positive and negative feedback lead to marked behavioural change' and (p. 155) 'there is no doubt that social reinforcement is a very powerful change strategy'. Systematic investigation of varieties of feedback source and feedback strategy is, however, common in the specialised literature. Thus many studies of microteaching have been carried out contrasting video-feedback with and without a tutor present, with and without feedback in the form of rating or category scores and so on. Unfortunately few concrete conclusions can be drawn from this flurry of research. Some studies (Perrott,

1972; McDonald & Allen, 1967; Gregory, 1971; McIntyre & Duthie, 1977; Tuckman & Oliver, 1968) for example show that tutor presence affects student performance while others (McKnight, 1971; Olivero, 1965; Orme, 1966; Forge, 1973) show it to be unimportant although it is a consistent finding that students prefer the presence of a supervising tutor. As we noted in Chapter 2 there is other evidence (Hargie, 1980; Tucker & Acheson, 1971) which suggests that the most effective feedback is feedback which is closely tied in to previous modelling and sensitisation experiences. The tutor's role may, therefore, lie less in the simple provision of ratings or other analyses than in guiding trainees towards comparison of their own performance with that of the model. This is congruent with the notion (Borg, 1970) that modelling continues throughout the SST cycle and with McIntyre's (1977) suggestion that the most important thing SST accomplishes is the extension and refinement of trainees' available repertoires of alternative strategies for behaviour.

The search for the 'active ingredients' of SST is clearly fraught with difficulties and, as has been shown, evidence can be found for the potency of each of the traditional elements of the training cycle namely, sensitisation, practice and feedback. Comparisons between them and attempts to discern their relative contributions to training outcomes are particularly hazardous and conclusions may well be masked by differences in the detail of their implementation or indeed by differences in individual trainees, tutors and situations. Different skills may also require different procedures for maximum improvement.

We have tried to offer simple guidelines for the matching of procedures to programme objectives and trainees in Chapter 2, but on the whole we would continue to recommend that all SST programmes use some form of sensitisation, practice and feedback. Results of variations in procedures with particular groups should also be closely monitored since their success or failure may be more relevant for the development of appropriate programmes for succeeding similar groups than the results of investigations designed for general applicability.

(4) In What Circumstances and for Whom Can SST be Recommended?

We have demonstrated that SST does change trainees, that the measurement of these changes is not as well-related to the best available models of social skill as it might be and that no one aspect of training is clearly more important than another. How then can the potential trainer judge whether SST is viable in his circumstances?

It is likely that such viability will depend in part upon the extent to which it can be modified to meet the needs of relevant trainees (and trainers) and in part upon the intervention with which it is being contrasted. Experimental studies of SST outcomes frequently employ 'no treatment' groups as controls, but potential innovators are more likely to be interested in comparison between SST outcomes and the outcomes of existing practice. SST outcomes need to be substantially better than existing practice to warrant the upheaval attendant upon change.

A number of studies in remedial SST have, in fact, compared SST with other therapeutic strategies with moderately favourable results for SST. Jackson and Oei (1978) for example showed that SST was more effective in the short-term than 'cognitive restructuring' although the difference was no longer significant on follow-up. Curran (1975) and Hall and Goldberg (1977) demonstrated the superiority of SST over systematic desensitisation and several other studies have shown it to be superior to 'traditional hospital treatment' which may be supposed to imply some form of helpful intervention.

It may be, however, that results from these studies are in part the result of the patients selected. Trower *et al.* (1978b) for example show that for phobic patients systematic desensitisation and SST are equally effective while for patients described as having a 'primary deficiency' in social skill SST is the superior treatment. Trower argues from these results, as do Marzillier and Winter (1978) and Griffiths and Gillingham (1978), that individual differences in patients' diagnoses must be taken more account of not only in the evaluation of SST but also in the design of programmes.

Comparative studies have also been undertaken in microteaching (Kallenbach & Gall, 1969; Davis & Smoot, 1970; Harris *et al.*, 1970) and micro-counselling (Evans *et al.*, 1975; Welch, 1976; Hearn, 1976) with broadly favourable results for both forms of SST; but again methodologies are open to criticism (Turney *et al.*, 1973; Ivey & Authier, 1978) and there is need for further investigation.

More impressive perhaps than these rather limited comparisons is the simple fact that (as detailed in Chapter 1) SST has been adapted and applied across a very wide spectrum of trainers, trainees, settings and circumstances and that its use continues to spread.

Social skill training may be criticised as relatively artificial: it occurs in a controlled environment; clients may be real or simulated; and there is almost certain to be some element of role-playing required from the trainee. None the less the face-validity of the exercise is high. It is practical rather than theoretical. It seems to trainers, trainees and informed observers to be about real things. Its face-validity is only inferior to real life which, in the case of specialised SST, is practical work in the professional agency, classroom or the client's home. An important comparison, therefore, would be between SST and supervised internship.

One aspect of this comparison concerns cost. Kallenbach and Gall (1969) costed microteaching and supervised teaching practice, and found microteaching to be cheaper. We have costed SST for our professional groups against supervised practice in clinics, agencies and homes and have again found SST to be appreciably cheaper for similar, but ill-quantified, experiences and results. Thus staff time in administration of, travel to and from, and supervision of practice, plus travel expenses, far exceeds the initial investment in and depreciation of CCTV equipment and the time spent in SST procedures.

Such comparisons fall down, of course, in identifying a similar metric of student achievement for each. Supervised practice in professional training is notoriously weak on clear objectives and reliable and valid assessment procedures. Evaluation studies of comparable rigour to those undertaken of SST are rare and confined to isolated studies of aspects of teaching practice.

The potential trainer can judge for himself whether his circumstances and intended trainees would allow him to design a programme within the guidelines of Chapter 2. If he shares our sense of excitement tempered by empirical caution he will want to go ahead – but he will want to monitor outcomes carefully and to use them in continuing modification of skills and acquisition procedures.

Conclusion and Recommendations for Further Research

As has been demonstrated, evaluation of the effectiveness of SST is not simple and results are, in some areas, mixed. Enough positive evidence has been amassed, however, to merit its continued use and refinement as an intervention strategy and its exploitation as an arena in which hypotheses relevant to the theory of social interaction may be refined and tested. Specifically, the following advantages can be recorded.

(1) Short-term effects are consistently reported.

(2) Trainees' attitudes towards the experience are positive.
(3) Results (short and long-term) are at least as positive as most comparable interventions.
(4) It engenders debate among theorists, practitioners and trainees about the nature and contexts of interaction.
(5) It is a relatively short, inexpensive intervention strategy which proved viable across a wide range of trainees and settings.
(6) The face-validity of the exercise is high. Other activities with similar face-validity are far more expensive and, to date, lack any comparably rigorous evaluation.

As must be clear from the preceding sections of this chapter, a number of issues remain to be resolved and will only be resolved after some considerable research effort: effort which we would argue is worthwhile.

We would urge that such research take place under three broad headings. They are: first, research which refines and elaborates existing models of interaction and which applies such refinements to the procedures of SST; secondly, research which evaluates training as a general procedure useful in many contexts or features of training common to many contexts; and, thirdly, research which evaluates specific programmes in specific contexts.

(1) Models of Interaction

Practitioners of SST have been slow to recognise their own theoretical antecedents (let alone those of practitioners in other settings) and both principles and practices have suffered as a result. Recently, however, there has been a marked increase in the number of studies which cross the boundaries of theoretical approach and applied setting and it seems likely that implicit and explicit models will benefit accordingly. Specifically, there is need for research which explores the potential of multilevel skill analysis using high- and low-inference behavioural units; for observation and experimental study of the organisation and sequencing of such units and related cognitive processing; for empirical testing of hypotheses about such processing and, finally, for more consideration of the influence of situations upon social behaviour. Work is already in progress in each of these areas and it is pleasing to report that it is at least influenced by practitioners of SST.

(2) General Evaluation

As should be clear from the preceding sections of this chapter, research has suffered from the variety of investigative designs and procedures as well as from the inevitable variety of training programmes themselves. A first recommendation for this type of investigation thus remains the replication and, if possible, explication of existing studies. A number of specific issues stand out however as prime targets for further (or indeed initial) enquiry. These include the following.

(1) Validation of assessment procedures in individualised SST.
(2) Development of skill analyses and observation systems in specialised SST.
(3) Further investigation of procedural variations in SST.
(4) Investigation of the validity of role-play/simulation and its effect upon performance.
(5) Investigation of cognitive changes taking place during and after SST (and their relationship to skill generalisation and transfer).
(6) Development and validation of generalisation training.
(7) Further investigation of the relationship of individual differences to the success of training.

Again work is in progress in most of these areas – but more is needed.

(3) Evaluation of Specific Programmes

It is difficult to make recommendations under this heading since by definition each programme has its own needs. We would, however, simply recommend that trainers do monitor their procedures as closely as possible and that they share their findings as widely as possible with others. There is a particular need for dissemination of findings on supervision and feedback procedure and, perhaps more importantly, on the long-term effects of training. Monitoring may be specific to a programme and even to a group of trainees but it should not stop short at the point where those trainees leave the unit.

It would appear then that the emperor is, indeed, decently clad. However, the texture of the material and the function of the apparel need further investigation. And we still lack an adequate theory of clothing.

CONCLUSION

We began by emphasising the scientific aspirations of SST. Classically SST essays a robust empiricism whereby skilled behaviour should be observed, recorded and analysed and trainees should imitate models until, with the help of feedback, they can reproduce, as appropriate, the skills originally observed. This model has been criticised as naively positivistic, insensitive to the meanings created by participants and destructively reductionist in its skill analysis. None the less it continues, like Dr Johnson's stone, to refute sophisticated critiques: it works and it can be seen to work.

There are, of course, aspects of the model and the practice which should be improved. Both the investigation of social skill and the devising of training programmes need theoretical and methodological sophistication.

The central thrust of SST is behaviourist. Behavioural data, however, is necessary but by no means sufficient for the understanding of human actions and experience. SST must take more account of internal processes not themselves observable. In particular three directions might be followed. First there must be an elaboration of that part of the social skill training model which refers to perception, information processing and the plans which give structure and organisation to behaviour. Secondly, as a practical consequence of this, there should be increased emphasis on SST as a focus and stimulus for cognitive remodelling. There are many pointers to the notion that SST succeeds in affecting human behaviour not so much through behavioural practice but through the effect this behavioural practice and, in particular, the sensitisation phase, has upon the cognitions and plans of participants. Thirdly more emphasis must be given to the meanings which trainers and trainees attribute to social exchange in real life and in the controlled environment of SST. As an example of this shift of emphasis social skill trainers might conceive their process as an exercise in the reorientation of constructs. Psychometric instruments with a phenomenological orientation, such as the repertory grid test (Kelly, 1955) might chart these shifts.

Interpersonal exchanges, verbal and non-verbal, occur within boundaries set by physical circumstances, psychological expectations and social norms. The study of social skills in these situations is already under way (Argyle & Furnham, 1980) and should add a further dimension to training procedures.

SST has always involved the reduction of the complex to the simple, the conglomerate to the element. While further work may yield more convincing elements there is a pressing need for studies of their organisation – both hierarchical and sequential.

SST develops social skills over a relatively short period, say ten weeks in a typical course. But how do social skills develop through a lifetime? Social skill development in this sense is a relatively unresearched area. What stages, if any, characterise social skill development? What is the relationship between social skill development and intellectual and moral development?

The theory and method of SST originates, primarily, in psychology. The influence of other academic disciplines has so far been slight. Apart from contributions from sociology, anthropology and ethology, we would predict an increasing cross-fertilisation with linguistics, particularly that area of the discipline known as discourse analysis. Discourse analysis is concerned with the linguistic analysis of everyday speech and communication: the connection with SST should be obvious.

These five areas:

(1) cognition and social skills;
(2) situations for social skills;
(3) linguistic analysis of social skills;
(4) articulation and organisation of social skill; and
(5) social skill development;

seem to us to offer the most fruitful elaboration of the existing model. Thus the classic Argyle (1967) model (Figure 1.1, p. 24) would take on additional dimensions of space (situation), time (skill sequence and development) and internal elaboration (cognition, organisation of skills).

Critique of the model upon which SST is largely premised was one aim of this book. We also set out to overview current practice in what we have called developmental, remedial and specialised settings for SST. We have noted the lamentable lack of cross-fertilisation between these areas and hope that we may have stimulated practitioners in each to consider the literatures of the others. Remedial practitioners, for example, might profit from the observation systems and detailed investigations of sensitisation and feedback typical of specialised SST.

Trainers in specialised settings might exploit the single-subject methodologies and individual assessment techniques of remedial SST.

Developmental SST is, in our view, the weakest area in its atheoretical eclecticism and polarisation into, on the one hand, ill-defined social education and on the other overly-rigid behaviour modification. The area is an important one bringing a new dimension to formal schooling and in many cases bridging school and work, immaturity and adulthood. It deserves better.

We aimed particularly to offer a practical guide for would-be trainers. For them we have provided a blend of anecdote, description, analysis, principles and exhortation. We hope it proves useful.

Our own practical experience has been in the area of professional training. This will be clear not only from the case studies but also from the emphasis we have given to a curriculum model within which SST finds a place. In unguarded moments we may reveal an almost evangelical fervour for SST as *the* example of how the grail of professional training – the integration of theory and practice – might be achieved.

Bruner (1966) has described education as a process whereby we discover man's distinctive features and strive to develop them. It is a cliché to describe man as a social animal. But endemically communicative and interminably interactive he is. Social skill training helps people to become more effective socially and thus more fully human.

We have found the development of social skill training challenging academically, effective practically and rewarding personally. We hope this book will enable others to share these satisfactions.

APPENDIX 1: MICROTEACHING AND LINKED PSYCHOLOGY IN THE FETC

Weeks	Microteaching 20 x 2 hours	Observation and analysis of teaching behaviour 20 x 2 hours	The learner 20 x 2 hours
1 & 2	General orientation and familiarisation with equipment.	Impressionistic assessment and comment on VTR exemplars. Principles and problems of objectivity in observation of interaction situations	Introduction to selves as learners: aims and objectives of the course, introduction to studentship, techniques of study
3	'Pre-experience' recording and impressionistic evaluation of that recording	For each microteaching skill exemplars of the appropriate teacher behaviour ('models') will be viewed in a preceding observation and analysis session. An appropriate measuring instrument will be developed and practised	Sensation and perception; attention
4 & 5	'Stimulus variation'		Concept formation
6 & 7	'Questioning'		Language and concept formation; meaningful/rote learning feedback
8 & 9	'Reinforcement'		Motivation; classical and instrumental conditioning
10 & 11	'Conceptual variation'		Classroom learning model; individual differences; language and class
12 & 13	'Illustration and use of examples'		Discovery and reception learning; concept formation; cognitive style; modelling and imitation in learning
14 & 15	'Set induction'		Motivation; learning set and transfer
16 & 17	'Closure'		Memory
18/19 & 20	Integration of skills 'Post-experience' recording		Tactics and strategies of teaching

APPENDIX 2: BEd DEGREE WITH HONOURS IN EDUCATION: CURRICULUM OUTLINE

		Part 1				Part 2			
		Year I		Year II		Year III		Year IV	
		Semester A	B	C	D	E	F	G	H
		Semester wks (poly. 17)	16	16	11	12	16	16	12
MODULES	1	A.1 Sociological studies	B.1 Main subject domestic science or physical education or communication studies	C.1 Main subject	D.1 Main subject	E.1 Main subject	F.1 Main subject	G.1 Option within main subject	H.1 Option within main subject
	2	A.2 Psychological studies	B.2 Main subject	C.2 Main subject	D.2 Main subject	E.2 Main subject	F.2 Main subject	G.2 Main subject	H.2 Main subject
	3	A.3 (i) Philosophy of community service A.3 (ii) Methods of social investigation	B.3 Practical teaching observation placement	C.3 Practical teaching communication	D.3 Practical teaching organisation for learning	E.3 Practical teaching planning and evaluation	F.3 Educational studies educational research	G.3 Practical teaching curriculum development	H.3(i) Practical teaching curriculum development H.3(ii) Educational studies curriculum studies
	4	A.4 Economic and social history	B.4 Educational studies psychology, soc. psych., sociology	C.4 Educational studies psychology, soc. psych.	D.4 Educational studies psychology economics	E.4 Educational studies psychology philosophy sociology	F.4 Educational studies philosophy of education	G.4 (i) Educational studies discipline option G.4 (ii) Curriculum studies	H.4 Educational studies discipline option
	5	A.5 Foundation studies	B.5 Soc. & comm. studies	C.5 Soc. & comm studies	D.5 Soc. & comm. studies	E.5 Soc. & comm. studies	F.5 Project	G.5 Project	H.5 Project
Teaching practice					5 weeks	5 weeks			5 weeks

APPENDIX 3: BEd DEGREE WITH HONOURS – MICROTEACHING AND LINKED THEORY

Skill	Psychology	Social Psychology
(1) Arousing	Sensation and perception; sensory deprivation and sensory overload; perceptual organisation and perceptual set	Elements of social interaction; teacher 'enthusiasm'
(2) Questioning	Language and thinking; language and social class; a taxonomy of classroom questions	Communication patterns in classroom groups; pupil involvement and teacher expectancies
(3) Reinforcement	Reinforcement in classical and instrumental conditioning; feedback and motivation; programmed learning	Social reinforcement; management styles in teaching
(4) Explaining	Studies of concept formation and concept attainment in children and adults; attempts to accelerate the acquisition of concepts	Verbal moves in interaction; classroom studies of 'effective' explanation
(5) Illustration and use of examples	The value of positive and negative instances in concept learning; role of the teacher in emphasising relevant attributes	Comprehension cues and studies of teachers' sensitivity to them
(6) Set induction	Attention; arousal; transfer of training; mental set	Role and leadership in classroom interaction
(7) Closure	Short-term and long-term memory; the interference theory of forgetting; influence of various learning strategies on memory	Studies of teachers' informal assessment behaviour
(8) Integration of skills	Relating learning to existing cognitive structures; meaningful and rote learning	Classroom climate and affective variables in learning

APPENDIX 4: HEALTH VISITING PROGRAMME

Exemplar Role Plays

Exemplar One

Interviewer. Mrs . . ., a 45-year-old middle-class housewife, has been making many excuses recently to visit her GP and he suspects her real difficulty is an alcohol problem. He has referred the family to you for surveillance and you decide to interview Mrs . . . to assess the situation for yourself.

Interviewee. You are a 45-year-old middle-class housewife, and recently you have been visiting your GP more than usual with minor complaints. Your real problem, however, is an increasing liking for alcohol, and of late you find yourself making more and more excuses for secretive drinking in the house. You have three teenage children, a spotless comfortable home, and a husband who tends to become more and more involved in his job. The GP has asked the health visitor to call and interview you as he feels your visits to the surgery are really cries for help for an underlying problem.

Suggest you act co-operatively!

Exemplar Two

Interviewer. You are making a routine visit to Mrs White who has a baby of nine months, a son of three years, and a daughter aged six years. During the interview, Mrs White confides she is worried about her six-year-old daughter. Probe, assess situation, and offer any help required.

Interviewee. You are the mother of three children; your eldest a girl aged six years started off well at school, but this past year has been doing badly according to school reports. She is also difficult at home, i.e. you find you have to shout at her a few times before she hears you. You are concerned about her as she is usually a good child, and apart from having mumps last year, very healthy. You are glad the health visitor called, as this presents an opportunity for you to discuss your problem.

Exemplar Three

Interviewer. Mr . . ., a 40-year-old labourer, has been involved in a bomb incident and has lost a leg. He has been referred to you for follow-up through the hospital liaison health visitor. You visit to establish a relationship, and assess him for a rehabilitation programme. You find him alone in a country cottage type dwelling.

Interviewee. You are Mr . . ., a 40-year-old labourer and you have recently been involved in a bomb incident, after which you lost a leg. You are a bachelor, living alone in the country. The health visitor has called to establish a relationship and assess you for a rehabilitation programme.

Log-book Guidelines

Assessment of SST will be in the form of a log-book which you will be required to submit at the end of the course. The log-book will be a record of your SST work and experience.

Format

(1) A looseleaf binder with a firm cover would be most suitable.
(2) Your lecture notes should be clearly separated from your log.
(3) With your lecture notes you will find it useful to keep copies of journal articles which you have found useful.
(4) You *must* record details of what reading you have done as you go along and when your log-book is completed it must include a bibliography in the standard form.

Content

Your log section should contain:
(1) An analysis of the rationale for SST.
(2) A summary of each of the social skills studied together with anticipated implication for professional interaction.
(3) An evaluation of these skills in the light of your experience in the SST Unit in the Polytechnic generally and in your fieldwork practice.
(4) A summative analysis (evaluation) of your SST work and experience.
(5) Any innovatory ideas which have occurred to you, e.g. a social skill not included in the programme which you consider to be important in health visiting practice.

Procedure

(1) You must write up your lecture notes and your analysis of the

practical sessions as you go along, otherwise you will be confronted with an impossible task.

(2) You should take your log-book with you on fieldwork practice and discuss its content with your fieldwork teacher at regular intervals.

(3) Any difficulties encountered in the practice sessions or in compiling your log should be discussed with your studies adviser as soon as possible.

(4) You will be given specific tasks to undertake during your block placements, in relation to the families you will be visiting.

(5) Material from your log can be extracted and incorporated with your health visiting studies.

Rating for Health Visitor Skill Sequence

Skill	*Rating focuses*
Reinforcement	Variety (verbal reinforcement) Frequency (verbal reinforcement) Use of non-verbal reinforcement Development of client responses Partial/delayed reinforcement
Questioning	Wording Types of question (open, closed, etc.) Sequence and structure Probing and prompting Attending to responses
Set induction	Establishing working relationship (creature comfort, friendly approach etc.) Stating goals Links with previous knowledge Providing resources
Closure	Summarisation Invitation of questions Link with future Indication of appreciation Closure markers (verbal and non-verbal)
Sustaining	Attention paid to client Time given to client

	Appreciation of feeling
	Redirection (redirecting and re-focusing clients' ideas)
Reflection of feeling	Choice of vocabulary
	Accuracy
	Conciseness
	Reflectivity (how free of interpretation was the reflection?)
Paraphrasing	Choice of vocabulary
	Conciseness
	Specificity
	Accuracy
	Factuality (how free of interpretation was the paraphrase?)
	Feedback (did the client accept the paraphrase?)
Explaining	Planning
	Use of appropriate language
	Clarity
	Emphasis
	Summary
	Obtaining feedback
Demonstration	Planning
	Introduction
	Presentation
	Positioning of group
	Feedback (questions, group participation etc.)

APPENDIX 5: SPECIFICATIONS OF CCTV EQUIPMENT IN THE ULSTER POLYTECHNIC SST SUITE

Each Unit Comprises

1 Sony U-Matic type VO-2630 with remote control panel
1 National 22" colour receiver type TC2203
1 Hitachi GP5 colour camera
1 Fujinon Motorised zoom lens
1 Hitachi Pan and Tilt head
1 Hitachi Control Unit for above
1 Phillips EL/6033/10 omnidirectional microphone
1 Eagle Pro M5 lapel microphone
1 Koss headphones
1 Eagle telephone hand set intercom
1 Set of red, green, amber lights plus control unit
1 Stop clock

Studio Equipment

1 Hitachi GP7 studio colour camera
1 Operating Panel for above
1 Tripod for above
1 Vel mini-mixer
1 Berky studio lights (4)
4 Eagle pro M5 lapel microphones
2 AKG omnidirectional microphones
1 Shure audio-mixer

Classroom Equipment

2 Korting 26" colour receiver/monitors
2 Sony U-matic type VO-2360 video-cassette recorders

BIBLIOGRAPHY

Alberti, R. and Emmons, M. (1974) *Your Perfect Right; A Guide to Assertive Behaviour*, 2nd edn (San Luis Obispo, California, Impact)

Allen, D. and Fortune, J. (1966) 'The Stanford Summer Microteaching Clinic' in Cooper, J. and Stroud, T. (eds.) *Microteaching: A Description*, Stanford Teacher Education Programme (Stanford, Stanford University Press)

Allen, D.W. and Clark, R. (1967) 'Microteaching: Its Rationale', *The High School Journal, 51*, 75-9

Allen, D. and Ryan, K. (1969) *Microteaching* (Reading, Mass., Addison-Wesley)

Allen, D. *et al*. (1967) 'A Comparison of Different Modelling Procedures in the Acquisition of a Teaching Skill', *ERIC* (Education Resources Information Centre) ED:011 261

Allen, W. (1972) 'An Experimental Study Comparing Microteaching and the Traditional Method of Instruction' (Unpublished EdD thesis, East Texas State University)

Anastasi, A. (1978) *Psychological Testing* (New York, Wiley)

Annett, J. (ed.) (1974) *Human Information Processing Part 1*. Units 10-11, Open University DS261 (Milton Keynes, Open University Press)

Argyle, M. (1967) *The Psychology of Interpersonal Behaviour* (Harmondsworth, Penguin)

Argyle, M., Bryant, B. and Trower, P. (1974) 'Social Skills Training and Psychotherapy', *Psychological Medicine, 4*, 435-43

Argyle, M. and Cook, M. (1976) *Gaze and Mutual Gaze* (Cambridge, Cambridge University Press)

Argyle, M., Graham, J., Campbell, A. and White, P. (1979) 'The Rules of Different Situations', *N. Zealand Psychologist, 8*, 13-22

Argyle, M. and Furnham, D. (1980) *Social Situations* (Cambridge, Cambridge University Press)

Arkowitz, H. (1977) 'Measurement and Modification of Minimal Dating Behaviour' in Hersen, M., Eisler, R. and Miller, P. (eds.) *Progress in Behaviour Modification*, volume 5 (New York, Academic Press)

Austad, C.A. (1972) 'Personality Correlates of Teacher Performance in a Microteaching Laboratory', *J.Expmtl. Edn, 40*, 1-5

Ausubel, D. (1968) *Educational Psychology: A Cognitive View* (New

York, Holt, Rinehart and Winston).

Authier, J. and Gustafson, K. (1976) 'The Application of Supervised and Non-supervised Microcounselling Paradigms in the Training of Registered and Licensed Practical Nurses', *J. Cons. & Clin. Psychology, 44*, 704-9

Bales, R. (1950) *Interaction Process Analysis* (Reading, Mass., Addison-Wesley)

Bandura, A. (1969) *Principles of Behaviour Modification* (New York, Holt, Rinehart and Winston)

—— (1971) *Social Learning Theory* (New York, General Learning Press)

—— (1977) *Social Learning Theories* (Englewood Cliffs, New Jersey, Prentice Hall)

Barrios, B. and Shigetomi, C. (1979) 'Coping Skills Training for the Management of Anxiety: A Critical Review', *Beh. Therapy, 10*, 491-522

Bartlett, F. (1932) *Remembering* (Cambridge, Cambridge University Press)

Beattie, G. (1980) 'The Skilled Art of Conversational Interaction' in Singleton, W., Spurgeon, P. and Stammers, R. (eds.) *The Analysis of Social Skill* (New York, Plenum)

Beck, S., Forehand, R., Wells, K. and Quante, A. (1978) 'Social Skills Training with Children: An Examination of Generalization from Analogue to Natural Settings' (Mimeo, University of Georgia)

Becker, W. (1973) 'Applications of Behaviour Principles in Typical Classrooms' in Thoresen, E. (ed.) *NSSE Yearbook for 1973* (Chicago, Chicago University Press)

Becker, W., Madsen, C., Arnold, C. and Thomas, D. (1967) 'The Contingent Use of Teacher Attention and Praise in Reducing Classroom Behaviour Problems', *J. Spec. Ed., 1*, 287-307

Bellack, A. (1979) 'A Critical Appraisal of Strategies for Assessing Social Skill', *Behavioural Ass., 1*, 157-76

Bellack, A. and Hersen, M. (1977) *Behaviour Modification: An Introductory Textbook* (Baltimore, Williams and Wilkins)

—— (1979) *Research and Practice in Social Skills Training* (New York, Plenum)

Bellack, A., Hersen, M. and Turner, S. (1976) 'Generalization Effects of SST in Chronic Schizophrenic Patients', *Behav. Res. and Therapy, 14*, 391-8

—— (1978) 'Role Play Tests for Assessing Social Skills: Are They Valid?', *Behaviour Therapy, 9*, 448-61

Berger, R. and Rose, S. (1977) 'Interpersonal Skill Training with Elderly Institutionalized Patients', *J. Gerontol., 32, 3*, 346-53

Berliner, D. (1969) 'Microteaching and the Technical Skills Approach to Teacher Training' (Technical Report No 8, Stanford Center for Research and Development in Teaching; Stanford, Stanford University Press)

Berne, E. (1976) *Games People Play* (Harmondsworth, Penguin)

Bilodeau, E. and Bilodeau, I. (1966) *Skill Acquisition* (New York, Academic Press)

Bjerstedt, A. (1967) 'CCTV and Video-recordings as Observation Amplifiers in Teacher Training', *Educational Television International, 1*, 300-12

Bloom, M. (1976) 'Analysis of the Research on Educating Social Work Students', *J. of Edn for Social Work, 12, 3*, 3-10

Borg, W. (1970) *A Microteaching Approach to Teacher Education* (London, Collier Macmillan)

—— (1971) 'The Mini-course: A Milestone on the Road to Better Teaching', *B.J. Ed. Tech, 2*, 14-23

Bornstein, M., Bellack, A. and Hersen, M. (1977) 'Social Skills Training for Unassertive Children: A Multiple Baseline Analysis', *J. App. Behav. Anal., 10, 2*, 183-95

Bower, S., Amatea, E. and Anderson, R. (1976) 'Assertiveness Training with Children', *Elementary Sch. Guidance and Counselling, 10, 4*, 236-45

Bower, T. (1977) *The Perceptual World of the Child* (Cambridge, Mass., Harvard University Press)

Bradley, C. (1976) 'Interpersonal Communication Skills: The Marriage of Interaction Analysis and Microcounselling', *J. Indust. Teacher Edn, 13, 4*, 16-26

Brannigan, G. and Young, R. (1978) 'Social Skills Training with the BMD Adolescent', *Acad. Therapy, 13, 4*, 401-4

Brewer, C. and Lait, J. (1980) *Can Social Work Survive?* (London, Temple Smith)

Britton, R. and Leith, G. (1971) 'An Experimental Evaluation of the Effects of Microteaching on Teaching Performance' in Packham, D., Cleary, A. and Mayes, T. (eds.) *Aspects of Educational Technology* (London, Pitman)

Bronfenbrenner, U. (1967) *Two Worlds of Childhood: USA and USSR* (New York, Russell Sage Foundation)

Brown, G. (1975) *Microteaching: A Programme of Teaching Skills* (Methuen, London)

—— (1976) 'Introducing and Organizing Microteaching', *Ed. Media International, 2*, 21-9
Bruner, J. (1966) *Towards a Theory of Instruction* (Cambridge, Mass., Harvard University Press)
Brusling, C. (1972) 'An Experiment on Microteaching at the Gothenburg School of Education' (Mimeo, Gothenburg, Sweden, School of Education)
Bush, R. (1966) 'Microteaching: Controlled Practice in the Training of Teachers', *Communication, 48*, 201-7
Butler, P. (1976a) 'Assertive Training', *Psychotherapy: Theory Research and Practice, 13, 1*, 56-60
—— (1976b) 'Techniques of Assertive Training in Groups', *Int. J. of Group Psychotherapy, 26, 3*, 361-71
Callner, D. and Ross, S. (1978) 'The Assessment and Training of Assertive Skills with Drug Addicts: A Preliminary Study', *Int. J. of the Addictions, 13, 2*, 227-30
Carkhuff, R. (1971) *The Development of Human Resources* (New York, Holt, Rinehart and Winston)
Cartledge, G. and Milburn, J. (1978) 'The Case for Teaching Social Skills in the Classroom: A Review', *Rev. Ed. Res., 1, 1*, 133-56
Chittenden, G. (1942) 'An Experimental Study in Measuring and Modifying Assertive Behaviour in Young Children', *Monogr. Soc. Res. Ch. Dev.*, *7*, 1-87
Clark, J. (1973) *A Family Visitor* (London, Royal College of Nursing)
Claus, K. (1969) 'Effects of Modelling and Feedback Treatments on the Development of Teachers' Questioning Skills' (Technical Report No. 6, Stanford Center for Research and Development in Teaching, Stanford, Stanford University)
Cobb, J. (1970) *Survival Skills and First Grade Academic Achievement* (Report No. 1, University of Oregon, Contract No. NPECE-70-005, OEC 0-70-4152 (607) US Office of Education; Eugene, Oregon, Oregon Research Institute)
Cobb, J. and Hops, H. (1973) 'Effects of Academic and Survival Skills Training on Low-achieving First Graders', *J. Ed. Res., 67*, 108-13
Cohen, L. (1969) 'Students' Perceptions of the School Practice Period', *Res. in Edn, 2*, 52-8
Combs, M. and Slaby, D. (1977) 'Social Skills Training with Children' in Lakey, B. and Kazdin, A. (eds.) *Advances in Clinical Child Psychology*, Vol. 1 (New York, Plenum)
Cooper, J. and Stroud, T. (1966) *Microteaching: A Description* (Stanford Teacher Education Program, Stanford, Stanford University Press)

Cooper, T. and Mangham, I. (1971) *T Groups* (London, Wiley)
Cope, E. (1971) 'Teacher Training and School Practice', *Educ. Res., 12*, 87-98
Council for the Education and Training of Health Visitors (1979) *Syllabus for the Examination of Health Visitors in the United Kingdom* (London, CETHV)
Crowley, T. and Ivey, A. (1976) 'Dimensions of Effective Interpersonal Communications', *J. Couns. Psychology, 23*, 267-71
Curran, J. (1975) 'SST and Systematic Desensitization in Reducing Dating Anxiety', *Beh. Res. & Ther., 13*, 65-8
Davies, B. (1979) 'In Whose Interests?' (Occasional Paper No. 19, Leicester, National Youth Bureau)
Davis, O. and Smoot, B. (1970) 'Effects on the Verbal Teaching Behaviours of Beginning Secondary Teacher Candidates' Participations in a Program of Laboratory Teaching', *Ed. Leadership* (Res. Supplement), *28*, 165-9
Davis, R. (1970) 'The Effectiveness of Microteaching and Videotapes in Training Prospective Elementary Teachers', *Dissertation Abstracts International, 20*, 4303A
Department of Education and Science (1979) *Annual Report of the FE Curriculum Review and Development Unit* (London, HMSO)
Dickson, D. (in preparation) 'An Investigation of the Development and Retention of Interviewing Skills included in a Microcounselling Programme' (Newtownabbey, Ulster Polytechnic)
Dingwall, R. (1977) *The Social Organisation of Health Visitor Training* (London, Croom Helm)
Duncan, S. and Fiske, D. (1977) *Face to Face Interaction* (New York, Wiley)
Durlak, J. and Mannarino, M. (1977) 'The Social Skills Development Programme: A School-based Preventive Mental Health Programme for High-risk Children', *J. Clin. Child Psychology, 6, 3*, 48-52
Ebert, M. (1970) 'The Effect of Modelling and Feedback on the Learning of Questioning Behaviours' (Unpublished PhD, University of California; *Dissertation Abstracts International*, 31/A5244.5)
Edelstein, B. and Eisler, R. (1976) 'Effects of Modelling and Modelling with Instruction and Feedback on the Behavioural Components of Social Skills', *Behaviour Therapy, 4*, 382-9
Eisler, R. (1976) 'Assertive Training in the Work Situation' in Krumboltz, J. and Thoresen, C. (eds.) *Counseling Methods* (New York, Holt, Rinehart and Winston)
Eisler, R., Miller, P. and Hersen, M. (1973a) 'Components of Assertive

Behaviour', *J. Clin. Psychology, 29*, 295-9

Eisler, R., Hersen, M. and Miller, P. (1973b) 'Effects of Modelling on Components of Assertive Behaviour', *J. Beh. Ther. and Expmtl Psychiatry, 4*, 1-6

—— (1974) 'Shaping Components of Assertiveness with Instructions and Feedback', *Am. J. Psychiatry, 131*, 1344-61

Eisler, R., Hersen, M., Miller, P. and Blanchard, E. (1975) 'Situational Determinants of Assertive Behaviours', *J. Cons. and Clin. Psychology, 43*, 330-40

Ekman, P. and Friesen, W. (1975) *Unmasking the Face* (Englewood Cliffs, New Jersey, Prentice Hall)

Ellett, L. and Smith, E. (1975) 'Improving Performance and Self-evaluation', *A V Communication Review, 23*, 277-88

Ellis, A. (1958) 'Rational Psychotherapy', *J. General Psychology, 59*, 35-49

Ellis, R. (1972) 'Skills in Context', *Times Higher Ed. Suppl.* (October 25)

—— (1974b) 'Skills in Context: A Model for Applied Psychology Courses', *Bull. Assn. for the Teaching of Psychology, 2*, 162-76

—— (1977) 'Propositions, Prescriptions and Performance', Annual Conference of the BPS, N. Ireland Branch (Mimeo, Newtownabbey, Ulster Polytechnic)

—— (1980) 'Social Skills Training for the Interpersonal Professions' in Singleton, W., Spurgeon, P. and Stammers, R. (eds.) *The Analysis of Social Skill* (New York, Plenum)

Ellis, R. and Whittington, D. (1972) 'Contexts for Microteaching', *J. APLET, 2*, 37-46

—— (1979) 'Skills in Context: A Model for the Speech Therapy Curriculum', *Proc. 5th IUT Conference*, University of Maryland (Maryland, IUT)

Evans, D., Uhlemann, M. and Hearn, M. (1975) 'Microcounselling and Sensitivity Training with Hotline Workers' (Mimeo, London, Ontario, University of Western Ontario)

Falloon, I., Lindley, P. and McDonald, R. (1974) *Social Training: A Manual* (London, Maudsley Hospital)

Falloon, I., Lindley, P., McDonald, R. and Marks, I. (1977) 'Social Skills Training of Out-patient Groups', *B.J. Psychiatry, 131*, 599-609

Fiedler, D. and Beach, L. (1978) 'On the Decision to be Assertive', *J. Cons. and Clin. Psychology, 46*, 537-46

Finch, B. and Wallace, C. (1977) 'Successful Interpersonal Skills Training with Schizophrenic Inpatients', *J. Cons. and Clin. Psychology, 45*, 885-90

Fischetti, M., Curran, J. and Wessberg, H. (1977) 'Sense of Timing: A Skill Deficit in Socially Anxious Heterosexual Males', *Behav. Modification, 1, 2*, 179-94

Fitts, P. and Posner, M. (1967) *Human Performance* (Monterey, Brooks-Cole)

Flanders, N. (1970) *Analysing Teaching Behaviour* (Reading, Mass., Addison-Wesley)

Flowers, J. (1975) 'Roleplaying and Simulation Methods' in Kanfer, F. and Goldstein, A. (eds.) *Helping People Change* (New York, Pergamon)

Forge, H. (1973) 'Comparison of Three Variations of Microtraining in Teaching Basic Interviewing Skills to Counsellor Trainees' (Unpublished dissertation, Kansas City, University of Missouri)

Fortune, J., Cooper, J. and Allen, D. (1967) 'The Stanford Summer Microteaching Clinic, 1965', *J. Teacher Edn., 18, 4*, 389-93

Foy, D., Eisler, R. and Pinkston, S. (1975) 'Modelled Assertion in a Case of Explosive Rage', *J. Beh. Ther. and Exp. Psychiatry, 6*, 135-7

Freeman, J. and Davis, O. (1975) 'Relationships of Self-concept and Teaching Behaviours of Secondary Teacher Candidates in Microteaching', *Contemp. Edn., 16*, 215-18

Friedman, P. (1971) 'The Effects of Modelling and Roleplaying on Assertive Behaviour' in Rubin, R., Fensterheim, H., Lazarus, A. and Franks, C. (eds.) *Advances in Behaviour Therapy* (New York, Academic Press)

Fyffe, A. and Oei, T. (1979) 'Influence of Modelling and Feedback Provided by the Supervisors in a Microskills Training Programme for Beginning Counsellors', *J. Clin. Psychology, 35*, 3-10

Galassi, J., Kostka, M. and Galassi, M. (1975) 'Assertiveness Training', *J. Couns. Psychology, 22*, 451-2

Gay, M., Hollandsworth, J. and Galassi, J. (1975) 'An Assertiveness Inventory for Adults', *J Couns. Psychology, 22*, 340-4

Gilmore, S. (1977) 'The Effects of Positive and Negative Models on Student-Teachers Questioning Behaviours' in McIntyre, D., Macleod, G. and Griffiths, R. (eds.) *Investigations of Microteaching* (London, Croom Helm)

Gluckstern, N. (1973) 'Training Parents as Drug Counselors in the Community', *Personnel and Guidance Journal, 51*, 676-80

Goldberg, E. (1970) 'Effects of Models and Instructions on Verbal Behaviour' (Unpublished PhD dissertation, Philadelphia, Temple University)

Goldfried, M. and Goldfried, A. (1975) 'Cognitive Change Methods', in Kanfer, F. and Goldstein, A. (eds.) *Helping People Change* (New York, Pergamon)

Goldman, B. (1969) 'Effect of Classroom Experience and Videotape Self-observation upon Undergraduate Attitudes Towards the Self and Towards Teaching', Proc. Am. Psychology Assocn. *ERIC* (Education Resources Information Centre) ED: 038 359

Goldsmith, J. and McFall, R. (1975) 'Development and Evaluation of an Interpersonal Skill Training Program for Psychiatric Patients', *J. Abnorm. Psychology, 84*, 51-70

Goldstein, A. (1973) *Structured Learning Therapy: Toward a Psychotherapy for the Poor* (New York, Academic Press)

Goldstein, A., Martens, J. Hubben, J., Van Belle, H., Shaaf, W., Wiersma, H. and Goldhart, A. (1973) 'The Use of Modelling to Increase Independent Behaviour', *Beh. Res. and Therapy, 12*, 295-340

Goldstein, A., Sprafkin, R. and Gershaw, N. (1976) *Skill Training for Community Living* (New York, Pergamon)

Goldthwaite, D. (1969) 'A Study of Microteaching in the Pre-service Education of Science Teachers', *Dissertation Abstracts International, 29*, 3021A

Gottman, J. (1977) 'The Effects of a Modelling Film on Social Isolation in Children', *Child Dev., 48*, 179-97

Gottman, J., Gonso, J. and Rasmussen, B. (1975) 'Social Interaction Social Competence and Friendship in Children', *Child Dev., 46.*, 709-18

Gottman, J. Gonso, J. and Schuler, P. (1976) 'Teaching Social Skills to Isolated Children', *Child Dev., 47*, 179-97

Grayson, M., Nugent, C. and Owen, S. (1977) 'A Systematic and Comprehensive Approach to Teaching and Evaluating Interpersonal Skills', *J. Medical Edn., 52, 11*, 906-13

Gregory, I. (1971) 'Microteaching in a Preservice Education Course for Graduates', *B.J. Ed. Tech., 2*, 24-32

Griffiths, R. (1974) 'The Contribution of Feedback to the Microteaching Technique', *Programmed Learning and Ed. Tech., 2*, 87-94

—— (1980) 'Social Skills and Psychological Disorder' in Singleton, W., Spurgeon, P. and Stammers, R. (eds.) *The Analysis of Social Skill* (New York, Plenum)

Griffiths, R., Macleod, G. and McIntyre, D. (1977) 'Effects of Supervisory Strategies in Microteaching' in McIntyre, D., Macleod, G. and Griffiths, R. (eds.) *Investigations of Microteaching* (London, Croom He

Griffiths, R. and Gillingham, P. (1978) 'The Influence of Videotape Feedback on the Self-assessments of Psychiatric Patients', *B.J. Psychiatry, 133*, 156-61

Gutride, M., Goldstein, A. and Hunter, G. (1973) 'The Use of Modelling and Role Play to Increase Social Interaction among Psychiatric Patients', *J. Cons. and Clin. Psychology, 40*, 408-15

Guttman, M. and Haase, R. (1972) 'The Generalisation of Microcounselling Skills from Training Period to Actual Counselling Setting', *Counselor Edn and Supervision, 12*, 98-107

Halford, K. (1978) 'Cognitive Restructuring in Social Skills Training', *Austr. Psychologist, 13, 2*, 278-86

Hall, R. and Goldberg, D. (1977) 'The Role of Social Anxiety in Social Interaction Difficulties', *B.J. Psychiatry, 131*, 610-15

Hannum, J. and Smith, P. (1978) 'Developing Social Skills through Self-control', *J. Am. Couns. Health Assn., 26, 5*, 256-9

Hargie, O. (1977a) 'Microteaching with Pre-service Special Education Teachers', *Remedial Edn., 12*, 22-9

—— (1977b) 'The Effectiveness of Microteaching', *Ed. Review, 29*, 205-9

—— (1978) 'The Reactions of Special Education Teachers to Microteaching' (Mimeo, Newtownabbey, Ulster Polytechnic)

—— (1980) 'An Evaluation of a Microteaching Programme' (Unpublished PhD dissertation, Newtownabbey, Ulster Polytechnic)

Hargie, O. and Dwyer, E. (1979) 'The Reactions of Special Education Teachers to Microteaching: A Follow-up Study' (Mimeo, Newtownabbey, Ulster Polytechnic)

Hargie, O. and Maidment, P. (1979) *Microteaching in Perspective* (Belfast, Blackstaff)

Hargie, O., Dickson, D. and Tittmar, H-G. (1977) 'Mini-teaching', *B.J. Teacher Edn, 4*, 113-18

—— (1979) 'The Determinants of Students' Attitudes to Microteaching', *PLET, 16*, 150-7

Hargie, O., Saunders, C. and Dickson, D. (1981) *Social Skills in Inter-Personal Communication* (London, Croom Helm)

Hargie, O., Tittmar, H-G. and Dickson, D. (1978a) 'Extraversion/Introversion and Student Attitudes to Microteaching', (Mimeo, Newtownabbey, Ulster Polytechnic)

—— (1978b) 'Personality Correlates of Student Attitudes to Microteaching', *Contemp. Edn, 50*, 39-47

Harris, W., Lee, V. and Pigge, S. (1970) 'Effectiveness of Microteaching Experiences in Elementary Science Methods Classes', *J. Res. in*

Science Teaching, *7*, *1*, 31-3
Hayman, P. and Cope, C. (1980) 'Effects of Assertion Training on Depression', *J. Clin. Psychology*, *36*, *2*, 534-43
Hearn, M. (1976) 'Three Modes of Training Counsellors' (Unpublished dissertation, London, Ontario, University of Western Ontario)
Hersen, M. and Bellack, A. (1976a) 'Social Skill Training for Chronic Psychiatric Patients', *Comp. Psychiatry*, *17*, 559-80
—— (1976b) 'A Multiple Baseline Analysis of Social Skills Training in Chronic Schizophrenics', *J. App. Behav. Anal.*, *9*, 239-45
—— (1977) 'Assessment of Social Skills' in Ciminero, A. (ed.) *Handbook of Behavioural Assessment* (New York, Wiley)
Hersen, M., Eisler, R. and Miller, P. (1973a) 'Development of Assertive Responses: Clinical, Measurement, and Research Considerations', *Beh. Res. & Therapy*, *11*, 505-21
Hersen, M., Eisler, R., Miller, P., Johnston, M. and Pinkston, S. (1973b) 'Effects of Practice, Instructions and Modelling on Components of Assertive Behaviour', *Beh. Res. & Therapy*, *11*, 443-51
Hersen, M., Eisler, R. and Miller, P. (1974) 'An Experimental Analysis of Generalisation in Assertive Training', *Beh. Res. & Therapy*, *12*, 295-310
Hersen, M., Turner, S., Edelstein, B. and Pinkston, S. (1975) 'Effects of Phenothiazines and SST in a Withdrawn Schizophrenic', *J. Clin. Psychology*, *31*, 588-9
Hess, R. and Torney, J. (1967) *The Development of Political Attitudes in Children* (New York, Aldine)
Higgins, M., Ivey, A. and Uhlmann, M. (1970) 'Media Therapy' A Programmed Approach to Teaching Behavioural Skills', *J. Couns. Psychology*, *17*, 20-6
Higgins, R., Alonso, R. and Pendleton, M. (1979) 'The Validity of Role-Play Assessments of Assertiveness', *Beh. Ther.*, *10*, 655-62
Hirsch, S., Von Rosenberg, R., Phelan, C. and Dudley, H. (1978) 'Effectiveness of Assertiveness Training with Alcoholics', *J. of Studies on Alcohol*, *39*, *1*, 89-97
Holding, D. (1965) *Principles of Training* (Oxford, Pergamon)
Hops, H. and Cobb, J. (1973) 'Survival Behaviours in the Educational Setting' in Hammerlynk, L. (ed.) *Behaviour Change* (Champaign, Illinois, Research Press)
Hymel, S. and Asher, S. (1977) 'Assessment and Training of Isolated Children's Social Skills' (Paper presented at the biennial meeting of the Society for Research in Child Development, New Orleans, Louisiana, March; New York, Society for Research in Child

Development)
ILEA (1978) *A Syllabus for Work, Life and Communication Skills* (London, ILEA)
Ivey, A. (1971) *Microcounselling: Innovations in Interviewing Training* (Springfield, Illinois, Charles Thomas)
Ivey, A. and Authier, J. (1978) *Microcounselling*, 2nd edn. (Springfield, Illinois, Charles Thomas)
Ivey, A., Normington, C., Miller, C., Morrill, W. and Haase, R. (1968) 'Microcounselling and Attending Behaviour: An Approach to Pre-Practicum Counsellor Training', *J. Couns. Psych., 15*, 1-12
Jackson, P. and Oei, T. (1978) 'Social Skill Training and Cognitive Restructuring with Alcoholics', *Drug and Alc. Dependency, 3*, 5-9
Jensen, L. and Young, J. (1972) 'Effect of Televised Simulated Instruction on Subsequent Teaching', *J. Ed. Psychology, 63, 4*, 368-73
Kallenbach, W. and Gall, T. (1969) 'Microteaching Versus Conventional Methods of Training Elementary Intern Teachers', *J. Ed. Res., 63, 3*, 136-41
Kanfer, F. (1975) 'Self Management Methods' in Kanfer, F. and Goldstein, A. (eds.) *Helping People Change* (New York, Pergamon)
Kanfer, F. and Goldstein, A. (eds.) (1975) *Helping People Change* (New York, Pergamon)
Kaseman, B. (1976) 'An Experimental Use of Structured Techniques in Group Psychotherapy', *Group Psychotherapy, Psychodrama and Sociometry, 29*, 33-9
Kazdin, A. (1974) 'Effects of Covert Modelling and Model Reinforcement on Assertive Behaviour', *J. Abn. Psychology, 83*, 240-52
—— (1975) 'Recent Advances in Token Economy Research' in Hersen, M., Eisler, R. and Miller, P. (eds.) *Progress in Behaviour Modification* Vol. 1 (New York, Academic Press)
—— (1976) 'Effects of Covert Modelling, Multiple Models and Model Reinforcement on Assertive Behaviour', *Beh. Therapy, 7*, 211-22
Keller, M. and Corlson, P. (1974) 'The Use of Symbolic Modelling to Promote Social Skills in Pre-school Children with Low Levels of Social Responsiveness', *Child Dev., 45*, 912-19
Kelley, J. (1971) 'The Use of Reinforcement in Microcounselling', *J. Couns. Psychology, 18*, 268-72
Kelly, G. (1955) *The Psychology of Personal Constructs* (New York, Norton)
Kennedy, K. (1975) 'An Analysis of the Costs of Microteaching', *Res. Intelligence, 2*, 54-7

Kerrebrock, R. (1971) 'Application of the Microcounselling Method to the Training of Teachers in Basic Counselling Techniques' (Unpublished PhD dissertation, UCLA; Dissertation Abstracts International, 32, 740A; *Univ. Microfilms* No. 71-21, 470)

Kieviet, F. (1972) 'A Dutch Study on Microteaching' (International Microteaching Symposium, Tubingen, West Germany, University of Tubingen)

Kirby, F. and Toler, H. (1970) 'Modification of Pre-school Isolate Behaviour: A Case Study', *J. Appl. Beh. Anal., 3*, 309-14

Kissock, C. (1971) 'A Study to Test the Value of Microteaching in a Programme of Video-modelling Instruction' (Unpublished PhD dissertation, Minnesota, University of Minnesota)

Koran, J. (1969) 'The Relative Effects of Classroom Instruction and Subsequent Observational Learning on the Acquisition of Questioning Behaviour by Pre-service Elementary Science Teachers', *J. Res. in Science Teaching, 6*, 217-23

—— (1971) 'A Study of the Effects of Written and Film Mediated Models on the Acquisition of a Science Teaching Skill by Preservice Elementary Science Teachers', *J. Res. in Science Teaching, 8*, 45-50

Koran, M. (1969) 'The Effects of Individual Differences on Observational Learning in the Acquisition of a Teaching Skill' (Unpublished PhD dissertation, Stanford University; Dissertation Abstracts International, 30A, 1450-1)

Korsch, B. and Negrette, V. (1972) 'Doctor-patient Communication', *Scientific Amer. 227*, 66-74

Kremer, L. and Perlberg, A. (1971) 'The Use of Microteaching to Train Student Teachers in Stimulating Learners' Questions' (Mimeo, Haifa, Israel, Technion Institute)

Kuna, D. (1975) 'Lecturing, Reading and Modeling in Counselor Restatement Training', *J. Couns. Psychology, 22*, 542-6

La Greca, A. and Santogrossi, D. (1980) 'Social Skills Training with Elementary School Students', *J. Cons. and Clin. Psychology, 48, 2*, 220-7

Lane, C. (1973) 'Comparative Effectiveness of Feedback Through Videotape, Purdue Teacher Evaluation Scale and Normal Supervisory Practice on Student Teacher Attitudes', *Dissertation Abstracts International, 33*, 5602A

Lange, A. and Jakubowski, P. (1976) *Responsible Assertive Behaviour* (Champaign, Illinois, Research Press)

Levine, J. and Zigler, E. (1973) 'The Essential/Reactive Distinction in

Alcoholism: A Developmental Approach', *J. Abn. Psychology, 81*, 242-9

Lewinsohn, P. (1975) 'The Behavioural Study and Treatment of Depression' in Hersen, M., Eisler, R. and Miller, P. (eds.) *Progress in Behaviour Modification*, Vol. 1 (New York, Academic Press)

Lewinsohn, P. and Shaffer, M. (1971) 'The Use of Home Observations as an Integral Part of the Treatment of Depression', *J. Cons. and Clin. Psychology, 37*, 87-94

Ley, P. (1977) 'Psychological Studies of Doctor-patient Communication' in Rachman, J. (ed.) *Contributions of Medical Psychology* (Oxford, Pergamon)

Liberman, R. (1975) *Personal Effectiveness* (Champaign, Illinois, Research Press)

Libet, J. and Lewinsohn, P. (1973) 'The Concept of Social Skill with Special Reference to the Behaviour of Depressed Persons', *J. Cons. and Clin. Psycholigy, 40*, 304-12

McDonald, F. (1973) 'Behaviour Modification in Teacher Education' in Thoresen, E. (ed.) *NSSE Yearbook for 1973* (Chicago, Chicago University Press)

McDonald, F. and Allen, D. (1967) 'Training Effects of Feedback and Modelling Procedures on Teaching Performance' (Unpublished Report, Stanford, Stanford University)

McFall, R. and Lillesand, D. (1971) 'Behaviour Rehearsal with Modelling and Coaching in Assertion', *J. Abn. Psychology, 77*, 313-23

McFall, R. and Marston, A. (1970) 'An Experimental Investigation of Behaviour Rehearsal in Assertive Training', *J. Abn. Psychology, 76*, 295-303

McFall, R. and Twentyman, C. (1973) 'Four Experiments on the Relative Contributions of Rehearsal, Modelling and Coaching to Assertion Training', *J. Abn. Psychology, 3*, 199-218

McIntyre, D. (1973) 'Three Approaches to Microteaching: An Experimental Comparison' (Mimeo, Stirling, Dept of Education, Stirling University)

McIntyre, D. and Duthie, J. (1977) 'Students Reactions to Microteaching' in McIntyre, D., Macleod, G. and Griffiths, R. (eds.) *Investigations of Microteaching* (London, Croom Helm)

McKinlay, T. (1978) 'Teaching Assertive Skills to a Passive Homosexual Adolescent: An Illustrative Case Study', *J. Homosexuality, 3, 2*, 163-70

McKnight, P. (1971) 'Microteaching in Teacher Training: A Review of Research', *Res. in Ed., 6*, 24-38

McTear, M. (1978) 'Some Issues in the Analysis of Discourse', *Papers in Linguistics, 12, 3*, 47-59

—— (1979) ' "Hey! I've got Something to Tell you": A Study of the Initiation of Conversational Exchanges by Preschool Children', *J. Pragmatics, 3*, 321-36

McWhirter, E. (1976) 'Psychology in Professional Courses', *Bull. BPS, 29*, 211-17

Macleod, G. and McIntyre, D. (1977) 'Towards a Model for Microteaching' in McIntyre, D., Macleod, G. and Griffiths, R. (eds.) *Investigations of Microteaching* (London, Croom Helm)

Madsen, C., Becker, W. and Thomas, D. (1968) 'Rules, Praise and Ignoring', *J. App. Behav. Analysis, 1*, 139-50

Mahoney, M. (1974) *Cognition and Behaviour Modification* (New York, Ballinger)

Mandia, R. (1974) 'Sales Training: As Simple as PAC', *Training and Dev. J., 28, 11*, 15-20

Marlatt, G. and Perry, M. (1975) 'Modelling Methods' in Kanfer, F. and Goldstein, A. (eds.) *Helping People Change* (New York, Pergamon)

Marzillier, J. and Winter, K. (1978) 'Success and Failure in Social Skills Training: Individual Differences', *Behav. Res. and Therapy, 16*, 67-84

Marzillier, J., Lambert, C. and Kellett, J. (1976) 'A Controlled Evaluation of Systematic Desensitisation and Social Skills Training', *Behav. Res. and Therapy, 14*, 225-38

Matson, J. and Stephens, R. (1978) 'Increasing Appropriate Behaviour of Explosive Chronic Psychiatric Patients with a Social Skills Training Package', *Behav. Modification, 2, 1*, 61-76

Matson, J. and Zeiss, R. (1979) 'Group Training of Social Skills in Chronically Explosive Severely Disturbed Psychiatric Patients', *Behav. Engineering, 5, 2*, 41-50

Medley, D. and Mitzel, H. (1963) 'Measuring Classroom Behaviour' in Gage, N. (ed.) *Handbook of Research on Teaching* (Chicago, Rand McNally)

Meichenbaum, D. (1977) *Cognitive Behaviour Modification: An Integrative Approach* (New York, Plenum)

Melhuish, E. (1980) 'An Approach to Teaching Doctors Social Skills' in Singleton, W., Spurgeon, P. and Stammers, R. (eds.) *The Analysis of Social Skill* (New York, Plenum)

Miller, N. and Dollard, J. (1941) *Social Learning and Imitation* (New Haven, Yale University Press)

Minor, B. (1978) 'A Perspective for Assertiveness Training for Blacks', *J. of Non-white Concerns in Guidance, 6, 2*, 63-70

Mishel, M. (1978) 'Assertion Training with Handicapped Persons', *J. Couns. Psych., 25, 3*, 238-41

Monti, P., Curran, J., Corriveau, D., Delaney, A. and Hagerman, S. (1980) 'Effects of SST Groups and Sensitivity Training Groups with Psychiatric Patients', *J. Cons. and Clin. Psychology, 48, 2*, 241-8

Monti, P., Fink, E., Norman, W., Curran, J., Hayes, S. and Caldwell, A. (1979) 'Effect of SST Groups and Social Skills Bibliotherapy with Psychiatric Patients', *J. Cons. and Clin. Psychology, 47*, 189-91

Moreland, J., Ivey, A. and Phillips, J. (1973) 'An Evaluation of Microcounselling as an Interviewer Training Tool', *J. Clin. and Cons. Psychology, 41*, 294-300

Moreland, J., Phillips, J., Ivey, A. and Lockhart, J. (1970) 'A Study of the Microtraining Paradigm with Beginning Clinical Psychologists' (Mimeo, Amherst, Mass., University of Massachusetts)

Moreno, J. (1959) *Psychodrama* (New York, Beacon House)

Morgan, R. (1980) 'Analysis of Social Skills: The Behaviour Analysis Approach' in Singleton, W., Spurgeon, P. and Stammers, R. (eds.) *The Analysis of Social Skill* (New York, Plenum)

Morris, T. (1971) *The Work of Health Visitors in London* (London, Greater London Council)

Morrison, A. and McIntyre, D. (1971) *Schools and Socialisation* (Harmondsworth, Penguin)

—— (1973) *Teachers and Teaching*, 2nd edn (Harmondsworth, Penguin)

Morton, T. (1978) 'Intimacy and Reciprocity of Exchange: A Comparison of Spouses and Strangers', *J. Pers. and Soc. Psychology, 36*, 72-81

Nuffield Provincial Hospitals Trust (1950) *Inquiry into Health Visiting* (London, Nuffield Provincial Hospitals Trust)

Nuttall, E. and Ivey, A. (1978) 'Research for Action: The Tradition and its Implementation' in Goldman, L. (ed.) *Research and the Counselor* (New York, Wiley)

O'Connor, R. (1969) 'Modification of Social Withdrawal Through Symbol Modelling', *J. Appl. Behav. Anal., 2*, 15-22

—— (1972) 'Relative Efficacy of Modelling, Shaping and the Combined Procedures for Modification of Social Withdrawal', *J. Abnormal Psych., 79*, 327-34

Oden, S. and Asher, S. (1977) 'Coaching Children in Social Skills for Friendship Making', *Child Dev., 48*, 495-506

O'Donnelly, N. and Colby, L. (1979) 'Developing Managers Through Assertiveness Training', *Training, 16, 3*, 36-41

Olivero, J. (1965) 'The Use of Video-recordings in Teacher Education', *ERIC* (Education Resources Information Centre) ED 011 074

Onoda, L. and Gassert, L. (1978) 'Use of Assertion Training to Improve Job Interview Behaviour', *Pers. and Guidance Journal* (April), 492-5

Oratio, A. (1977) *Supervision in Speech Pathology* (Baltimore, University Park Press)

Orme, A. (1966) 'The Effects of Modelling and Feedback Variables on the Acquisition of a Complex Teaching Strategy' (Unpublished PhD dissertation, Stanford University; Ann Arbor, Michigan, University Microfilms Inc.)

Panepinto, R. (1976) 'Social Skills Training for Verbally Aggressive Children' (Unpublished masters thesis, W. Virginia, University of W. Virginia)

Patterson, G. (1973) 'Reprogramming the Families of Aggressive Boys' in Thoresen, E. (ed.) *NSSE Yearbook for 1973* (Chicago, Chicago University Press)

Pendleton, D. and Furnham, A. (1980) 'Skills: A Paradigm for Applied Social Psychological Research' in Singleton, W., Spurgeon, P. and Stammers, R. (eds.) *The Analysis of Social Skill* (New York, Plenum)

Perrott, E. (1972) 'Course Design and Microteaching in the Context of Microteaching' (Paper delivered at the International Microteaching Symposium, Tubingen, West Germany, University of Tubingen)

Perrott, E., Applebee, A., Heap, B. and Watson, E. (1975) 'Changes in Teaching Behaviour after Completing a Self-instructional Microteaching Course', *J. APLET, 12, 6*, 348-63

Perry, M. (1975) 'Modelling and Instructions in Training for Counselor Empathy', *J. Couns. Psychology, 22*, 173-9

Peters, G., Cormier, S. and Comier, W. (1978) 'Effects of Modelling, Rehearsal, Feedback and Remediation on Acquisition of a Counseling Strategy', *J. Couns. Psychology, 25, 3*, 231-7

Phillips, E.L. (1980) 'Social Skills Instruction as Adjunctive/Alternative to Psychotherapy' in Singleton, W., Spurgeon, P. and Stammers, R. (eds.) *The Analysis of Social Skill* (New York, Plenum)

Priestley, P., McGuire, J., Flegg, D., Hemsley, V. and Welham, D. (1978) *Social Skills and Personal Problem Solving* (London, Tavistock)

Rackham, N. and Morgan, T. (1977) *Behaviour Analysis in Training*

(Maidenhead, Berks., McGraw Hill)

Randall, G. (1976) 'A Management Skills Approach to Developing People and Organisations' (Paper to NATO Conference on Co-ordination and Control of Groups and Organisational Performance)

Randall, R. (1972) 'The Effects of Microteaching on the Self-Concepts of Social Studies Student Teachers', *Dissertation Abstracts International, 33*, 2225A

Rathus, D.C. (1973) 'A 30-item schedule for assessing assertive behaviour', *Beh. Therapy, 4*, 398-406

Rathus, S. (1972) 'An Experimental Investigation of Assertive Training in a Group Setting', *J. Behav. Ther. & Exp. Psychiatry, 3*, 81-97

Raushbaum-Selig, M. (1976) 'Assertive Training for Young People', *School Counselor, 24, 2*, 115-22

Rehm, L. and Marston, A. (1968) 'Reduction of Social Anxiety Through Modification of Self-reinforcement', *J. Cons. and Clin. Psych., 32*, 565-74

Rich, A. and Schroeder, H. (1976) 'Research Issues in Assertiveness Training', *Psych. Bull., 83*, 1081-96

Rinn, R. and Markle, A. (1979) 'Modification of Skills Deficits in Children' in Bellack, A. and Hersen, M. (eds.) *Research and Practice in Social Skills Training* (New York, Plenum)

Rodgers, A. (1974) *The Seven Point Plan* (London, NIIP)

Roff, M., Sells, S. and Golden, M. (1972) *Social Adjustment and Personality Development in Children* (Minneapolis, University of Minneapolis Press)

Rosenshine, B. (1971) *Teaching Behaviours and Student Achievement* (Slough, NFER)

Salter, A. (1949) *Conditioned Reflex Therapy* (New York, Farrar, Strauss and Giroux)

Sanchez, V., Lewinsohn, P. and Larson, P. (1980) 'Assertion Training: Effectiveness in the Treatment of Depression', *J. Clin. Psych., 36, 2*, 526-9

Sarason, I. and Ganzer, V. (1973) 'Modelling and Group discussion in the Rehabilitation of Juvenile Delinquents', *J. Couns. Psych., 20*, 442-9

Saskatchewan Newstart (1972) *Life Skills Coaching Manual* (Prince Albert, Saskatchewan, Dept of Manpower and Immigration)

Saunders, C. and Saunders, E. (1979) 'Assessment of Teaching Practice Supervisors' Frames of Reference' (*Proc. Irish Education Conference*, Dublin, University College), Mimeo available from Educational Studies Association of Ireland, Officina Telegraphica, POB 36, Galway

Saunders, E. and Saunders, C. (1977) 'Research, Development and Implementation of a Curriculum Innovation' (Proc. Irish Education Conference, Cork, University College), Mimeo available from Educational Studies Association of Ireland, Officina Telegraphica PO Box 36, Galway

Schaffer, R. (1974) *The Growth of Sociability* (Harmondsworth, Penguin)

—— (1978) *Mothering* (London, Open Books)

Scroggins, W. and Ivey, A. (1976) 'An Evaluation of Microcounselling as a Model to Train Resident Staff' (Mimeo, Alabama, University of Alabama)

Secondy, M. and Katz, V. (1975) 'Factors in Patient-Doctor Interaction', *J. Med. Edn., 50, 7*, 689-91

Shady, G. and Kuc, S. (1977) 'Preparing the Hard-core Disadvantaged for Employment: Social Skills Orientation Course: An Evaluation', *Canadian J. Criminology, 19, 3*, 303-9

Shaw, M. and Rutledge, P. (1976) 'Assertiveness for Managers', *Training & Dev. J., 30, 9*, 8-14

Shepherd, G. (1977) 'Social Skill Training: The Generalisation Problem', *Behav. Therapy, 8*, 362-4

—— (1978) 'SST: The Generalisation Problem – Some Further Data', *Behav. Res. & Therapy, 16*, 287-8

Simon, A. and Bowyer, G. (eds.) (1970) *Mirrors for Behaviour*, 2nd edn (Philadelphia, Research for Better Schools Inc.)

Singleton, W., Spurgeon, T. and Stammers, R. (eds.) (1980) *The Analysis of Social Skill* (New York, Plenum)

Skinner, B. (1953) *Science and Human Behaviour* (New York, Macmillan)

Snyder, M. (1974) 'Self-monitoring of Expressive Behaviour', *J. Pers. & Social Psych., 30*, 526-37

Spence, S. (1979) 'Social Skills Training with Children and Adolescents: A Trainers' Manual' (Mimeo, Tennal School, Birmingham)

Stones, E. and Morris, S. (1972) *Teaching Practice* (London, Methuen)

Stott, D. (1966) *Studies of Troublesome Children* (London, Tavistock)

Stufflebeam, D., Foley, W., Gephart, W., Guba, E., Hammond, R., Merryman, H and Provus, M. (1971) *Educational Evaluation and Decision Making* (Ithaca, Illinois, Peacock)

Swenson, G., Brady, T. and Edwards, K. (1978) 'The Effects of Attitude Pretraining on Assertion Training with Christian College Students', *Bull. of the Christian Assoc. for Psychological Studies, 4*, 14-17

Tiegerman, S. and Kassinove, H. (1977) 'Effects of Assertive Training and Cognitive Components of Rational Therapy on Assertive Behaviours and Interpersonal Anxiety', *Psychological Reports, 40*, 535-42

Tittmar, H-G., Hargie, O and Dickson, D. (1977) 'Social Skills Training at Ulster College', *PLET, 14*, 300-2

Tizard, B. (1973) 'Do Social Relationships Affect Language Development?' in Connolly, K. and Bruner, J. (eds.) *The Growth of Competence* (London, Academic Press)

Trower, P. (1980a) 'How to Lose Friends and Influence Nobody: An Analysis of Social Failure' in Singleton, W., Spurgeon, P. and Stammers, R. *The Analysis of Social Skill* (New York, Plenum Press)

Trower, P. (1980b) 'Situational Analysis of the Components and Processes of Behaviour of Socially Skilled and Unskilled Patients', *J. Cons. & Clin. Psychology, 48, 3*, 327-39

Trower, P., Bryant, B. and Argyle, M. (1978a) *Social Skills and Mental Health* (London, Methuen)

Trower, P., Yardley, K., Bryant, B. and Shaw, P. (1978b) 'The Treatment of Social Failure', *Behaviour Modification, 2, 1*, 41-60

Tucker, P. and Acheson, K. (1971) 'Videotape versus Written Instruction and Videotape versus Audiotape Feedback in a Minicourse on Higher-order Cognitive Questioning' (Report No. A71-18, Far West Laboratory for Educational Research and Development, Stanford, Stanford University)

Tuckman, B. and Oliver, W. (1968) 'Effectiveness of Feedback to Teachers as a Function of Source', *J. Ed. Psychology, 59*, 297-301

Turney, C., Clift, J., Dunkin, M. and Traill, R. (1973) *Microteaching: Research Theory and Practice* (Sydney, Sydney University Press)

Twentyman, T. and Martin, B. (1978) 'Modification of Problem Interaction in Mother Child Dyads by Modelling and Behaviour Rehearsal', *J. Clin. Psych., 34, 1*, 138-43

Ullman, C. (1957) 'Teachers, Peers and Tests as Predictors of Adjustment', *J. Ed. Psychology, 48*, 257-67

Van Hasselt, V., Hersen, M. and Milliones, J. (1978) 'Social Skills Training for Drug Addicts and Alcoholics: A Review', *Addictive Behaviour, 3, 4*, 221-32

Van Hasselt, V., Hersen, M., Whitehill, M. and Bellack, A. (1979) 'Social Skill Assessment and Training for Children: An Evaluative Review', *Beh. Res. & Therapy, 17*, 413-37

Wagner, A.C. (1973) 'Changing Teaching Behaviour: A Comparison of Microteaching and Cognitive Discrimination Training', *J. Ed. Psychology, 64*, 299-305

Waimon, N. and Ramseyer, G. (1970) 'Effects of Video Feedback on the Ability to Evaluate Teaching', *J. Teacher Edn, 21*, 92-5

Waterson, N. and Snow, C. (eds.) (1978) *The Development of Communication* (London, Wiley)

Weathers, J. (1978) 'Guide to Assertive and Social Skills', *Comm. Educ., 27, 2*, 94-6

Weissman, M. and Paykel, E. (1974) *The Depressed Woman: A Study of Social Relationships* (Chicago, University of Chicago Press)

Welch, C. (1976) 'Counsellor Training in Interviewing Skills' (Unpublished Dissertation Montreal, McGill University)

Welford, A. (1968) *Fundamentals of Skill* (London, Methuen)

—— (1980) 'The Concept of Skill and its Application to Social Performance' in Singleton, W., Spurgeon, T. and Stammers, R. (eds.) *The Analysis of Social Skill* (New York, Plenum)

Wells, K., Hersen, M., Bellack, A. and Himmelhoch, J. (1979) 'Social Skills Training in Unipolar Non-psychotic Depression', *Am. J. Psychiatry, 10*, 1331-3

Westefeld, J., Galassi, J. and Galassi, M. (1980) 'Effects of Role-playing Instructions on Assertive Behaviour', *Behav. Therapy, 11, 2*, 271-7

Whitehall, M. (1978) 'A Conversation Skills Training Programme for Socially Isolated Children: An Analysis of Generalisation' (Unpublished masters thesis, Pittsburgh, University of Pittsburgh)

Whittington, D. (1974) 'Skills in Context: The Model Applied in Teacher Training', *Bull. of the Assn for the Teaching of Psychology, 2*, 170-8

—— (1977) 'SST: A Case Study' (Annual Conference of the BPS N. Ireland Branch, mimeo, Newtownabbey, Ulster Polytechnic)

Williams, M. (1977) 'Group Social Skills for Chronic Psychiatric Patients', *Eur. J. Beh. Anal. & Modification, 1, 14*, 223-9

Wolpe, J. (1958) *Psychotherapy by Reciprocal Inhibition* (Stanford, Stanford University Press)

Wolpe, J. and Lazarus, A. (1966) *Behaviour Therapy Techniques* (New York, Pergamon)

Young, D.A. and Young, D.B. (1972) 'The Practicum Crescendo' (Paper delivered to Tubingen International Microteaching Conference, mimeo, Maryland, University of Maryland, Education Center)

Young, D.B. (1967) 'The Effectiveness of Self-instruction in Teacher Education Using Modelling and Videotape Feedback' (Unpublished PhD dissertation, Stanford University; *Dissertation Abstracts Inter-*

national, 28/4520A)

Young, E., Rimm, D. and Kennedy, T. (1973) 'An Experimental Investigation of Modelling and Verbal Reinforcement in the Modification of Assertive Behaviour', *Behav. Res. & Ther., 11*, 317-34

Zielinski, J. and Williams, L. (1979) 'Covert Modelling versus Behaviour Rehearsal in the Training and Generalisation of Assertive Behaviours: A Crossover Design', *J. Clin. Psych., 35, 4*, 855-63

Zigler, E. and Phillips, L. (1960) 'Social Effectiveness and Symptomatic Behaviour', *J. Abn. & Soc. Psychology, 61*, 231-8

AUTHOR INDEX

SUBJECT INDEX